*The Afterlife of Enclosure*

# THE AFTERLIFE OF ENCLOSURE

*British Realism, Character, and the Commons*

Carolyn Lesjak

Stanford University Press
Stanford, California

STANFORD UNIVERSITY PRESS
Stanford, California

© 2021 by the Board of Trustees of the Leland Stanford Junior University. All rights reserved.

No part of this book may be reproduced or transmitted in any form or by any means, electronic or mechanical, including photocopying and recording, or in any information storage or retrieval system without the prior written permission of Stanford University Press.

Printed in the United States of America on acid-free, archival-quality paper

Library of Congress Cataloging-in-Publication Data
Names: Lesjak, Carolyn, 1963- author.
Title: The afterlife of enclosure : British realism, character, and the commons / Carolyn Lesjak.
Description: Stanford, California : Stanford University Press, 2021. | Includes bibliographical references and index.
Identifiers: LCCN 2020035328 (print) | LCCN 2020035329 (ebook) | ISBN 9781503615083 (cloth) | ISBN 9781503627819 (paperback) | ISBN 9781503627826 (epub)
Subjects: LCSH: English fiction—19th century—History and criticism. | Commons in literature. | Inclosures in literature. | Working class in literature. | Realism in literature. | Dickens, Charles, 1812-1870—Criticism and interpretation. | Eliot, George, 1819-1880—Criticism and interpretation. | Hardy, Thomas, 1840-1928--Criticism and interpretation.
Classification: LCC PR878.C635 L47 2021  (print) | LCC PR878.C635  (ebook) | DDC 823/.809357—dc23
LC record available at https://lccn.loc.gov/2020035328
LC ebook record available at https://lccn.loc.gov/2020035329

Cover design: Rob Ehle

Typeset by Kevin Barrett Kane in 10/15 Sabon

*For Sophie and Mia*

# Contents

*Illustrations* ix
*Acknowledgments* xi

INTRODUCTION
Realism and the Commons
1

CHAPTER 1
The Persistence of the Commons, The Persistence of Enclosure
15

CHAPTER 2
Dickensian Types and a Culture of the Commons
44

CHAPTER 3
Eliot, Cosmopolitanism, and the Commons
88

CHAPTER 4
The Typical and the Tragic in Hardy's Geopolitical Commons
125

AFTERWORD
Old and New Enclosures
171

*Notes* 175
*References* 211
*Index* 227

# Illustrations

Figure 1. George Cruikshank, "London Going Out of Town, or the March of Bricks & Mortar" (1829)    16

Figure 2. Henry Heath, "Swing!" (1830)    27

Figure 3. Title page. From Henry Wilson and James Caulfield, *The Book of Wonderful Characters: Memoirs and Anecdotes of Remarkable and Eccentric Persons in all Ages and Countries* (1869 [1829])    53

Figure 4. The Wonderful Miss Atkinson. From Henry Wilson and James Caulfield, *The Book of Wonderful Characters: Memoirs and Anecdotes of Remarkable and Eccentric Persons in all Ages and Countries* (1869 [1829])    55

Figure 5. Daniel Dancer. From Henry Wilson and James Caulfield, *The Book of Wonderful Characters: Memoirs and Anecdotes of Remarkable and Eccentric Persons in all Ages and Countries* (1869 [1829])    57

Figure 6. Joana Southcott. From Henry Wilson and James Caulfield, *The Book of Wonderful Characters: Memoirs and Anecdotes of Remarkable and Eccentric Persons in all Ages and Countries* (1869 [1829])    59

Figure 7. Cover of *Bleak House* by Charles Dickens, with illustrations by H. K. Browne, No. X. (1852–53)    68

Figure 8. Edward Henry Corbould, "Dinah Morris Preaching on the Common" (1861)    107

# Acknowledgments

This book took shape as Occupy reclaimed public space, and squares, parks, and plazas became for a time a commons. It has been completed in the midst of a global pandemic and the resurgence of Black Lives Matter protests in response to the murder of George Floyd. My deepest gratitude goes to all the people whom I will never know who continue to fight for a better world.

In the spirit of this book and its belief in the "many," I feel very lucky to have so many people to thank. I thank all those at Simon Fraser University for offering me a new home mid-career; I am grateful, as well, for the support of my department, and the university, in the form of grants and sabbatical time to complete this project.

Many thanks as well to all my friends and colleagues who keep me going and remind me on a daily basis how nice it is to be part of a collective: Caren Irr, Phil Wegner, Susan Hegeman, Andy Neather, Martine DeVos, Margaret Linley, Miguel Mota, Kristin Mahoney, David Coley, Clint Burnham, Rob Seguin, Liz Blasco, Matt Hussey, Vanessa Haney, Paul Jaskot, Elaine Freedgood, Julie Crawford, Liza Yukins, and Amy Friedlander. A special thanks to Lisa Cohen for her friendship and her fierce acuity as a reader—and for being there at all stages of the book to talk ideas and read drafts, and to encourage and inspire me. I am indebted to all the scholars, too numerous to name, whose work has informed my thinking and become part of this book. I am also deeply grateful to my editor, Faith Wilson Stein, and to the anonymous readers for Stanford University Press, for their invaluable insights and commentary, which I hope I have made good on.

With gratitude for their constant support, I thank my father, Jim Lesjak, and my sister, Catherine Lesjak.

## ACKNOWLEDGMENTS

For a book about the commons, the writing itself was quite solitary, save for the unceasing love and companionship of Christopher Pavsek, for whom there simply are not words enough to thank for seeing me through it all, and my two lovely and spirited daughters, Sophie and Mia, to whom this book is dedicated.

*   *   *

A portion of Chapter 1 was published as "1750 to the Present: Acts of Enclosure and Their Afterlife," in *BRANCH: Britain, Representation and Nineteenth-Century History*, edited by Dino Franco Felluga, Extension of *Romanticism and Victorianism on the Net*, 2015. A section of Chapter 2, framed differently, appeared as "'Done because we were too menny': The Poor, the Bad, and the Utopian," in *Politics/Letters*, edited by James Livingston and Bruce Robbins, 2018. Part of Chapter 3 was originally published as "George Eliot and Politics," in *The Blackwell Companion to George Eliot*, edited by Amanda Anderson and Harry Shaw, 2012.

*The Afterlife of Enclosure*

# Introduction
## Realism and the Commons

THE HISTORICAL RECORD leaves no doubt that the Victorian period, despite claims to the contrary, was an age neither of equipoise nor of innocence. Violence and inequality, ceaseless war and famines, colonial dispossession, the development and consolidation of a capitalist world order and its attendant forms of alienation and dispossession—all make good on Walter Benjamin's dictum that "there is no document of civilization which is not at the same time a document of barbarism" (256).[1] But there is also another history folded within this one that has received scant critical attention within literary studies: the history of enclosure and what Peter Linebaugh refers to as its antonym, the commons ("Enclosures" 11). This is the history that informs this book. It is a story not of the victors, but of those over whom history ran roughshod: the anonymous, the commoner, those whom "civilization" seemingly left behind, the necessary detritus in the progressive narrative of modernity. Linebaugh calls this form of historiography a "bottom-up history," which "requires that we pay attention to the cranny in the wall, as Bottom the Weaver expressed it in *A Midsummer Night's Dream*." As he interprets Bottom's approach, "we must attend not to the completeness of the wall but to its chinks" ("Enclosures" 25).

For Linebaugh, as a social historian, the chinks in the wall are to be found by documenting those voices previously left out of history, work begun by the History Workshop in the late 1960s when its founder, new left historian Raphael Samuel, walked the countryside around Oxford talking to elderly residents about their experiences of class struggle in nineteenth-century Oxfordshire. What approach then might a bottom-up *literary* history take, given the absence of such voices? In *The Afterlife of Enclosure: British Realism, Character, and the Commons*, I argue that these openings are to be found in classic British realist texts, hiding, as it were, in plain sight, given the considerable critical scholarship on realism. Attending to them, I wager, is revelatory on two fronts: it not only unsettles existing accounts of realism, and of the British realist novel, in particular, that too seamlessly align the novel with the victors, but also brings to the fore the significant contribution realist novels make to the history of the commons and, more pointedly, to a dialectical reading of that history.

The fate of realism seems to be perennially in the balance, its death repeatedly foretold. Reflecting on realism's sad state, Rachel Bowlby wittily writes in the foreword to *Adventures in Realism*, "Poor old realism. Out of date and second-rate. Squashed in between the freshness of romanticism and the newness of modernism, it is truly the tasteless spam in the sandwich of literary and cultural history" (xi). Bowlby's opening sally sums up the broad challenge at the heart of this book—namely, to show how realism has been misperceived in the ways that it has, and how we might reconceive it more productively given the ongoing relevance of its concerns. After all, as Bowlby and others in *Adventures in Realism* stress in their respective attempts to save realism from the dustbin of history and give it new life, realism is far less naive in its representational practices than critics from Virginia Woolf on would have it.[2] Zombie-like, it refuses to die, as our obsession with documenting our every moment and meal on endlessly proliferating internet platforms testifies.[3] Whereas many of these current resuscitations focus on the complexities of realist representation, I propose a rereading of realism with a more overtly political aim in mind: to consider how realist novels help us think about our own present and future with the tools realism offers to hand. In this regard, my analysis shares a thrust common to recent accounts of realism that emphasize its generative possibilities and transformative or even radical politics, such as Lauren Goodlad's *The Victorian Geopolitical Aesthetic: Realism, Sovereignty, and Transnational Experience* (2015), Isobel Armstrong's *Novel Politics: Democratic Imaginations in Nineteenth-Century Fiction* (2016), and Anna Kornbluh's *The Order of Forms: Realism, Formalism, and Social Space* (2019).[4] Specifically, *The Afterlife of Enclosure* reconfigures our understanding of British realism by placing at the center of its project two fundamental thematics that have been neglected or undervalued in literary criticism in recent decades. On the one hand, the book brings into view anew the connection between depictions of the *common*—the ordinary, common characters; the commonplace events; and the seemingly unremarkable *mise-en-scène* of everyday life that are the lifeblood of realism—and the historical existence of the literal *commons*—those shared lands that were once a defining feature of the British landscape and political imaginary. On the other hand, it argues for the enduring presence within nineteenth-century realism of utopian energies, which both hark back to the commons and point forward to a transformed society, and which thereby give the lie to those critical assessments of realism that see in it the mere reproduction and affirmation of the given world and the status quo, a view, as Goodlad, Kornbluh, and others note, that continues to hold sway as a "still influential set of assumptions" (*The Victorian Geopolitical Aesthetic* 5) or "deeply held critical truisms" (*Order of Forms* 16).[5] The three realist writers who are the focus of this study—Charles Dickens, George Eliot, and Thomas Hardy—each trace out a series of figurations of the common in the wake of the destruction of the physical or literal commons, endowing both the historical trauma that was enclosure and the utopian spirit that the commons embodied with an afterlife, an afterlife that reveals a radical politics at the heart of the work of the British nineteenth century's most canonical writers.

## Histories Past, Present, and Future

In her book on the Paris Commune, *Communal Luxury: The Political Imaginary of the Paris Commune*, Kristin Ross, following Benjamin, notes that "there are moments when a particular event or struggle enters vividly into the figurability of the present, and this seems to me to be the case with the Commune today" (2). The same, I believe, can be said today about the enclosure of the historical commons in Britain and the responses and resistance to it. Multiple movements and conversations, including Occupy in North America, Indigenous campaigns around the globe centered on decolonization and the return of land, ecological movements grounded in a call to renew a "global commons," and discussions of the newly emergent forms of common life (and the ever-looming threat of their privatization) in the digital realm, have brought to the fore a contemporary politics of the commons as well as critiques of the new forms of enclosure that have accompanied neoliberalism. All of these movements quite powerfully suggest that the commons and its enclosure have an afterlife that extends far beyond the reach of the nineteenth century. They further suggest that now is an opportune time to devote serious scholarly attention to enclosure's prior figurations.

What form, then, do such figurations take in the nineteenth-century novel? This book will explore this matter at length; for now a well-known passage from Eliot's *Middlemarch* begins to elucidate what I call the worldly ethics at the heart of the language of the common, an ethics that is given shape less in direct representations of enclosure, in more traditional appeals to specific political goals, or in explicit political programs than in *figures* for the common.[6] In this passage, the narrator writes of her heroine, Dorothea Brooke,

> We are all of us born in moral stupidity, taking the world as an udder to feed our supreme selves: Dorothea had early begun to emerge from that stupidity, but yet it had been easier to her to imagine how she would devote herself to Mr. Casaubon, and become wise and strong in his strength and wisdom, than to conceive with that distinctness which is no longer reflection but feeling—an idea wrought back to the directness of sense, like the solidity of objects—that he had an equivalent centre of self, whence the lights and shadows must always fall with a certain difference. (211)

Eliot paradoxically links the most immaterial of perceptions or sensations—feeling—to the concreteness of things, to the "the solidity of objects." Such an equation gives to feeling a materiality that feeling itself would seem to belie, and connects this "thingness" or solidity to nothing less than psychological interiority, on the face of it one of the least solid attributes of selfhood. Additionally, this meeting of subject and object implies an ethics: through a reorientation of her self to the world, Dorothea emerges from her "moral stupidity," an ignorance that follows from assuming the self as supreme rather than on the level with or of the world. In other words, selves here gain their worldliness. Likewise, the world, no longer an udder, now takes on its own materiality as a solid force capable of resistance, refusing to "feed our supreme selves" or be subsumed by us.

By granting even the thoroughly unlikeable Edward Casaubon an "equivalent centre of self," this passage is a bold provocation on Eliot's part to move her readers toward a vision of a world peopled by "equivalent selves": selves that are materially and ethically indebted to one another, bound by the shared common conditions that she examines throughout her oeuvre. This image of equivalent selves is but one figure among others for the common in Eliot's work (I explore further examples in Chapter 3) and represents one way in which her writing works through the demise of the literal, material basis of common culture in the nineteenth century—a history that Eliot witnessed firsthand growing up in the Midlands as the pastures on the Arbury estate where her father worked as a land agent were enclosed. Over the course of this passage, a complex set of materialist relations emerges that looks both back to the eighteenth century in its echoing of John Locke and forward to a new Dorothea, and by extension a new "we," able to navigate a world filled with equivalent selves.

This expansive vision of "extending relationships" is not limited to Eliot but rather spans the nineteenth century and foregrounds a disregarded aspect of nineteenth-century realism by illuminating the collective nature of its project and its political aspirations.[7] In their respective reinventions of the common, each writer in this study eschews mere nostalgia and experiments instead with new forms of communal relations that undercut the association between realism and liberalism and its attendant individualist ideology. Against claims such as Terry Eagleton's that "liberalism and the realist novel are spiritual twins" (*The English Novel* 164), or Alex Woloch's formulation of realism as an *opposition* between "the one" (the unique individual) and "the many" (homogenized society), Dickens, Eliot, and Hardy attempt to reconfigure the relationship between individuals and their social world as mutually constitutive rather than oppositional: social unity appears as an ensemble of rich individuality, and individuality finds its richness in its social being. Dialectical rather than dualistic, this relationship involves reimagining the one *as* the many. Again, as in the passage from *Middlemarch*, social unity of this sort is neither a given nor recoverable from the past, but instead something to be achieved—with difficulty, no less, as the need to include Casaubon enforces—in a future that has yet to come, then and now.[8]

With the benefit of hindsight, the resonances of this "we" with the Occupy movement of the early twenty-first century seem nothing short of prescient: like the realization that Eliot hopes Dorothea can come to, Occupy's claim "We are the 99 Percent" involves humility and a willingness to associate oneself with a collective *in the making*.[9] Marco Roth characterizes this identification, as enacted in online testimonials, as "not just a gesture, but a speech act": "By writing 'I am the 99%' or in some cases 'We are the 99%' . . . the individuals who have chosen to post their post-industrial miseries on the web are doing something that Americans of recent generations have been averse to doing. They are actually creating class consciousness, for themselves and those around them" (26–27). These resonances also give concrete expression to the "uninterrupted narrative," the "single vast unfinished plot" (*The Political Unconscious* 20) that Fredric Jameson, drawing on Marx, identifies as the fundamental history the political unconscious of texts makes available to us: "the collective struggle to wrest a realm of Freedom from a realm of Necessity" (19).

That history has largely been examined in nineteenth-century literary analyses through the lens of industrialization and modernization.[10] What has gone missing from such accounts is the persistence of enclosure and its effects in the attention that nineteenth-century realism affords to the notion of the common and its elevation as a subject worthy of literature and culture. This history is one that nineteenth-century realists are uniquely positioned to narrate precisely because they witnessed the destruction of the commons and the profound transformations of a whole social world and set of values that this destruction entailed, summed up by Georg Lukács as the "rationalization" of modern life (*History and Class Consciousness* 68), or, by Max Weber, as simply "the spirit of capitalism."[11] As a result, they were cognizant—in ways we can no longer be—of the historical existence of a relationship to land and property alternative to that which came to prevail over the course of the nineteenth century, and of an alternative set of social and historical relations inhering in common rights and the commons more generally.¹² Indeed, for theorists of the commons, part of the difficulty in imagining a contemporary commons, as David Bollier notes, rests in the fact that enclosures "eclipse the history and memory of the commons, rendering them invisible," such that the "impersonal, individualistic, transactional-based ethic of the market economy becomes the new normal" (*Think Like a Commoner* 79). With a foot in both of these worlds, and with the recognition that there can be no going backward, Dickens, Eliot, and Hardy instead work to reinvent a new culture of the commons in their novels that works within the constraints of the present in which they lived. Following Bollier, my gambit in rereading realism in this way is that "by naming the commons, we can learn how to reclaim it" (3).

## Representing Enclosure and the Commons

How then did nineteenth-century writers represent enclosure, and why have these representations remained largely opaque to twenty-first-century readers? As *The Afterlife of Enclosure* demonstrates, this question is challenging for two primary reasons. First, the historical processes of enclosure involve at once a series of parliamentary acts, local actions, and far more amorphous events that have occurred over many centuries. As a result, even the seemingly simple act of dating enclosure proves difficult; without a signal moment when enclosure can be said to have begun, and with no clear endpoint—enclosure continues apace today—enclosure's time frame threatens conventional modes of telling history and storytelling. Moreover, the effects of this process are multiple, varied, and often deferred and diffuse, marked only tenuously by their connection to the initial event that induced them. Therefore, as an *event* enclosure defies our commonsense understandings of a historical event as discrete, locatable, and temporally bounded. To conceive of the representational challenges such a "slow" event poses, I draw on the work of Rob Nixon, who sees in contemporary environmental disasters and climate change a similar problematic: such events are "attritional catastrophes" (7) that perpetrate a "slow violence" (2). In the context of enclosure, this problematic is articulated in the attentiveness British realism affords to the constitutive violence of capitalism and the processes of primitive accumulation that drove enclosure.¹³ Slow rather than spectacular, this form of violence constitutes the world as we now know it; wending its way through the ubiquity of the everyday, it makes itself known in the least conspicuous of manners: the workaday world, the seemingly natural hedgerow, the constitution of ourselves as individuals, the weather.

Second, all three writers discussed here are fully aware of the pejorative senses of commonness as low, vulgar, and coarse; hence they must actively advocate for the common against its derogatory associations, which, as Raymond Williams argues, gain force over the course of the nineteenth century.[14] In their advocacy, they grapple with the tension at the heart of what it means to be *common*. With its etymological roots in the French "*commune*," and its ties to the notion of land or other resources belonging to or shared by all (later a *commonwealth*), *common* is descriptively neutral; in its connection with "the common people, as distinguished from those of rank or dignity," the ordinary, the unrefined or the general mass, it also becomes a derisive term with definite class connotations. As Williams writes, by the late nineteenth century, "'her speech was very *common*' has an unmistakable ring, and this use has persisted over a wide range of behaviour" (72). It is no accident that contemporaneous reviews of all three writers single out their "commonplace" characters for criticism (Henry James, for example, bemoans how Dickens "*reconciles* us to the commonplace" ["*Our Mutual Friend*" 787, emphasis added]), nor is it surprising that Eliot feels the need to interrupt the narrative of *Adam Bede* with a spirited defense of her own characters, described variously by the "idealistic friend" she constructs as her interlocutor as "coarse," "vulgar," "low," "clumsy," and "ugly." All three novelists directly and indirectly contest these associations, and in each commonness becomes a ground for a politics and ethics of the public good. To be sure, not all forms of commonness are to be celebrated. There are forms that reproduce rather than challenge the status quo, such as the common prejudices and ideologies—of class, race, gender, and so forth—that all three novelists work to unsettle and dismantle.

For each, as well, the reach of the public good at times extends beyond the borders of England to a vision of a potentially global common figured variously as the multitude or "the many," as forms of cosmopolitanism or a commonwealth, or as a geopolitical commons.[15] (Paradoxically, Dickens is perhaps the least visionary in this regard despite his seemingly more modern urban sensibilities as a novelist of the city, a point I return to in Chapter 2.) In keeping with its original derivation, an expansive view of the *common* strives to retain and enlarge upon the obligations and duties that come with the Latin *munis* in *communis,* to aspire to what Jedidiah Purdy, in the context of articulating what a new commonwealth might look like today, calls "the commonwealth ideal": a global community in which "no one gets their living by degrading someone else, nor by degrading the health of the land or the larger living world," a "way of living in deep reciprocity as well as deep equality" (xiii). The premise of the common, of being shared by *all,* "of living in deep reciprocity as well as deep equality," demands nothing less; that such a life in common is still in the making, its fulfillment hard to fathom, its contours hard to draw, bespeaks the enormity of the undertaking in which realist writers were engaged in their respective commitments to the common and how it might be envisioned.

In the face of these formidable representational demands, each writer's work, I suggest, needs to be seen not as a completed project so much as an ongoing thought experiment that attempts to come to terms with the history of enclosure and with the challenge of enclosure's figurability via new forms of realism that each uses to capture the lived experience of enclosure and its aftermath and the largely invisible structural and global relations of which it is a part.

To be sure, enclosure enters nineteenth-century literature and nonfiction in myriad ways, and, at times, is directly referenced. There are numerous references to the literal commons in novels ranging from Elizabeth Gaskell's *North and South,* where Margaret Hale walks on the "broad commons," to Anthony Trollope's *The Way We Live Now* and its description of Roger Carbury's estate, whose "acreage has been extended by the enclosure of the commons" (45). Enclosure also figures centrally in sensation literature; *Lady Audley's Secret,* for example, links the enclosure of land to the enclosure of women's bodies, in what Elizabeth Langland terms "a dialectic between freedom and enclosure, privilege and confinement" (64).

Nonfiction and poetry also directly address enclosure. William Cobbett traveled the southern English countryside on horseback during the years 1821 to 1826 observing the changing conditions of farmers and laborers, which he then recorded in *Rural Rides*. Cobbett witnesses firsthand the results of the commons being enclosed, referring polemically to enclosure as part of the "rage for improvements . . . the rage for what empty men think was an augmenting of the *capital* of the country" (101). The English Romantic poet John Clare, too, captures the intimate, lived experience of enclosure and its literal reroutings of the self and the land. Whereas his village of Helpston was organized in a circular manner when still an open-field parish (the open fields radiating from the village hub), with enclosure that space becomes, as John Barrell characterizes it, linear. The haunts of Clare's childhood are made inaccessible, and the rituals attached to them destroyed. For example, a poem about two fountains, Round Oak and Eastwell Fountain, describes how

> In my own native field two fountains run
> All desolate and naked to the sun;
> The fell destroyer's hand hath reft their side
> Of every tree that hid and beautified
> Their shallow waters in delightful clumps,
> That sunburnt now o'er pebbles skips and jumps. (*Poems of John Clare* 297–98)

Clare's biographer, Jonathan Bate, notes that Eastwell Fountain became private property after enclosure, thus ending Clare's and the other village children's custom of drinking from it for good luck on Whit Sunday (49). He comments more generally that, in Helpston, "The final enclosure, the Award of 1820, enumerated the ownership of every acre, rood and perch, the position of every road, footway and public drain. Fences, gates and No Trespassing signs went up. Trees came down. Streams were stopped in their course so that the line of ditches could be made straight" (48).[16]

But more often than not, the literal enclosure of land does not make its way into classic nineteenth-century realist novels in such a direct manner, as a discrete event to be narrated. Instead, faced with the challenges of representing the social and political consequences of enclosure and the loss of the commons, nineteenth-century realist writers produce *figurations* of the commons. These figurations find expression in the language of common characters and types; in visions of common culture and the common good; and in the language of common relations. They work through and figure the afterlife of enclosure as it appears in the continuing trauma of the decollectivization of the commons as well as in the utopian-collective spirit that it embodied, and that continues to resonate, however meekly, in their historical present.

In large part, this narrative of the commons has been obscured by our tendency to read the present as an inevitable outcome of the past, to read history, as per Linebaugh, in terms of "the completeness of the wall" rather than the crannies. In the case of nineteenth-century literary studies, such a teleological view has helped to perpetuate a narrative in which individualism *necessarily* won out over collective ties as England moved from a rural to an urban economy and from feudal to capitalist social relations.[17] Deeply colonialist at its core, this history reinforces a hierarchy in which common interests are seen to be less developed than individual ones, just as common lands are seen to be "undeveloped" and "empty" (as in the doctrine of *terra nullius*), and hence free to be colonized. Exploring this hierarchy in the colonial context, Brenna Bhandar stresses its racialized nature, noting that "ideas of what constitutes use and improvement ... encapsulate an articulation of modern rationales for ownership and modern conceptualizations of racial value" (181). There is nothing natural or inevitable about this view of improvement; rather, the "notion that land requires improvement because its inhabitants are also in need of civilizational uplift, and vice versa, is no accident of history" (181).

Within accounts of realism, specifically, an analogous hierarchy privileges psychologically "developed" characters over character types, round characters over so-called flat ones.[18] The reconceptualization of the relationship between the individual and the social that the commons occasions, however, prompts us to rethink the use of character types in realism. For, in different ways, Dickens, Eliot, and Hardy all continue to construct their characters as *types*, the very method of characterization that critics have often dismissed as inferior, and that realism supposedly discounts and supersedes as it ostensibly flattens out individual psychological complexity.

Against this prevailing view, these writers require us to expand our understanding of the forms of typification employed by realist writers and to appreciate the model of character to which typification aspires in a more nuanced fashion. Although *type* today is largely synonymous with Georg Lukács's elaboration of the concept, nineteenth-century novelists also drew significantly on an earlier tradition of typification found in a genre of writing associated primarily with the eighteenth century, known variously as "characteristic writing," "eccentric biographies," and "character books." While this connection is most directly seen in Dickens's work, in which actual "characters" from these books appear, Eliot and Hardy also mobilize notions of character as material type(s). To recall the passage from *Middlemarch*, to conceive of character as material type, as the narrator encourages Dorothea to do in relation to Casaubon, is to grant to others a solidity like that of objects, which, in turn, establishes a reciprocal and mediated relation of equivalence, not only between subjects, but between subjects and objects. It is the claim of independence—of the subject from the object—as Theodor Adorno powerfully asserts, that "heralds the claim of dominance" and that constitutes the alienated subject under capitalism: "Once radically separated from the object, the subject reduces it to its own measure; the subject swallows the object, forgetting how much it is an object itself" ("Subject and Object" 499). Common types dispel any such claims of dominance: to be a type in the materialist sense that Eliot et al. mean is to refuse the possessive "supreme self," the subject that "swallows the object, forgetting how much it is an object itself."[19] In their various experiments with "character-building," all three writers in this study at once reinvent older traditions of type and envision future forms of typical character that gesture toward a lifeworld freed from the tenets of private property and the various forms of dispossession concomitant with privatization and market-dependence.[20] In short, the inventive use of type both to capture the social totality, as in the Lukácsian model of realism, and to develop a new political imaginary grounded in the commons makes these nineteenth-century "thought experiments" anything but outmoded and antiquated, stale or tasteless.

Instead, in its twinned emphasis on the materiality of character and the materiality of the world, the language of the commons articulates a profound ethical insight. As Silvia Federici contends in another context, "[N]o common is possible unless we refuse to base our life and our reproduction on the suffering of others, unless we refuse to see ourselves as separate from them" ("Feminism"). Dickens, Eliot, and Hardy all share a version of this ethic, each reinforcing the ineluctably collective nature of social life in their own unique manner. Dickens creates nineteenth-century "collective biographies" that unsettle the very meaning of an individual life and lay the ground for a vision of universal equality. Eliot renders our collective life through the metaphorics of indebtedness to others that encompasses nothing less than the commonwealth of all. And Hardy brings the global home, as it were, by conceiving even the most private details and intricacies of daily life in Britain as an intimate part of a far larger process unfolding across the globe in the nineteenth century, poignantly described as "the great web of human doings then weaving in both hemispheres, from the White Sea to Cape Horn" (22), as he writes in *The Woodlanders*.

Each of these attempts to gesture toward or reinvent the commons is simultaneously an implicit, and sometimes explicit, attempt to imagine a social utopia that has overcome the "suffering of others." Far from a naive utopianism, all three novelists recognize the deeply unequal economic and social structures defining their present, and they recognize that any viable solution will have to address the inescapably economic basis of social relations and provide for those whom Eliot calls in *Romola* the "vast multitudes" of the "common lot." In this regard, the common lot of Eliot's multitudes, as well as those of Dickens and Hardy, enrich contemporary accounts of the commons, such as Michael Hardt and Antonio Negri's, which, as Federici notes, "[skirt] the question of the reproduction of everyday life" ("Feminism").[21] More generally, realism's emphasis on the "reproduction of everyday life" takes on new meaning: it not only allows us to see that any possible common future must be grounded in the nitty-gritty details of material life—those very details at the heart of realist representation—it also expands the reach of that everyday life to include both the individual and the hemispheric, to echo Hardy. For Hardy knows, and wants us to know, that even as his characters exist in what appear to be the most intensely local or regional of environments, "their lonely courses formed no detached design at all"; part of a much larger design, his task and ours, is to discern the "pattern" without losing sight of either the individual isolated life or "the great web of human doings." Both the individual and the hemispheric are meant to loom large despite their difference in relative size, an equivalence Hardy beautifully images by opening this passage with yet another pattern: "They went out together," Hardy's narrator specifies, "the pattern of the air-holes in the top of the lantern being thrown upon the mist overhead, where they appeared of giant size, as if reaching the tent-shaped sky" (21). Needless to say, keeping both "patterns" in our sight is no easy feat. In fact, we could do worse than identify this challenge as *the* problematic of nineteenth-century realism.

My hope, then, is that we can learn from the ways nineteenth-century realism dealt with this problematic, because it is a problematic that equally, if differently, marks our current moment. The deeply entwined crises of global capitalism and ecological catastrophe, and the slow violence each has wrought, require that we keep the far and the near equally close at hand, and that we refuse to be debilitated and immobilized by the picture that then comes into view—or worse, that we succumb to the truisms of the present.[22] That our deeds, as Eliot would have it, "carry terrible consequences . . . consequences that are hardly ever confined to ourselves" (*Adam Bede* 217) cannot help but reverberate with renewed force in the Anthropocene, an age literally named for our ability to alter and even destroy the earth itself. But what also reverberates with renewed force is a faith in common people and the commons, whose history has as long a pedigree as the violent history of dispossession with which we began.

CHAPTER 1

# The Persistence of the Commons, The Persistence of Enclosure

IT MIGHT SEEM STRANGE to return to the history of enclosure and its status as a movement, a set of practices, a politics, and an ideology, given its rootedness in a landscape and a population that is now on the path to extinction. If the period from approximately the fifteenth to the nineteenth centuries marks the beginning of the depopulation of the British countryside, developments today signal its global end. "The global countryside," Mike Davis reports in *Planet of Slums*, "has reached its maximum population and will begin to shrink after 2020" (2). Hardly natural phenomena, the burgeoning growth of megacities and megaslums and the consequent shift in the world's population from the countryside to these urban centers is occurring, much like it did in nineteenth-century Britain and earlier, through a complex set of intertwined social, political, geographical, and economic factors, processes, parliamentary acts, and governmental actions—and inaction. Also, as in the nineteenth-century, this shift in population goes both ways, as urbanization also extends *to* the countryside. Davis comments about developments in southern China, for example, that "[i]ndeed, in many cases, rural people no longer have to migrate to the city: it migrates to them" (9). Two centuries ago, in 1829, George Cruikshank anthropomorphized this same dynamic visually in an etching titled "London Going Out of Town, or the March of Bricks & Mortar," in which animated haystacks, trees, and fences bemoan the onslaught of "Mr. Goth brickmaker in Brixton" and the destruction his bricks and mortar bring: an uprooted tree cries, "I must leave the field," while another tree reckons, "Our fences I fear will be found to be no defense against these Barbarians who threaten to . . . destroy us in a 'manor' of ways," punning on the Lord of the Manor's attempt at the time to pass a bill to enclose the fields of Hampstead (see Figure 1).

CHAPTER ONE

FIGURE 1. George Cruikshank, "London Going Out of Town, or the March of Bricks & Mortar" (1829). Source: © Museum of London. Reprinted with permission.

While it may seem a long way from the British countryside to the *chawls* and *favelas* of today's megacities and megaslums, we can see today's "urban climacteric" as the logical outcome of the set of practices and policies that coalesced around acts of enclosure in Britain. This perspective allows us to understand how enclosure was at once a local phenomenon, and one that, from its outset, had a potentially global reach, if not the fully realized means to impose its order on a global scale.[1] Cruikshank's bricks and mortar, for example, did not stop at the English countryside; the twin processes of enclosure and deforestation extended across the British empire and beyond, providing, among other things, the wood for English furniture—a process that Elaine Freedgood traces in her analysis of *Jane Eyre* and its references to the mahogany that comes from Madeira and Britain's colony, Jamaica. Enclosure, she writes, "requires deforestation; deforestation in turn guarantees the legible demarcation of space—its visibility and its representability" (*The Ideas in Things* 39).

A long view also usefully reminds us that what was destroyed by the centuries-long history of enclosure—the commons, common right, communal wastes and forests, a certain form of labor independence—contained a nascent worldview too, but one that envisioned a radical alternative to what has now come to pass in our "planet of slums." The lived experience of the commons captured by the poet John Clare, for example, and shared by his fellow laboring commoners, constituted nothing short of an alternative epistemology, a "different ecology . . . dependent on the unenclosed," according to Peter Linebaugh ("Enclosures" 18–19). Clare himself equates the "lawless law" (one of his terms for enclosure) with the destruction of the "rights of freedom," rights figured in a range of spatial registers both local and expansive, from the felling of an individual elm tree that "barked of freedom" ("The Fallen Elm," "*I AM*" 142) to the "right to roam" (Jonathan Bate's phrase), which not only names Clare's immediate experience of what was lost when his native village of Helpstone (now Helpston) was enclosed, but implies, as well, a profoundly different relationship to the geography of social space and our place within it.[2] Bate approvingly cites E. P. Thompson's claim that "Clare may be described, without hindsight, as a poet of ecological protest: he was not writing about man here and nature there, but lamenting a threatened equilibrium in which both were involved" (Bate 50). Finally, a return to the "event" of enclosure also forces us to think metacritically about the very notion of an event and, most important and pressing, about the distinct representational challenges centuries-long historical events pose both for the fiction and nonfiction writers living through enclosure and its aftermath in the latter part of the nineteenth century and for criticism today.

In relation to a different nineteenth-century event, the "event of the Second Reform," Herbert Tucker directly addresses what constitutes a historical event and how we might understand its status. He asks, "*Event:* what's the long and the short of it?" Part of the answer for Tucker involves recognizing how "fungible events and their ordering are in the construction of histories" and how they inevitably entail a two-way street between past and present in which the event takes on profoundly different meanings. As he explains, "To the degree we conceive an event as an *outcome* (which is what etymology tells us it is), we write it up as the result or effect of what or where it came from, pushed as it were from behind, expelled by the agencies whose force it manifests and signifies." When that same event is seen "as a *coming-forth* (and etymology supports this concept equally)," however, "the event comes to us as much more a thing unto itself, a newborn necessarily dependent on its parentage but still instinct with promise for the future." When we see "the event as a miraculous infancy," Tucker reflects, it "verges on Claude Romano's mediation on eventfulness in *L'événement et le monde*, a richly ramified thought experiment that wonders what might happen if we substituted for the category of *event* that of *advent*," a change in orientation that might move "our basic thinking about time towards *l'avenir, l'avventura*, the *to-come*." Such an "adventualist orientation" allows for the possibility of a more candid acknowledgment as to why we "shape history this way rather than that." As a still ongoing movement that is also punctuated by identifiable events such as particular riots and momentous turning points, enclosure is at once event and advent, outcome and "the to-come," a recognition, I will argue, nineteenth-century writers put into practice in their respective attempts to refigure the commons in the midst of their own lived experience of enclosure. My own treatment of enclosure and its aftermath as represented in nineteenth-century realist fiction likewise hopes to look both backward and into the future and to unearth in the wake of the enclosure movement and its destruction of the literal commons the imagined alternatives found in British realism's invocations to the common. But before turning to these fictional projects, it is important to get a better sense of the kinds of challenges—temporal, representational, spatial, experiential—enclosure presented then and continues to present now.

### The Longue Durée of Enclosure

The ability to connect the British countryside and urban slums is not limited to a retrospective history of enclosure. Contemporaneous riots and other forms of resistance to specific acts of enclosure and the fact of enclosure, more broadly, register how deeply entwined the fate of the country and the future of the city were.[3] Certainly divisions—especially the central division forming the title of Raymond Williams's *The Country and the City*—have, historically, obscured such connections, so much so that Williams's overall aim, registered by his titular "and," was precisely to show how this division as such never existed and instead to chart the deep interconnectedness of the countryside and the city in the development of nineteenth-century agrarian capitalism. As he comments,

> [M]ost obviously since the Industrial Revolution, but in my view also since the beginning of the capitalist agrarian mode of production, our powerful images of country and city have been ways of responding to a whole social development. That is why, in the end, we must not limit ourselves to their contrast but go on to see their interrelations and through these the real shape of the underlying crisis. (297)

Nonetheless, the operative nature of the division between country and city cannot be underestimated, enforced, as it has been, in numerous ideological ways by the left and right alike. On the one hand, as Ian Dyck points out in *William Cobbett and Rural Popular Culture*, critical studies of this period's labor politics have been more interested in industrial workers, aided by age-old stereotypes of the rural laborer as constitutionally incapable of a radical politics. The figure of Hodge (a fourteenth-century invention), whom Thomas Hardy describes in his essay "The Dorsetshire Labourer," typifies the limitations of the rural laborer in the urban imagination. "This supposed real but highly conventional Hodge," Hardy notes,

> is a degraded being of uncouth manner and aspect, stolid understanding, and snaillike movement. His speech is such a chaotic corruption of regular language that few persons of progressive aims consider it worthwhile to enquire what views, if any, of life, of nature, or of society, are conveyed in these utterances. Hodge hangs his head or looks sheepish when spoken to, and thinks Lunnon a place paved with gold. Misery and fever lurk in his cottage, while, to paraphrase the words of a recent writer on the labouring classes, in his future there are only the workhouse and the grave. He hardly dares to think at all. He has few thoughts of joy, and little hope of rest. His life slopes into a darkness quite "quieted by hope." (38–39)[4]

Karl Marx and Frederick Engels in large part share this view, a view famously perpetuated in their reference to "the idiocy of rural life"

(40)—although "idiocy" here, as Eric Hobsbawm clarifies in his introduction to *The Communist Manifesto*, actually refers to "the narrow horizons" of rural life rather than to "stupidity," as it is commonly understood. Hobsbawm nonetheless acknowledges that Marx "shared the usual townsman's contempt for—as well as ignorance of—the peasant milieu" (11).[5]

Yet in practice, peasant farmers and industrial laborers often joined together, as they did in June 1791 in response to a Private Enclosure Act that redistributed six thousand acres of commons to local landlords, freeholders, and tithe-owners. The mob that ensued, composed of both those farmers being driven from their land and industrial laborers (whose numbers would soon include many of those newly landless farmers), embodied, as Robert Anderson argues, the close connection between enclosure and industrial capitalism.[6] If we return to an earlier moment, when the first bills of enclosure were being passed in Parliament in 1621, the complex nature of enclosure as a twinned agricultural and urban process is clear. Discussing the debates around the bill, Christopher Hill notes that enclosure "affected more than the profits of individuals. If the English economy was to continue to expand, a more specialised division of labor was essential. More food would have to be grown to feed the industrial areas, food prices must be lowered, and corn import ended" (18). The fact that enclosure would lead to the depopulation of the countryside was understood: up until 1597, the Tudor government had passed bills to prevent enclosure on precisely these grounds, as Hill documents. Later, as well, the anti-Jacobin turned radical journalist and editor of the *Political Register* William Cobbett, riding through the rural English countryside in the 1820s, continually links the worsening conditions of the farm laborers he sees to the "infernal stock-jobbing system" (184), a link materialized for him in an old oak table being sold at auction in the Weald of Surrey.[7] The table, at which a "Master Charington" used to sit down with his farm laborers, is no longer needed, as communal food and board, previously staples provided by farmers to their workers, have been replaced by a system of wages alone. As Cobbett queries rhetorically, "[I]f the farmer now shuts his pantry against his labourers, and pays them wholly in money, is it not clear, that he does it because he thereby gives them a living *cheaper* to him; that is to say, a *worse* living than formerly?" (183). In Cobbett's telling, the Master has now become the "Squire," his daughters the "*Miss* Charingtons . . . a species of mock gentlefolks" (183), and the table destined to make its way "to the bottom of a bridge that some stock-jobber will stick up over an artificial river in his cockney-garden." This particular encounter so incenses Cobbett that he decides to purchase the table himself and "keep it for the good it has done in the world" (184). Had he not, who knows but it might have become part of the drawbridge to Wemmick's Walworth castle in Charles Dickens's *Great Expectations*, providing passage between London and its growing suburbs—which developed in the mid- to late nineteenth century and are equally part of the afterlife of enclosure.[8] By 1912, with working- and middle-class suburbs absorbing the burgeoning masses of a vast metropolitan London, the working-class writer Edwin Pugh writes in *The City of the World* that the suburbs "feed the City" while making suburbanites into "black-coated hordes" (quoted in Hapgood 177).

Whether in its earliest moments or later suburban incarnations, the dynamic of enclosure necessarily included at its center what Philip Corrigan and Derek Sayer refer to as the "great 'freeing' of labor" (96), a dynamic explicitly theorized by Marx in *Capital I*, in the chapter "The Secret of Primitive Accumulation"—a conceptual framework, significantly, that has received renewed attention by contemporary theorists such as Alexander Kluge and Oskar Negt, specifically in relation to the current processes of globalization. Against those who would see primitive accumulation as a discrete event that occurred in the past, Kluge and Negt argue that primitive accumulation is an ongoing process that continues to underpin capitalist development today. But to return to Marx, and a passage on enclosure and its relationship to the expropriation of property, worth quoting at length:

> Communal property—always distinct from the State property just dealt with—was an old Teutonic institution which lived on under cover of feudalism. We have seen how the forcible usurpation of this, generally accompanied by the turning of arable into pasture land,

begins at the end of the 15th and extends into the 16th century. But, at that time, the process was carried on by means of individual acts of violence against which legislation, for a hundred and fifty years, fought in vain. The advance made by the 18th century shows itself in this, that the law itself becomes now the instrument of the theft of the people's land, although the large farmers make use of their little independent methods as well. The parliamentary form of the robbery is that of 'Bills for Inclosure of Commons,' in other words decrees by which the landlords grant themselves the people's land as private property, decrees of expropriation of the people. (*Capital* I 885)

Marx identifies a number of key aspects of the enclosure movement here. First is the actual timeline of enclosure, which extends from the end of the fifteenth century to the mid-nineteenth century and, as I will argue, therefore defies commonsense understandings of historical events as discrete, locatable, and terminal—especially given that communal property continues to be fought over and expropriated beyond Marx's own time and right into the present. How then to capture the historical process of enclosure without doing damage to its "non-eventual" aspects, or "slow violence" (to borrow Rob Nixon's suggestive term for capturing the processes of climate change), perpetrated over the course of multiple centuries but not visible in any simple, transparent way? Second is the importance of the eighteenth century within this long timeline, given the shift in political relations that occurs in which "the law itself becomes now the instrument of the theft of the people's land," via Acts of Parliament, also known as "Bills for Inclosure of Commons." And as Marx goes on to clarify, the sleight of hand involved in claiming communal property as private property is evident in the very need for parliamentary acts and the ideological warfare against the "expropriated poor" accompanying them. Regardless of which side one was on, however, nothing less than a "redefinition of agrarian property itself" was at issue, as E. P. Thompson underscores: "But what was 'perfectly proper' in terms of capitalist property-relations involved, none the less, a rupture of the traditional integument of village custom and of right: and the social violence of enclosure consisted precisely in the drastic, total imposition upon the village of capitalist property-definitions" (*The Making of the English Working Class* 238).⁹

Finally, Marx directly links the expropriation of land and the expropriation of people, tying rural laborers and urban workers to one another, and making clear that enclosure and industrial revolution go hand in hand. In an earlier passage, for instance, he stresses, "Nowhere does the antagonistic character of capitalist production and accumulation assert itself more brutally than in the progress of English agriculture (including cattle-breeding) and the retrogression of the English agricultural labourer" (*Capital* I 828). This "progress," moreover, has a long history, which Marx traces in the chapters following his chapter on the "secret" of primitive accumulation. Writing about Francis Bacon's history of Henry VII, Marx notes how the very arguments Bacon uses to contest the increased frequency of enclosures in the fifteenth century and to support an act signed by Henry VII in 1489 to forbid "depopulating inclosures, and depopulating pasturage" in fact highlight why, in the end, these arguments were unsuccessful. "Bacon, without knowing it" Marx wryly comments,

> reveals to us the secret of their [small farmers' and peasants'] lack of success. "The device of King Henry VII," says Bacon . . . "was profound and admirable, in making farms and houses of husbandry of a standard; that is, maintained with such a proportion of land unto them as may breed a subject to live in convenient plenty and no servile condition, and to keep the plough in the hands of the owners and not mere hirelings." (*Capital* I 880)

But of course, Marx adds, "What the capitalist system demanded was the reverse of this: a degraded and almost servile condition of the mass of the people, their transformation into mercenaries, and the transformation of their means of labour into capital" (881). This history, "the history of [these 'freed' men's] expropriation," as Marx powerfully describes it, "is written in the annals of mankind in strokes of blood and fire" (*Capital* I 875).¹⁰

It is a history regularly repeated over the course of the enclosure movement, albeit with a number of identifiable peaks. Linebaugh identifies Bacon's moment and the "Elizabethan leap" (when land ownership shifts from the church and monasteries to private ownership—an event to which I will return further on) as one key peak in this history, with another peak in the eighteenth and nineteenth centuries. He dramatically characterizes the enclosures that followed King Henry III's dissolution of the Catholic monasteries in 1536 as "a massive act of state-sponsored privatization. More than any other act in the long history of enclosure," Linebaugh continues, "it made the English land a commodity" (*The Magna Carta Manifesto* 49). In *Empire of Capital*, Ellen Meiksins Wood also emphasizes the singular role of the state. "The effect of English social property relations," she asserts, "was to create that kind of market dependence [in which the market acts as a 'regulator' or functions as an imperative], polarizing the rural population into those who succeeded in competitive conditions, and those who failed to do so and were driven off the land" (17). This process was simply not possible "without the support of the state, which, by means of judicial interventions and legislation, helped to make property rights market-dependent. From the beginning, too, intervention by the state has been needed to create and maintain not only the system of property but also the system of propertylessness" (18).[11] The role of the state is clearly on display in the period from 1750 to 1850, which, as the historian J. M. Neeson argues, bookends the first wave of parliamentary enclosures and the doing away of common right. Like Marx, Neeson links the expropriation of land and people, noting that, in this intense period of enclosure, "only common right stood between the survival of the common-field peasantry and its proletarianization" (34).

The numbers alone bear out these claims. If enclosure in the sixteenth century was largely "by agreement" and, in fact, condemned by both the church and the government, who sided with the commoners' claims regarding "common rights," by the 1750s the government had taken the lead and over the course of the period 1750–1830 passed over four thousand Acts of Enclosure, resulting in over 21 percent of the land (approximately 6.8 million acres) being enclosed. As Neeson puts it, "Much of England was still open in 1700; but most of it was enclosed by 1840" (5). By the end of the century virtually all the open fields in Britain were gone. How this looked and was experienced of course varied from parish to parish, region to region within Britain, the detailed social history of which, in recent years, has been increasingly well documented, as new archival research and new access to archives, as well as a "localist" turn within nineteenth-century scholarship, have brought renewed attention to the individual particulars of enclosure and to individual landowners. These "small stories" are indispensable to the social history of enclosure, as are the individual responses to enclosure that works such as Cobbett's rides or Clare's poetry record. At the same time, however, these local histories risk losing the long view in their necessarily synchronic approach to history. In contrast, a reading across an extended swath of time and space—marked by the very sort of unevenness that defines the history of enclosure—allows for a diachronic reading of history in which structural determinations and limitations (of geography, of capitalist logic) can emerge and be made visible, even as they seem to defy historical representation by dint of their scope, nature, and lack of "eventfulness."

The historical record regarding the actual parliamentary acts that destroyed the commons, as well as forests and wastes, and the riots that often followed are well documented and provide us with a good picture of what the Annales School refers to as the history of "events" (historians and sociologists such as Fernand Braudel and Francois Simiand call this *histoire évènementielle* or "evental history") rather than long-term structures (Braudel 25–54). Representative, and perhaps most well-known, are the Swing Riots of 1830 (so called in reference to the fictitious tenant farmer "Captain Swing," whose signature appended threatening letters to landowners) in which agricultural workers in Elham Valley, near Kent, destroyed threshing machines, burned ricks, smashed barns and workhouses, and maimed cattle—in short, attacked the visible signs of the new capitalist relations being imposed on agrarian production and rural life more broadly.[12] But as with the larger challenge to representing enclosure, these objects must also stand in, inadequately, for a centuries-long process of impoverishment and dispossession, an impoverishment no less recognized by lords than by commoners. Lord Carnarvon, for example, noted in Parliament in 1830 that enclosure, "by making the agricultural labourer dependent for the payment of his hardly-earned wages on poor-rates, miserably and churlishly doled out, had rendered the condition of the poor of the country more abject than that of the poor of any other nation . . . with the farmers . . . no longer able to feed and employ their labourers" (reported in Hansard). Or as the labor historians John and Barbara Hammond put it, "Before enclosure the cottager was a labourer with land; after enclosure he was a labourer without land." The Hammonds also detail the specific changes in the crucial sixty-year period from 1770 to 1830, changes that surely resonate with neoliberal doctrines today and their effects on working conditions across the economy. Such changes included the move from yearly contracts to shorter- and shorter-term contracts of as little as a day; from payment in kind, which included meals, to payment in cash; from working alongside one's employer to being a "free labourer" with no security. Likewise, existing social safety nets such as poor relief were gradually reduced, and the burden of church titles increased, as they, like other forms of payment, moved from in kind to cash allotments that were very high for the poor. All of these factors came into play in the Swing Riots, in which rioters demanded higher wages, lower tithes, and the destruction of threshing machines; all of these actions were replayed countless times during the *longue durée* of enclosure (see Figure 2).

As my reference to the *longue durée* of enclosure suggests, however, enclosure was at once a series of discrete events and something akin to an "attritional catastrophe"—the term Nixon uses to describe catastrophes such as climate change that "overspill clear boundaries in time and space" and "are marked above all by displacements—temporal, geographical, rhetorical, and technological displacements that simplify violence and underestimate, in advance and in retrospect, the human and environmental costs" (7).[13] In short, the changes wrought by enclosure were violent, and its long-term human and environmental costs high—and in no way captured by events such as parliamentary acts or riots. Enclosure, in essence, did away with an entire way of life, and to recognize this is not synonymous with being nostalgic for an older traditional mode of living now lost. Rather, such a recognition begins to address the constitutive violence of capitalism and the often "uneventful" local ways in which it was resisted and alternative forms of life fought for. Neeson, for example, argues in this vein that rural laborers have been seen as passive in the face of enclosure largely because their actions were under the radar of conventional

FIGURE 2. Henry Heath, "Swing!" (1830). Source: © The Trustees of the British Museum. Reprinted with permission.

historians, even left-wing ones such as Neeson's own mentor, Thompson. Because opposition to enclosure often occurred at the most local level, innumerable campaigns on the part of commoners—ranging from refusals to consent and foot-dragging to petitions and threats to enclosers and/or their property—were left unrecorded, leaving a spotty archive, especially when it comes to understanding village arguments for common right and the patient, slogging work and strategies for preserving it (think community involvement today). "The unfolding village history of argument and obstruction that this longevity represents," Neeson argues, "is as instructive as the parliamentary record of petitions against enclosure and refusals to sign Bills, and the incidence of riots in enclosing villages—the kind of opposition historians have looked at most closely. If we neglect it we get a truncated view of protest, and we lose the history of wars of attrition waged skilfully over a decade or longer" (262). Similarly, we lose the kind of history Cobbett narrates, a history from below, in which the inevitability of capitalist production as the only way forward is not a given.[14] Common right in particular, as Neeson underscores, protected laborers from "wage dependence," thereby granting them a significant independence—from compulsory labor and its attendant structures of time, leisure, value, community, consumption, and property relations (41–42).

Crucially, there was also a gendered aspect to this socioeconomic and physical or spatial independence and its loss. As Silvia Federici writes, "The social function of the commons was especially important for women, who, having less title to land and less social power, were more dependent on them for their subsistence, autonomy, and sociality" (*Caliban and the Witch* 71). The issue of sociality in particular was not insignificant insofar as the commons was "the center of social life, the place where [women] convened, exchanged news, took advice, and where a women's viewpoint on communal events, autonomous from that of men, could form" (71–72, citing Clark). This loss of autonomy, and of the "web of cooperative relations" that the commons embodied, led as well to the gendered division between productive and reproductive labor as the economy moved from a subsistence-oriented to a market-oriented economy: "In the new monetary regime, only production-for-market was defined as a value-creating activity, whereas the reproduction of the worker began to be considered as valueless from an economic viewpoint and even ceased to be considered as work" (74–75). The ultimate result then of this "separation of production from reproduction," which followed directly from the privatization of land and the destruction of the commons, was the creation of "a class of proletarian women who were as dispossessed as men but, unlike their male relatives, in a society that was becoming increasingly monetized, had almost no access to wages, thus being forced into a condition of chronic poverty, economic dependence, and invisibility as workers" (75).

Again, the consequences of enclosure, and the specifically gendered differentiation of wage-laborers, need not lead to nostalgia for the past but instead can point toward a different future, in which new visions of the commons would be possible—at a time when our respective fates as members of a fully global world are more closely tied to one another than ever before. It does mean, however, that our conceptions of the commons must account for these gender differences—not to mention a whole host of other differences, from race and ethnicity to sexual orientation and class—and their overcoming within any future global commons. In particular, a feminist commons brings to the fore the necessity of envisioning and organizing new forms of social reproduction, for, as Federici insists, "we cannot build an alternative society and a strong self-reproducing movement unless we redefine our reproduction in a more cooperative way and put an end to the separation between the personal and the political, and between political activism and the reproduction of everyday life." Feminist struggles in the past to resist the destruction of communal or collective forms of everyday life, and the legacy and continuance of those struggles today, are and have been "an essential part of our resistance to capitalism"; they highlight the inextricably and necessarily twinned goals for any genuinely common future of "[undoing] the gendered architecture of our lives and . . . [reconstructing] our homes and lives as commons" ("Feminism").

Land rights and common rights, Linebaugh reminds us, have historically been connected to political rights. In *The Magna Carta Manifesto*, Linebaugh stresses that *two* charters made up Magna Carta: the charter we all know establishing juridical and individual political rights and the Charter of the Forest, guaranteeing the right to commoning (recovered in 1217), which in turn recognized subsistence rights, for example, the right to widow's estovers (wood needed for housing repairs, implements, and so on) and to subsistence usufructs (the temporary use of another person's land). Against the prevailing tendency to see commoning provisions as out of date, Linebaugh insists that they are more relevant than ever in the current neoliberal era. The parallel between economic and political rights in Magna Carta underscores for Linebaugh that

> political and legal rights can exist only on an economic foundation. To be free citizens we must be equal producers and consumers. What I shall call the *commons*—the theory that vests all property in the community and organizes labor for the common benefit of all—must exist in both juridical forms and day-to-day reality. (6)

It also speaks to a post-9/11 world in which Magna Carta liberties are at risk and need to be seen as inseparable from a planetary common:

> Capitalists and the World Bank would like us to employ commoning as a means to socialize poverty and hence to privatize wealth. The commoning of the past, our forebears' previous labor, survives as a legacy in the form of *capital* and this too must be reclaimed as part of our constitution. Chapter 61 [re: lawful rebellion in Magna Carta] giving liberty to the *communa totius terrae* provides the right of resistance to the reality of a planet of slums, gated communities, and terror without end" (279).[15]

Linebaugh here echoes the early Marx in his recognition that all capital is the congealed labor of past generations and appeals to the forgotten Charter of the Forest as a means forward in its invocation of the right to resist economic injustice. In this formulation, then, the commons becomes an activity; the labor of our forebears—commoning—has not only literally produced the world we live in but remains to be reclaimed in the present as communal rather than private wealth, in the commons rather than in capital.

## Representing the Commons and Enclosure

How then would eighteenth- and nineteenth-century writers grapple with the representational challenges of the *longue durée* of enclosure and the slow violence it entailed? Where did they represent the history and, in some cases, immediate experience of the destruction of the common? What were the larger implications of these representations for notions of the common and commoners? These are obviously enormous questions, which I will address over the course of this book. Here, I want simply to address some key concepts and representations of the commons and enclosure that set the stage for nineteenth-century writers and their respective invocations of the common as at once a reflection on a disappearing past and a vision of an alternative future.

## Property, Overpopulation, and the Poor

Advocates of enclosure certainly mounted their own case to support the destruction of the commons. At the center of these accounts were the intertwined issues of private property, fears of overpopulation, and the management of the poor. The influence of John Locke in these debates is inestimable: his labor theory of property defines open or undeveloped land as empty—*terra nullius*—and establishes property as a natural right.[16] Once conceived of as empty or unowned, land is made available for individual cultivation and ownership; what "Man . . . Improves" becomes "his Property" for Locke.[17] Perceived as unowned land in need of cultivation or ripe for more efficient methods of production as an "unused" or underused resource, the commons is essentially there for the taking, a vision that justifies and sustains not only the enclosures of the nineteenth-century countryside but European colonial and imperial projects more generally. In "Of Property," Locke includes the following qualifications regarding use. First, he enumerates the limitations of use, adding, "As much as anyone can make use of to any advantage of life before it spoils, so much by his labor he may fix a property in; whatever is beyond this, is more than his share, and belongs to others" (II. 5. 31).[18] Additionally, when he addresses property in relation to agriculture specifically, he clarifies that the enclosing and cultivating of property of which he speaks will not jeopardize the common good, "since there was still enough, and as good left; and more than the as yet unprovided could use." Premising his vision of private property on the analogy that "[n]o body could consider himself injured by the drinking of another man, though he took a good draught, who had a whole river of the same water left to quench his thirst" (II. 5.33.), Locke at once raises and skirts the contradiction at the heart of enclosure and its justification in the name of private property, namely that private property entails by its very logic the theft of the commons and the commonwealth.[19] Similarly, Locke claims that "he that leaves as much as another can make use of, does as good as take nothing at all" and further, that those dispossessed of the commons can in no way feel injured by those doing the dispossessing because, Locke assumes, there is always "enough" land. This claim, however, belies the fundamental dynamic of enclosure, namely its imperative to privatize commonly held lands and resources, and perpetuates the myth that the supply of land is effectively infinite.[20] Finally, as David Bollier argues, "the logic of res nullius justifies unchecked private plunder" without regard to prior inhabitants of the land and ecological integrity:

> Thus even though indigenous peoples and peasants have managed land, water, fisheries, forests and other natural resources as commons from time immemorial—without formal legal titles—Western imperialists have taken comfort in the legal fiction that *the land doesn't belong to anyone—so we can march right in and take it!* In this way, Locke's theory of private property deliberately ignores the prior use rights and customs of indigenous peoples, the rights of future generations and the inherent needs of nature itself. Using Lockean logic, it has become customary to talk about oceans, outer space, biodiversity and the Internet as if they too are resources that belong to no one. (*Think Like a Commoner* 105–6)[21]

Despite Locke's assurances that the common good was not in danger and that there was enough land and resources to go around, later accounts in support of enclosure whip up the diametrically opposed fear that overpopulation will deplete the land and resources—and rely on the benefits of private property to make their case. Bolstered by Malthusian claims, this line of argument targets the inefficiency of the open-field system and common rights and raises the specter of overuse (of commonly held resources as opposed to land held in private hands), which in turn will lead to the utter depletion of resources and the inability to feed a growing population. For Malthus, a "surplus population" inevitably results from the differential rates of growth of the population and of the food supply: whereas population increases at a geometric rate, food production increases at an arithmetic rate.[22] Within such a calculus, the poor suffer the most. While the rich have access to what Malthus called "preventive checks" to population—such as birth control—the overpopulated poor are at the mercy of "positive checks," namely, war, disease, and most prominently famine, to keep their numbers down. As Allen MacDuffie bluntly puts it, "Malthus was wrong about quite a lot, and his arguments about scarcity were inflected by his commitment to a ruinous *laissez-faire* economic doctrine. In his work, the burden and the moral responsibility fall upon the backs of the poor and almost nowhere else" (*Victorian Literature, Energy and the Ecological Imagination* 3). The Malthusian emphasis on overpopulation had a direct impact on thinking about the English Poor Laws, for part of this argument involved the belief that keeping the poor alive through poor relief only exacerbated the problem of a "surplus" or surfeit of poor people. Fittingly, Charles Dickens connected overpopulation and the poor laws in an introductory comment by Ebenezer Scrooge: refusing to contribute to a "fund to buy the Poor some meat and drink, and means of warmth" and invoking the presence of workhouses for those in need in the opening stave of *A Christmas Carol*, Scrooge retorts, "If they would rather die . . . they had better do it, and decrease the surplus population" (39).

Over the course of the eighteenth and nineteenth centuries, the conditions for receiving poor relief were made increasingly stringent, as workhouses replaced outdoor relief and the poor were viewed as morally flawed. Again, Locke plays a part here. As Anthony Brundage writes,

> [B]y the early eighteenth century attitudes towards the poor were beginning to harden in some quarters, as reflected in the views of commentators like John Locke, Bernard Mandeville, and Daniel Defoe. Labourers, increasingly seen as lazy, shiftless, and dissolute, could only be kept to their tasks by the relentless pressure of necessity. . . . In such circumstances the deterrent aspect of the workhouse came to the fore, and seemed an effective safeguard against the utter breakdown of labour discipline. (11–12)

Although put into practice less harshly in Locke's day, the workhouse test codified in the Parliament Act of 1723 predates the New Poor Law in 1834 by a century. This shift in policy, as Brundage argues, was "far-reaching": "Under its operation, poor law officials no longer needed to inquire into an applicant's character or situation. An 'offer' of the house would function as a self-acting test of destitution, a doctrine in tune with an advancing free market ethos" (12).[23] As we saw earlier in Wood's characterization of the state's need to ensure that laborers remain market dependent, the poor laws became instrumental in the "system of propertylessness" that sustains this free market ethos.[24] Later events such as the Swing Riots, also tied to the twin processes of enclosure and industrialization as we have seen, were concerned with the punitive measures being enacted against the poor. Far from mitigating their grievances, however, the government's response to the rioters was essentially to batten down the hatches in order to prevent such riots in the future. "The labourers," Brundage notes, "may have been partially chastened by the courts, but there was further disciplinary work to be done. And that required major reform of the poor laws" (60). The central purposes of the reformed bill were to make poor relief ever more demoralizing and difficult to obtain; to single out unwed mothers along Malthusian and moral grounds; and to guarantee that conditions within the workhouses, which were organized around Benthamite principles of panoptical discipline, were made unlivable.[25] In short, to echo Scrooge, if poor laborers would rather die than go to the workhouse, as these measures all encouraged, they should.

These issues concerning the poor, private property, and fears of overpopulation all come together in the context of enclosure and its processes of primitive accumulation, sometimes directly and sometimes indirectly. The means by which they fuel attacks on the commons is perhaps most powerfully and explicitly connected in the British economic writer William Foster Lloyd's *Two Lectures on the Checks to Population*, published in 1833. In Lecture 1, Lloyd addresses the difference between the commons and enclosed land, asking, "Why are the cattle on a common so puny and stunted? Why is the common itself so bare-worn, and cropped so differently from the adjoining inclosures?" (30). After dismissing the possibility that the difference could be the result of the land's poor fertility, Lloyd wagers that the difference comes down to a question of use, the nature of the ownership of the land, and what he refers to as a field's "point of saturation." Contrasting the use of an enclosed pasture to a common, he speculates that

> if a person puts more cattle into his own field, the amount of the subsistence which they consume is all deducted from that which was at the command, of his original stock.... But if he puts more cattle on a common, the food which they consume forms a deduction which is shared between all the cattle, as well that of others as his own, in proportion to their number, and only a small part of it is taken from his own cattle. (31)

Inevitably, for Lloyd, the common therefore reaches a point of saturation in which the cattle stock increases to such an extent that it "would be made to press much more forcibly against the means of subsistence" (32).

Following in the footsteps of Locke and Malthus, Lloyd raises the specter of the overuse of the commons, which, in his account and those of others, naturally leads to what the ecologist Garrett Hardin in 1968 famously called "the tragedy of the commons"—namely, the inevitable depletion of the commons by common rights and common use. In fact, Hardin relies on Lloyd's account in his own argument against the commons. For both of them, individual self-interest invariably supplants considerations of the common good, which in turn results in the overexploitation of the commons. Hardin's explanation echoes Lloyd's as he too begins dramatically with a hypothetical lone herdsmen, who, in his attempts "as a rational being" to "maximize his gain" incrementally adds one animal after another to the common land. "Picture a pasture open to all," Hardin conjures, and then add a group of herdsmen all acting "rationally," and the logical outcome—what Hardin names the "inherent logic of the commons"—is overgrazing and the eventual destruction of the commons. "Therein is the tragedy. Each man is locked into a system that compels him to increase his herd without limit—in a world that is limited. Ruin is the destination toward which all men rush, each pursuing his own best interest in a society that believes in the freedom of the commons. Freedom in a commons brings ruin to all" (1244).

A limited world confronted with what Hardin naturalizes as unlimited self-interest—"as a rational being, each herdsmen seeks to maximize his gain"—can only in such a scenario lead to ruin for all, a dire claim that powerfully sets the commons and common pool resources in opposition not only to individual interests and private property but to the survival of humans and the world *tout court*. Weighing these opposing interests, Hardin conclusively states that despite the fact that "our legal system of private property plus inheritance is unjust. . . . The alternative of the commons is too horrifying to contemplate. Injustice is preferable to total ruin" (1247). The power of Hardin's claim is such that, "for most of us, because of Hardin," as Derek Wall recognizes, "commons almost automatically mean tragedy" (19).[26]

### An Ecology of the Unenclosed

But neither in the past nor in our own present has this been the only narrative of the commons.[27] We began with John Clare's lived experience of the commons and the enclosing of the commons, and the idea that his poetry narrates "a different ecology . . . dependent on the unenclosed" (Linebaugh, (18–19). In poems such as "The Village Minstrel" and "The Moors," Clare's descriptions of his "open-field sense of space" (Barrell 103) revolve (literally) around the intimate connections between the social and the environmental and the actual circular organization of open-field parishes. Clare himself writes in "Sighing for Retirement," a poem composed while he was confined in the private High Beach asylum near Epping Forest (1837–41), that "I found the poems in the fields,/And only wrote them down."[28] In "The Village Minstrel" (1821), an early, autobiographical poem, Clare speaks of sitting on a molehill in his native Helpston

> To take a prospect of the circling scene,
> Marking how much the cottage roof's-thatch brown
> Did add its beauty to the budding green
> Of sheltering trees it humbly peeped between—
> The stone-rocked wagon with its rumbling sound,
> The windmill's sweeping sails at distance seen,

> And every form that crowds the circling round,
> Where the sky stooping seems to kiss the meeting ground. (*"I AM"* 35)²⁹

This "circling scene," soon to be destroyed "as curst improvement 'gan his fields inclose" (35), was rife with sound and song as "woodlarks carolled from each stumpy bush" (36), and a circular architecture with "lanes in nature's freedom dropt" and "paths that every valley wound" (36) open to exactly what the narrator is doing, namely roaming (to recall Bate's notion of the "right to roam").³⁰ Significantly this landscape is by no means devoid of people: the roof of the cottage adds to rather than detracts from "the budding green/Of sheltering trees it humbly peeped between"; "stone-rocked" wagons and windmills form part of the scene; and the narrator's wanderings through the landscape tie narrator and landscape to one another in an ever-changing relationship: "Surrounded thus [in a "new-revealing world"], not paradise more sweet,/Enthusiasm made his soul to glow;/His heart with wild sensations used to beat;/As nature seemly sang, his mutterings would repeat."

Likewise, in "The Moors," Clare recalls the "moory ground . . . Bespread with rush and one eternal green," and how

> Unbounded freedom ruled the wandering scene
> Nor fence of ownership crept in between
> To hide the prospect of the following eye—
> Its only bondage was the circling sky. (*"I AM"* 89)

This freedom is equally the freedom of the sheep and cows and larks and the "glad shepherd" and the poet as a boy; the fences of ownership equally imperil "men and flocks":

> Fence now meets fence in owners' little bounds
> Of field and meadow, large as garden grounds,
> In little parcels little minds to please
> With men and flocks imprisoned, ill at ease. (*"I AM"* 90)

Patrick Bresnihan characterizes the reciprocal relations threatened by fence meeting fence in terms of what he calls the "manifold commons":

"no single 'nature'" but instead "ongoing relations that constituted many different natures" (74). Significantly, this vision of "forms of common life" is not premised on the assumption of scarcity, which subtends Lockean property relations and Lloyd's and Hardin's Malthusian arguments against the commons (74). Instead Clare's poems gesture toward "a vision of the manifold commons which takes us away from the mutually reinforcing narratives of scarcity, liberal political economy and enclosure" (89). At the heart of Clare's poetry of protest rests a critique of property relations premised on ownership and a recognition of the different relationships an ecology of the unenclosed might proffer between individuals and the environment, identity and ownership, the one and the many, scarcity and excess, and their representation in poesy. Hugh Haughton aptly names Clare's practice "open field poetics" (66): for him, "The Mores" [also spelled "The Moors"] and "The Nightingale's Nest" exemplify this poetics, with the former being a "defiant celebration of the mobility of what it calls the 'following eye,' thriving on the inexplicit analogy between the unenclosed landscape of Clare's early life and the openness of the poem," and the latter "another instance of the 'following eye'; it gives us temporary access to the nightingale's world in all its privileged solitude—but leaves it intact" (66). Clare's "open field poetics" is equally an open field politics in the sense that it keeps the future open: it permits us to look forward from our own present rather than only backward to some lost pre-enclosure, seemingly pristine moment.[31]

Numerous poems of Clare's not only provide visions of an alternative ecology but also directly address the enclosing of open fields and wastes and the destruction of "forms of common life" and the commons. In "Helpstone" and "Helpstone Green," Clare laments that the landscape of his youth no longer exists, remarking in the latter poem, "The king kups yellow shades and all/Shall never more be seen/For all the cropping that does grow/Will so efface the scene,/That after times will hardly know/It ever was a green" (*John Clare* 63); in "The Lament of Swordy Well," Clare, in the voice of the titular piece of land—"I am the last/Of all the fields that fell;/My name is nearly all that's left/Of what was Swordy Well" ("*I AM*" 219)—tells the story of enclosure, observing,

> There was time my bit of ground
> Made freemen of the slave;
> The ass no pindar'd dare to pound
> When I his supper gave;
> The gypsies' camp was not afraid,
> I made his dwelling free,
> Till vile enclosure came and made
> A parish slave of me. ("*I AM*" 218)

And, after describing the "unbounded freedom" before enclosure in "The Moors," Clare likens the enclosure of the land to that of the land's laborers: "Enclosure came and trampled on the grave/Of labour's rights and left the poor a slave" ("*I AM*" 89). In this landscape, gypsies lie on the outskirts or margins, unenclosed and free—"The gypsies further on sojourn,/No parish bonds they like" ("*I AM*" 219)—and Swordy Well is "of all the fields" the "last/That my own face can tell," the only thing left after enclosure being the name of Swordy Well. For Clare, enclosure as a common lived experience is in the end not only the loss of an entire way of life but also a profound alteration of the very conditions of possibility for a common life, embodied in a view of land and labor that wasn't so much unclassed as unbound insofar as the world itself had a different shape and mobility—circular rather than linear, home to gypsies and wanderers, and "no friend to lawless work" nor "strife to buy and sell" ("*I AM*" 219). With his precise attention to detail and language—birds "flusker" and "flirt"—and the slow violence he pinpoints in the most particular and far-reaching incursions into a landscape and life, Clare both minutely and expansively names the changes that too smoothly fall under the heading of the move from a commons to a commodity culture.

My point here is not to give a full account of Clare and his moment so much as to adumbrate a possible politics of the commons and its conditions of possibility that ultimately exceed Clare's own moment.[32] Clare's response to enclosure is both deeply personal and illustrative insofar as it beckons toward alternative modes of relating to what, as Clare stresses time and time again, is a *social* geography. In its interplay between the human and nonhuman, individuals and the trees, birds, and fields, Clare's view of the "new-revealing world" need not be limited to Helpston and the attachment of place.[33] While for Clare, certainly, the particularities and specificities of Helpston were essential to his poetic vision, that vision equally extends beyond Helpston, as Sinclair and others have shown. Central to Clare's embodiment of a unenclosed, open-field view of the world is the reality of a different form of identity and an instantiation of a radical relationality or interdependence. Nineteenth-century novelists will continue to develop the notion of an unenclosed world as they reinvent the commons and the possibilities that might come with a commitment to the common—be it in the form of the common good, the commonwealth, common characters, or other myriad forms of the commons. As with Clare, nineteenth-century novelists will do so in full recognition of how the very notion of place and space and belonging is being radically transformed over the course of their own lifetimes.[34]

## Enclosure and Fossil Capital

With the benefit of hindsight, there can be no doubt that enclosure would eventually be realized on a global scale, radically transforming the world in ways that mirror the dynamics and experiences of enclosure within nineteenth-century imperial Britain. As Davis convincingly argues in *Planet of Slums*, many of the features of the original "event" of enclosure persist today around the globe: the conversion of public or common lands into private lands; the dispossession of local (often Indigenous) populations and their displacement from those lands; the "liberation" of the labor of those populations and their subjection to compulsory wage labor; the near-total destruction of ways of life intimately bound to the land; and the massive demographic shift from the country to the city. This history, as we can see in ways those living through its earlier incarnations could not, now extends to our lived environment: "[T]he carbon-saturated atmosphere we breathe today is, in both metaphorical and brutely chemical senses, the atmosphere of the British Empire" (Hensley and Steer 3). In formulating this history thus, Hensley and Steer aim to "coordinate the 'ecological' and the 'imperial' so as to see these two stories as one," and to show how "the nineteenth century . . . stands as the origin of not just the irreversible ecological degradation we have inherited from our forebears, but also the global interconnection and vast asymmetries of power that are the legacies of the British Empire in the present" (2–3). This "world-spanning" story, and the coincident development of our fossil economy and the climate change it brings in its wake, has its roots in the social and political history of enclosure, an event of such scale, duration, and reach that it can be hard to fathom, let alone represent.

Certainly the intimate causal relations between enclosure, the development of industrial capitalism, and global warming were not yet visible to those living then. Even today, four centuries later, the nature of these events and conditions make any attempt at a comprehensive view difficult. Andreas Malm opens *Fossil Capital* with the following scenario in order to highlight the particular challenges climate change raises in relation to issues of cause and effect:

> Global warming is the unintended by-product par excellence. A cotton manufacturer of early nineteenth-century Lancashire who decided to forgo his old waterwheel and invest in a steam engine, erect a chimney and order coal from a nearby pit did not, in all likelihood, entertain the possibility that this act could have any kind of relationship to the extent of Arctic sea ice, the salinity of Nile Delta soil, the altitude of the Maldives, the frequency of droughts on the Horn of Africa, the diversity of amphibian species in Central American rain forests, the availability of water in Asian rivers or, for that matter the risk of flooding along the Thames and the English coastline. (1–2)

The intricate and largely invisible connections Malm charts between industry and ecology, capital and climate—unified under the concept of fossil capital—underscore the twinned nature of the crises we currently face: namely global capitalism and climate change.[35]

For our purposes, Malm's history of fossil capital's development highlights how enclosure not only fundamentally changed the British landscape and land, labor, and property relations but also helped to "free" the fossil fuels that power our current fossil economy. For as land ownership shifted from the hands of feudal lords and the church to private interests during the "Elizabethan leap," it was not only the land but also the resources below the ground that were part and parcel of the "primitive" or capital accumulation Marx theorizes in *Capital*. After showing how the move to steam power in Britain was as much about controlling labor as it was about efficiency, and arose "as a form of power exercised by some people against others" (36), Malm connects the "fossil economy" that steam engenders to the enclosure movement, dating the mining of underground resources to the period during Elizabeth's reign: "Lords would simply appropriate land where they suspected that minerals lay buried. Several of the most high-profile enclosures of the seventeenth century were undertaken to prevent any interference with extraction, and much like their sheep walk twins, the coal encroachments provoked furious resistance" (323). Also "like their sheep walk twins," these encroachments essentially destroyed rural life and the social relations of the village, as copyholders feared the loss of their land should coal be discovered underground (324), and enforced the power of the state to separate laborers from the land:

> Already at this stage, landlords inclined to accumulate capital had secured the backing of a formidable state apparatus, thrashing the resistance in a thousand disputes; by the end of the seventeenth century, exclusive property to coal-rich lands had been conclusively enforced, the customary tenants and commoners deprived of virtually all of their rights. (324)[36]

Our current climate history is thus very much a product of the fossil economy whose origins lie with the enclosure movement; a history that can seem very far away, as Linebaugh suggests, has indeed come home ("Enclosures" 26).

Even without the terminology of "climate change" or "global warming," nineteenth-century writers were nonetheless grappling with these profound changes to the environment and yet still aware of the older relationships to land and property, and with them an alternative set of relations, both social and historical, inhering in common rights and the commons more generally.[37] Importantly, "one of the most insidious things about enclosures is how they eradicate the culture of commons and our memory of them.... The impersonal, individualistic, transactional-based ethic of the market economy becomes the new normal." For nineteenth-century writers following in the wake of Clare and his fellow Romantic poets enclosures had not yet fully rendered "the history and memory of the commons . . . invisible" (Bollier, *Think Like a Commoner* 79). Poised on the cusp of a full-scale commodity culture, however, realist writers also recognized that carrying this history forward would necessarily entail inventing a new "culture of commons" rather than recovering the lost commons. Still in the presence or with a memory of the literal commons on the one hand, and in the midst of a quickly consolidating capitalist system premised on private rather than collective property relations on the other hand, nineteenth-century realist writers, as we will see, were uniquely positioned to narrate a history of the commons able to incorporate both event and advent, past and future, and their own place within an ever fleeting common present.

CHAPTER 2

# Dickensian Types and a Culture of the Commons

ON THE FACE OF IT, Charles Dickens would not be the first novelist to come to mind when thinking about the history of enclosure and its afterlife.¹ He is often referenced as one of the few nineteenth-century realist novelists to set the majority of his novels in the city, and hence only to treat peripherally the towns beyond London, let alone the countryside—those are the places his characters come *from* to go *to* the city. Dickens's fiction is so tied to the city that Williams says about his writing, "It does not matter which way we put it: the experience of the city is the fictional method; or the fictional method is the experience of the city" (*The Country and the City* 154).² But to recall Mike Davis's prediction (discussed in Chapter 1), our present moment is witnessing the end of "the global countryside," so ways forward beyond the old and new enclosures and their afterlives will necessarily entail a reckoning with urban life and its forms of sociality. This is where, this chapter wagers, Dickens is revelatory. In particular, this chapter turns to Dickens's novelistic universe for a vision of an urban commons peopled by a distinctive Dickensian form of character that is collective in nature and intimately tied to his minor characters and a radical notion of type. Dickens's creation of an urban commons presciently anticipates Peter Linebaugh's recent demand that the "city itself must be commonized." While in our present context this is seen necessarily as a global project, "since the city, in the sense of law, force and commodity, has abolished the countryside commons and the 'bourgeois' nations destroyed the 'barbarian' ones" (*Stop, Thief!* 40), in Dickens it remains more circumscribed, as he tends to keep his sights set primarily on London and its environs. This does not, however, mitigate the force and foresight of Dickens's many articulations of the urban commons, but instead clarifies the need, today, for such a commons to encompass nothing short of the globe itself.³

In his response to *The Old Curiosity Shop*, William Thackeray declared that he "never read the Nelly part . . . more than once; whereas I have Dick Swiveller and the Marchioness by heart" ("Jerome Paturot" 387–88). This might seem to say more about poor little Nell and her long history of mockery at the hands of critics than about Dick Swiveller and the Marchioness. But as I will argue in this chapter, Thackeray is by no means alone when he identifies the life and appeal of Dickens's work in his minor rather than his major characters or, more broadly, his cast of eccentrics. Indeed, both in Dickens's time and our own, it is these characters, in both senses of the term, who largely define who Dickens is and the kind of writer he was.

These eccentric characters have consigned Dickens to a remarkably mixed reception history, which has at its center the varied critical assessments of these self-same characters. In his *A Course of English Literature* (1866), the Scottish novelist and journalist James Hannay, for example, lists the "Wellers, Skimpoles, Cuttles, Dombeys, Pecksniffs," and other such Dickensian figures as those who "most strike us." He acknowledges these "figures" as "more or less irregular specimens of humanity," refers to them as individuals not a "species," and, important for our purposes, emphasizes the role of memory in his assessment, prefacing his descriptions with "[i]f we turn over in our memories the figures of his fiction," what we find are characters that are "not unnatural at heart, but neither are they 'representative men,' such as occur in a few of the leading fictions of the world" (322). Likewise, Edwin P. Whipple, in "The Genius of Dickens," writes that "the reality of his personages comes from the vividness of his conceptions, and not from any photographic quality in his method of representation" (548). An unsigned review in the *London Review* (October 28, 1865) refers to Dickens's "power of creating characters which have, so to speak, an overplus of vitality," and goes on to say that "we perceive them to be full of potential capacities—of undeveloped action. They have the substance and freedom of actual existences. . . ." An unsigned review of *Our Mutual Friend* highlights, in particular, the Veneerings, the Podsnaps, the Lady Tippineses, the invisible Lord Snigsworth, the Brewers, Boots, and Buffers as "expressing in their persons the voice of society" ("Mr. Dickens's Romance" 459).

Negative reviews, too, stress the eccentricities at the heart of Dickens's characters, and weigh in as well on the question of their representativeness. To stay with *Our Mutual Friend*, E. S. Dallas in *The Times* writes that "Twemlow is described as a piece of furniture that went upon easy castors; and all through the novel we have to think of him and his associates not as men with the hearts of men, but as a species of knick-knacks."[4] Dallas is quick, however, to acknowledge that despite this failing, "the carefulness of the writing . . . in that passage contains sufficient evidence that Mr. Dickens has spared no pain in the exhibition of such knick-knacks" (6).[5] Less generous in its assessment, an unsigned review in *Saturday Review* comments,

> Nobody is admitted to the distinction of a place in *Our Mutual Friend* who is at all like the beings who have a place in the universe. The characters may be divided into two sets of people—those whom the writer intended to be faithful copies of ordinary persons or classes of persons, and those whom even the author must in his inner consciousness know to be immeasurably remote from the common experience of human life. But, in one set of people as much as in the other, the writer seems to notice nothing which is not odd and surprising and absurd. The people whom he does, equally with those whom he does not, intend to be curious and abnormal, are caricatured in the most reckless way. ("Reviews" 612)

Finally, Henry James labels "every character . . . a bundle of eccentricities." Whereas in earlier novels Dickens at least produced "exaggerated statements of types that really existed," in *Our Mutual Friend* "there is not one [among the grotesque creatures] whom we can refer to as an existing type" (787). As he asks, "[W]here are those exemplars of sound humanity who should afford us the proper measure of their companion's variations?" Without such exemplars, James concludes, Dickens "has added nothing to our understanding of human character . . . he reconciles us to what is commonplace, and he reconciles us to what is odd. The value of the former service is questionable. . . . The value of the latter service is incontestable, and here Mr. Dickens is an honest, an admirable artist" (787). But, as James then asks, "[W]hat is the condition of the truly great novelist? For him there are no alternatives, for him there are no oddities, for him there is nothing outside of humanity" (787).

Whether they celebrate or criticize his method of characterization, Dickens's contemporaneous critics circle around the relationship between types or caricatures as "bundles[s] of eccentricities" and the realistic representation of "human character," "actual existences," and "common humanity." Notably, both major and minor characters can be eccentric types within these assessments, and type can indicate either the realism of characters, "expressing in their persons the voices of society," or their total unreality—or, in James's case, both, depending on whether such a type exists or not. There is a comfort, in other words, with type itself that no longer exists. In the midst of explaining his influential distinction between round and flat characters in relation to Dickens, E. M. Forster, for example, pauses to acknowledge that "critics who have their eyes fixed severely upon daily life . . . have very little patience with such [flat] renderings of human nature" (70). But, he continues, "part of the genius of Dickens is that he does use types and caricatures, people whom we recognize the instant they re-enter, and yet achieves effects that are not mechanical and a vision of humanity that is not shallow." The need to mount such a case in 1927 speaks to the degree to which Dickens's flat characters had fallen out of favor between his own time and Forster's. Despite his final appeal that Dickens's "success with types suggests that there may be more in flatness than the severer critics admit" (72), Forster's prefatory clause—"Those who dislike Dickens have an excellent case. He ought to be bad"—has largely held sway. The revival of Dickens's reputation from roughly the 1930s onward tended to stress the seriousness of his work rather than exploring the "more" in flatness.

Part of thinking alongside Dickens—and nineteenth-century novelists more generally—entails rethinking typification and its relation to realism. And for Dickens, in particular, it involves expanding our understanding of the possible forms of typification at hand. While type today is largely synonymous with Georg Lukács's notion of type (to which I will return), Dickens also drew significantly on an earlier tradition of typification and caricature, specifically, found in what has been referred to variously as eighteenth-century "characteristic writing," "eccentric biographies," and "character books."[6] These books provide anecdotal stories about remarkable or curious characters and personalities, both historical and fantastical. With titles such as *The New Wonderful Museum*, the "Eccentric Magazine," and *R.S. Kirby's Wonderful Museum* (the full title of which is *R.S. Kirby's Wonderful and Eccentric Museum or Magazine of Remarkable Characters; Including All the Curiosities of Nature and Art, from the Remotest Period to the Present Time, Drawn from Every Authentic Source*), they turn their human characters into a collection of displayed objects, bringing to the study of character a brute solidity that we tend to reserve for objects alone. Significantly, too, the same characters who reappeared in numerous editions of these texts became so well known that when Dickens in *Our Mutual Friend* draws on John Elwes and Daniel Dancer, two of the misers regularly catalogued in the eccentric biographies, to portray Noddy Boffin, his readers would likely have recognized the original stories. (Dickens himself owned, among other eccentric biographies, F. Somner Merryweather's *Lives and Anecdotes of Misers, or the Passion of Avarice Displayed*.)[7]

Together, these kinds of books participate in what Deidre Lynch identifies as an eighteenth-century "typographical culture," so named for the connections it draws between textual production and literal forms of type and typeface. According to Lynch, this culture had "an interest in the material grounds of meaning and a fascination with the puns that could link the person 'in' a text to the printed letters (alphabetic symbols, or literal 'characters' in another sense) that elaborated that text's surface" (5–6). Dickens, I will argue, shares this interest in "the material grounds of meaning" with his eighteenth-century predecessors, but with a twist: by virtue of his belatedness in relation to typographical culture—his coming to it, as it were, after or at least during its passing—his practice of material character is recuperative *and* utopian. Putting old books to new ends, Dickens creates nineteenth-century "character books" whose materialism aims to capture the common ground, literally and figuratively, of an increasingly urban, far-flung world.

Via the form of the character book, Dickens's world and its cast of characters refigure the common by linking it to the memorable. In the midst of a world in which levelling sameness is ascendant—a sameness captured in eighteenth-century character books by the deadening objectification the railway brings in its wake—Dickens's novels produce the "singular," the "remarkable," the "peculiar," and the "extraordinary," all key terms of character books. They do so both directly, as when the set of travelling characters in *The Old Curiosity Shop* could be lifted straight out of a character book, and indirectly, in Dickens's vision of character as simultaneously odd and commonplace, material and memorable, exceptional and part of a common culture.[8] Less a pitting of the "one *vs.* the many," as Alex Woloch formulates the struggle between protagonists and minor characters within the "distributed field of attention" (17) that constitutes a narrative's character system, the common in Dickens involves a dialectical and utopian relationship figured in terms of the one *as* the many, an active problematic that motivates him as he navigates the destruction of one way of life and the creation of a new one.

To return to Thackeray: his claim to know the parts of Dick Swiveller and the Marchioness "by heart" is crucial to how we understand the common culture Dickens not only draws on in his mode of characterization but also actively creates in his readership and beyond. To reflect the extent of Dickens's reach, Juliet John, for instance, opts for the term "mass" rather than "popular" culture, which, she argues, best captures her "recognition that the desire to influence large numbers of people was what drove Dickens and 'lay [*sic*] the foundation of an endurable retrospect' for a posthumous audience" (25). This is not to suggest that he wasn't "for the people," as the term "popular culture" connotes; rather for John the distinction can only be "heuristic rather than absolute" (25) due to Dickens's concern for and advocacy of the people. The telling inflection for her is that "Dickens rejected the role of the radical writer, speaking primarily to a radical audience, preferring to address, as he saw it, 'the great ocean of humanity' rather than stagnant 'bye-ponds'" (25)—an orientation, as I will argue, that the capaciousness of the "common" encompasses, bringing together as it does Dickens's political vision, fictional method, and hopes for a future common culture of the people that would be popular, mass, and radical.[9] Dickens's appeal to the common is at once an appeal to a common cast of characters and an imagined common good akin to Raymond Williams's notion of a "subjunctive mode" in Dickens, of a "perspective which is not socially or politically available": "the notion of a quite different but attainable perspective, in which we could see all the forces and relationships differently. . . . The presence of that kind of subjunctive mode seems to me crucial; it is precisely the sense in which Dickens was connecting things that lay far ahead of him" (*Writing in Society*, 161).[10] The common in Dickens, as I hope to show, forms the basis for these connections—which both are future-oriented, as Williams suggests, and draw from Dickens's immediate literary past. It also provocatively unsettles our association of the common with the usual, the ordinary, the everyday, and the routine, since in Dickens the common comes to life, paradoxically, in the uncommon or the eccentric, and the pleasure such memorable eccentricity affords, a pleasure that, as Thackeray attests, arises from repetition and reproducibility, from knowing something "by heart."[11]

## Eccentric Biographies

In his classic formulation of the tenets of liberal individualism, J. S. Mill tellingly equates character with eccentricity. Noting that "the tyranny of opinion is such as to make eccentricity a reproach," Mill positions eccentricity as the means to "break through that tyranny." As he definitively states, "Eccentricity has always abounded when and where strength of character has abounded" (*On Liberty* 63). The lack of both, moreover, defines the weakness of contemporary British society. "That so few now dare to be eccentric," warns Mill, "marks the chief danger of the time" (63). Conformity, custom, and public opinion are to blame: together they reduce individuals to mass or "collective mediocrity" (62). All things in moderation, this collective intones, and the result is to "maim by compression, like a Chinese lady's foot, every part of human nature which stands out prominently, and tends to make the person markedly dissimilar in outline to commonplace humanity" (65). This description is striking on a number of counts: first, it gestures toward a vision of conformity as a material force that can literally "maim" character "by compression." In turn, "character" too becomes its own kind of matter, to be either maimed or quashed or, conversely, granted its individuality, should current social practices change in the ways Mill proposes. Just as this possibility is raised, however, Mill turns to simile: the maiming is "like" that of a Chinese lady's foot rather than the foot itself. Individuality as a material thing comes into view, and then, as quickly, disappears, a mere likeness of the material foot. Finally, Mill's language makes literal the notion of a character sketch, which, in turn, threatens to become a caricature: "every part of human nature which stands out prominently," whatever "tends to make the person markedly dissimilar in outline," is in danger.

Mill's concern with "strength of character" and his celebration of eccentricity bring to the fore exemplary Victorian concerns about the loss of individuality—and of the individual—within an increasingly mass culture.[12] Mill's "solution" to this problem harks back to an earlier period of greatness and a different kind of individual: "The greatness of England is now all collective; individually small, we only appear capable of anything great by our habit of combining. . . . But it was men of another stamp than this that made England what it has been; and men of another stamp will be needed to prevent its decline" (66). These men, for Mill, will be men of "genius," "mental vigour," and "moral courage" (63). Although he invokes the bodily, material aspects of character in his metaphors, then, the vision of individuality Mill ultimately endorses contains none of this material; instead the more visible and visceral signs of character are erased in favor of a discrete, fully singular individual defined by his or her mind and morals.[13]

In contrast, eccentric biographies see Mill's material invocations to their end. They take seriously the Chinese lady's foot, as it were, recognizing that character is always a material, collective endeavor in that it always involves an exchange between individuals and the world, one in which individuals are truly of the world instead of released from it. Organized as a series of vignettes or character sketches, these eccentric magazines, biographies, and wonderful museums offer the most literal version of this profoundly material understanding of character: they actually catalogue remarkable or curious characters and personalities, ranging from the down and out and non-normative—misers, persons with missing limbs and special talents, convicts, and so on—to famous historical personages, such as Napoleon and Frederick the Great.[14] Moreover, in most of these books, textual descriptions are coupled with engraved portraits, both real and fabricated. The wonderful Miss Atkinson, half pig, half woman—who was "born in Ireland," has "a 20,000 pound fortune, and is fed out of a silver trough"—finds her place here, as does Nice New, "a well-known character at Reading" whose "dress, like his person, was singularly remarkable" (Wilson and Caulfield 333). Abraham Newland, the Chief Cashier of the Bank of England from 1782 to 1807, Miss Margaret McAvoy, "an extraordinary blind girl" with "peculiar faculties" (202), and the misers, Dancer and Elwes, both of whom are described repeatedly as "remarkable" (39; 305), help round out the gallery, as do famous fanatics such as Joanna Southcott, and a panoply of odd performers with feats ranging from balancing spoons on their noses and eating stones to being an "astonishing pedestrian" (106), a famous "posture-master," and a notorious beggar (see Figures 3–6).

These books represent an early moment in the nineteenth century when people were treated as a collection of objects, their personalities and characters the goods collected in these "museums." In his study of eccentric biographies, James Gregory explains the connection between the biography and the museum. He lists the Reverend Nathaniel Wanley's *The Wonders of the Little World, or, A General History of Man in Six Books* (1678) as an ancestor of the eccentric biography with its study of "what man hath been from the first ages of the world to these times: in respect of his body, senses, passions, affections, his virtues"—which could, I would add, equally characterize realism as a project. Francis Bacon is key to this history, as well, as a means of conferring scientific value on these collections. His interest in "a collection . . . of the extraordinaries and wonders of human nature" tied eccentric biographies to "spaces arranged to display nature's extremes," an association carried forward in the reference to so many nineteenth-century versions of eccentric biography as "museums" ("Eccentric Lives" 74). George Eliot's turn to "natural history," as we will see in Chapter 3, can be seen as an equivalent borrowing from the language of scientific studies.

Initially, from our perspective, these collections might seem like one more way in which the museum as an archive reifies subjects and their cultural artifacts in negative ways.[15] But a closer look at how these books function suggests a more complex relationship between subject and object.

FIGURE 3. Title page. From Henry Wilson and James Caulfield, *The Book of Wonderful Characters: Memoirs and Anecdotes of Remarkable and Eccentric Persons in All Ages and Countries.* London: J.C. Hotten, (1869 [1829]). Source: Harvard Library.

As "wonderful" and "eccentric" museums, they turn human subjects into a collection of displayed objects less to "possess" them than to preserve their individuality, that is, their "character"—in the dual sense of representing the qualities of various people and specifically those who are particularly odd or eccentric. By imagining character as something collectible and hence materially palpable they gesture toward a model of selfhood that both generates a sense of individual difference and counters virulent forms of objectification. A kind of collective memory—of character types—is invoked, but significantly the repetition that brings it to mind does not threaten the individual but rather brings him or her into existence.[16] Unlike the repetitiveness that constitutes habits and that, as Athena Vrettos argues, threatens to mechanize individuals, this kind of repetition instead produces the eccentric, the remarkable, the curious.[17] This act of production and preservation takes different guises in different collections; in some, the stated purpose is avowedly moral, while in others the personalities and their portraits are left to speak for themselves.

These biographies first caught my attention in *Our Mutual Friend*, in which Noddy Boffin not only is fashioned after the misers in character books, as mentioned above, but also reads and collects these texts.[18] Among Boffin's collection are *Merryweather's Lives and Anecdotes of Misers, or the Passion of Avarice Displayed*, as well as other "wollumes" of character books, including Kirby's *Wonderful Museum*, and Caulfield's *Characters*, and Wilson's (473). (Boffin is particularly thrilled to discover that even the Annual Register contains a section devoted to "Characters" and quickly buys up "the whole set" and "[begins] to carry it home piecemeal, confiding a volume to Bella, and bearing three himself" [461]). An extensive detailing of the lives of a series of infamous misers, Merryweather's book presents avarice as a form of insanity, which Dickens then connects to the speculative craze of the "share-pushing sixties."

Merryweather describes the miser Daniel Dancer's "secret hoards" of money, and thoroughly reviews the many hiding places in his dilapidated house or "heap of ruins" where his money was found, including a dung-heap in the cowhouse with almost 2,500 pounds in it. Bundles, jackets, bowls, teapots, and chimneys all become secret containers for Dancer's hoards. (Boffin marvels about Dancer and his fellow misers,

FIGURE 4. The Wonderful Miss Atkinson. From Henry Wilson and James Caulfield, *The Book of Wonderful Characters: Memoirs and Anecdotes of Remarkable and Eccentric Persons in All Ages and Countries*. London: J.C. Hotten, (1869 [1829]). Source: Harvard Library.

"Such Characters, Wegg, such Characters! . . . It's amazing what places they used to put the guineas in, wrapped up in rags" [473]). Descriptions of Merryweather's other misers focus similarly on their hiding places and on the way in which money has corrupted not only their persons but their place within a system of exchange. For Merryweather, as well as Dickens, miserliness is an extreme example of the precarious balance between subjects and objects in which the scale has tipped dangerously toward objects to the detriment of their subjects.

Miserliness, in other words, threatens to make subjects one with their hoarded objects, the result of which is, in Dickens's striking phrase, something akin to a "pecuniary swoon." (A "pecuniary swoon" is exactly what Dickens hopes to avert with Bella Wilfer in *Our Mutual Friend*; in a test of her mercenary leanings—at one point she confesses to being "the most mercenary little wretch that ever lived in the world" [316]—she must fall in love with John Harmon a.k.a. Rokesmith without knowing of his wealth.) To be enraptured by objects is to prevent them from being seen at all. It is perhaps not an accident then that these catalogues of misers focus so intently on their respective hiding places. In any case, the miser's too-close intimacy with objects demonstrates how not to possess a thing. Unable to part with his or her money (famous women misers appear as well), the miser succumbs to the object rather than keeping it in circulation and maintaining its social value.

In George Eliot's rendering of her eponymous miser, Silas Marner, a similar confusion between subjects and objects occurs when Eppie first appears at Silas's cottage after he has lost all his gold. Able only to think about his money, and suddenly overcome by one of his cataleptic fits, Silas does not even notice when Eppie arrives and promptly falls asleep on his hearth. Recovering from his fit, he mistakes Eppie's hair for his pile of gold and imagines that the gold has returned on its own, only to discover as he reaches for it that "instead of hard coin with the familiar resisting outline, his fingers encountered soft warm curls" (167). Later the narrative expounds on the differences between Eppie and the gold:

> Unlike the gold which needed nothing, and must be worshipped in close-locked solitude . . . Eppie was a creature of endless claims

FIGURE 5. Daniel Dancer. From Henry Wilson and James Caulfield, *The Book of Wonderful Characters: Memoirs and Anecdotes of Remarkable and Eccentric Persons in All Ages and Countries*. London: J.C. Hotten, (1869 [1829]). Source: Harvard Library.

and ever-growing desires, seeking and loving sunshine, and living sounds, and living movements.... The gold had kept [Silas's] thoughts in an ever-repeated circle... but Eppie was an object compacted of changes and hopes that forced his thoughts onward, and carried them far away from their old eager pacing towards the same blank limit. (184)

Not only is the miserly Silas linked to the kinds of repetitive habits and fears of stagnation that Vrettos identifies with industrial culture, but the "ever-repeated circle" of his thoughts is, in turn, associated with a relentless work routine, making explicit the connection between routinized habits and soul-deadening labor: "The gold had asked that he should sit weaving longer and longer, deafened and blinded more and more to all things except the monotony of his loom and the repetition of his web" (184). For both Eliot and Dickens, subject-object relations form the crux of the analysis of a newly industrial culture in which distinctions between subjects and objects are unsettled or blurred, with miserliness serving as the extreme but by no means singular example. For both writers, as we will see, the goal is not to reassert the primacy of subjects over objects but rather to rethink the subject, as Eliot does with Eppie, as "an object compacted of changes and hopes."

Now, not all of the eccentric collections are about misers, and many of the "characters" Dickens borrows from these collections are not misers either. But my larger point is less about the specific attributes of the individuals forming the focus of these books and more about the very form in which they find expression. In short, their status as catalogues interests me, for the form of the catalogue makes these subjects—whether misers, dwarfs, mayors, or convicts—into objects. But rather than objectifying their subjects in the pejorative sense, this very cataloguing of characters preserves their eccentricity and difference, their inability to be subjected to the forces of homogenization that increasingly define nineteenth-century commodity culture and that would render such voluminous cataloguing obsolete. They become object lessons, as it were, in how to refuse the objectification that nullifies subjects. So even as Merryweather moralizes about his subjects and warns his readers to beware of their dangerous

FIGURE 6. Joana Southcott. From Henry Wilson and James Caulfield, *The Book of Wonderful Characters: Memoirs and Anecdotes of Remarkable and Eccentric Persons in All Ages and Countries*. London : J.C. Hotten, (1869 [1829]). Source: Author's collection.

propensities, the very form of his text produces an antithetical result: it turns his own subjects into objects in order to narrate their histories. In other words, they come alive to the extent that they are reified; their reification *revivifies* them rather than turning them into ossified commodities (as in Lukács's theory of reification). The same, I will suggest, is true of Dickens's catalogue of "characters." Describing the effect of the catalogue in a different context, that of Oscar Wilde's queerness, Neil Bartlett writes that "it gives an object the vigour of a body, and a body the purchasability of an object. The list itself is satisfying" (182). Bartlett goes so far as to assign to the catalogue an eroticism: "The eroticism of the catalogue is not surprising. Pornography too is a catalogue. It lists parts of the body and their attendant fetishes just as a catalogue might list rare and precious things, with an identical effect of intoxication. It is a naming of pleasures" (182). This naming of pleasures in the form of the catalogue, in both character books and Dickens's version of them alike, holds within it the possibility of carving out a wholly other kind of social space in which the boundary between subjects and objects is neither fully collapsed nor opposed—a space in which the "subject/object ratio" tilts provocatively toward objects, thereby allowing a newly animated subject to come into view, one formed in and inseparable from the collective, figured here in the literal and pleasurable form of the collection.[19]

If publication record is any indication, the Victorians did participate in the pleasure of these books. They were published throughout the nineteenth century, with almost sixty works in all published between 1790 and 1901 (leaving aside later reincarnations of them, such as Edith Sitwell's *The English Eccentrics* in 1933 [Gregory, "Eccentric Biography" 342]). Lynch notes that "the nineteenth century in fact saw an efflorescence of "sketchbooks," books of "remarkable characters," "eccentric magazines," and "caricature portfolios" (252).[20] The *New Wonderful Museum* boasted, in an advertisement, that it was read "by people of all classes and denominations throughout the kingdom, as well as in Ireland, Scotland, France and every country in Europe," and that its "fame has reached already to many other polished nations in the world."[21]

Wilfred Dvorak notes that "to readers who knew Merryweather's book (or knew lore about misers), it would have been obvious from Book

I of *Our Mutual Friend* that Dickens too meant Boffin to be a moral character whose behavior parodies that of the genuine miser like old Harmon" (130). There is equally a case to be made for their popularity on the basis of their content. Not only do these biographies catalogue peculiar characters, but the different editions of these books are often essentially the same: they are catalogues repeatedly cataloguing the same thing—but never as exact reproductions.[22] As a preface to one edition advertises,

> If there be any merit in communicating useful and curious information in a concise and portable form, this volume of REMARKABLE AND ECCENTRIC BIOGRAPHY has some claim to public approbation. Within a far less space than is sometimes devoted to the life of a single obscure individual, it gives authentic accounts of ONE HUNDRED AND TEN celebrated or singular persons . . . and that, too, without excluding any of the more important details contained in the original sources from which the materials of the work have been drawn. (Malcolm ix)

The content of these books is thus doubly peculiar: constituting practically a genre of its own, the eccentric biography makes claims to thoroughness and brevity—the preface goes on to say, "there is here concentrated in three hundred and seventy pages, the essence of twenty volumes"—at the same time that all the sketches and information provided are recycled and hence already familiar to readers. It is sameness with a difference. Books of the engraved portraits alone were also published, suggesting that these characters became so well known that their accompanying narratives were no longer needed. Within *Our Mutual Friend* they can be said to function much like Dickens's' references to *The Arabian Nights*: it is taken for granted that his readers will recognize them.

Certainly the kind of naming these biographies engage in treads tenuous ground. How, one might ask, is this different from pernicious forms of objectification? How to keep the catalogue from becoming yet one more commodity? How to keep the viewer complicit in the naming? Looking at a series of relations between narrative and objects, Susan Stewart, in *On Longing*, argues about grotesque bodies that they are ultimately a "freak of culture" rather than a "freak of nature" (109). The effect of this freakishness, for Stewart, is to create a spectacle from which the viewer is distant and, moreover, normalized in relation to the so-called freak, who can only be an aberration (109). Yet the effect of books like Merryweather's and others is quite different. Wilson and Caulfield, for example, preface their *Book of Wonderful Characters* with an essay in which they deplore the loss of individuality in modern society, a loss that they link to the uniformity and homogeneity brought about by the development of the railway:

> There is a great change, too, in the manners and customs of the people of England, that renders a book like this still more interesting at the present time. We have nearly lost all, and are daily losing what little remains of, our individuality; all people and all places seem now to be alike; and the railways are, no doubt, the principal cause of this change. For railway stations, all over the world, seem to have a strong, we might almost call it a family, resemblance to each other; while there was a great deal of difference, both in the localities and in the originality of the people you met with, at the old roadside or village inns where the coach stopped to change horses. . . . But now, when we go to a country town, there is nothing to be seen but a railway station, with its usual complement of guards, porters, policemen, &c., as like as two peas are to the one we left miles away. (i–ii)

Wilson and Caulfield link this plea for variety directly to a lost "spirit of individual exclusiveness" (ii). As they later suggest with respect to the fine arts (just one of their many examples), "Works designed for the halls and eyes of emperors, popes, and nobles, find their way in no poor representations, into humble dwellings, and sometimes give a consciousness of kindred powers to the child of poverty" (ii–iii). So in a bizarre twist of logic, the lives of pig-faced ladies, stone eaters, enormous babies, misers, and gluttons are meant to exemplify "individual exclusiveness," which is, in turn, "the great encourager of eccentricity of character." In part a reaction against the democratizing force of modernity, the stated purpose of these books makes them something other than your typical freak show.

But what they are, exactly, is another question. How, finally, does the stated purpose of these books relate to their effect? While Wilson and Caulfield frame their appeal in classist terms, the actual structure of these books supports a wholly different response—and one that Dickens will exploit to remarkable effect in his own novels. By putting eccentricity into circulation, in popular books that benefit precisely from the technological advances they bemoan in their introduction, Wilson and Caulfield successfully reproduce individual character, but in a "modern" form that undercuts their claim to "exclusivity" and, in turn, challenges older notions of subjectivity. By generating "freakishness" positively (rather than producing normativity negatively as Stewart posits), these books not only replace the upper classes as "encouragers of eccentricity" but equally alter the very terms of individuality. Individuality now comes in the form of the collection, which in essence means that it emerges by way of the object. Unlike the deadening objectification symbolized by the railway, this objectification brings subjects back to life: in the very midst of a world in which levelling sameness predominates, these texts produce the "remarkable," the "peculiar," and the "extraordinary." And these categories are hardly exclusive any longer, given their sheer proliferation in the texts themselves. Dispossessed by virtue of their objecthood, by being "given over" to others, these subjects travel alongside one another while yet remaining distinct and different in what now must be considered as "collective" rather than individual biographies. As collective biographies, they ask us to imagine being literally "beside ourselves"—in a state of being in which the touch of the material world, its objects, and other subjects make us something other than ourselves, something potentially "remarkable."[23] When we reconsider James's complaint about Dickens in this light, we can see that he did in fact unwittingly grasp what Dickens was all about when he asked, "[W]here are those exemplars of sound humanity who should afford us the proper measure of their companion's variations?" When Dickens is at his best, rather than his worst, as James thought, they no longer exist and that is precisely the point.

## More Is Better

"There's a vooden leg in number six, there's a pair of Hessians in thirteen, there's two pair of halves in the commercial, there's these here painted tops in the snuggery inside the bar, and five more tops in the coffee-room." With this list, *The Pickwick Papers*' Sam Weller inventories the residents of the house, bewildering Mr. Wardle and Mr. Pickwick with "the singular catalogue of visiters" (137) at the White Hart inn. Exemplifying a common and routinely remarked upon characteristic of Dickens's writing, shoes here stand in for their owners; things more generally link synecdochically to the people who possess them. Dorothy Van Ghent, most notably, ties this method of characterization to the processes of industrialization and its "uprooting and dehumanization of men, women and children by the millions." In her account, things and people exchange places in Dickens's world, a reflection of the reification and commodification of modern industrial life: "People were becoming things, and things (the things that money can buy or that are the means for making money or for exalting prestige in the abstract) were becoming more important than people. People were being de-animated, robbed of their souls, and things were usurping the prerogatives of animate creatures" (128). While there are certainly innumerable images and instances of the kind of alienation Ghent associates with the thing-like nature of people in Dickens, the inclusion of Dickens's debt to character books offers a different understanding of how and to what ends his method of characterization works. In particular, Ghent envisions the reversal between things and people creating "a picture of a daemonically motivated world in which 'dark' or occult forces or energies operate not only in people . . . but also in things" (128–29), a bleak vision that, to my mind, Dickens's novels as a whole simply do not sustain.

Ghent is certainly not alone: what has been left out of Dickens criticism almost entirely is the reference here in Weller's inventory and elsewhere to the specific tradition of eighteenth-century books, a tradition that Dickens alludes to, retools, and transforms throughout his oeuvre.[24] *The Pickwick Papers* overflows with references to it, whether in its descriptions of characters as "singular," "remarkable," "extraordinary," and "curious," or in its repeated allusions to the catalogues which housed these characters. The waterman whom Mr. Pickwick briefly meets, for example, "looked as if he were catalogued in some collection of rarities" (21); likewise, the fat men who multiply in one scene, distinguished only as "the fat man," "another fat man," and so on, not to mention the famous Fat Boy, the man with the wooden leg, the madman, the dismal man, and the two Misses Matinters, who are "single and singular" (482), all function as types, the mainstay of character books. In its very title, *The Old Curiosity Shop* announces its kinship with character books and also contains recognizable characters from them, including Sarah Biffen—born without arms and legs—who became a popular miniature portrait painter sponsored by the Earl of Morton and commissioned by the Royal Family. Biffen also turns up in *Nicholas Nickleby* and *Martin Chuzzlewit*. And obviously types, more generally, have been considered both central to Dickens's fictional universe and, for many critics, as we have seen, that which delimits its value.

As this range of references suggests, Dickens hardly outgrew his fascination with character books and their types, although the critical work on Dickens and the novel more generally would suggest otherwise: the linear, developmental model of the novel, which constructs a narrative of ever increasing complexity and individuation in the treatment of individual characters, enforces a view of character that assumes that not only Dickens but we, as his readers, should have progressed beyond types. That is certainly the line that criticism of the Jamesian variety has taken. And it pervades so many discussions of novelistic character that it feels as if the representation of character *had* to develop in the ways it did. J. W. Smeed, for example, in his discussion of Dickens's relationship to another, related tradition of character types, the Theophrastan "character," identifies the writing of "characters" not only in Dickens but also in Thackeray, as "part of the novelist's apprenticeship" (119).[25] Other major Victorian novelists are similarly apprenticed: Austen, Thackeray, Trollope, Bulwer Lytton, and even George Eliot, with her *Impressions of Theophrastus Such*, all move on from such static character types to full-blown novelistic characters. (In Eliot's case, the move back to Theophrastan character, according to Smeed, makes clear that this vision of character is not integral to her novels, a contention taken up in the following chapter.)

Against this teleological, developmental narrative, I want to suggest that Dickensian types and caricatures are not characters who have failed to achieve psychological depth, but instead refigure the radically material, thing-like nature of subjectivity on display in character books, a materiality that, like Judith Butler's notion of "dispossessed subjecthood," recognizes the embeddedness of characters in a profoundly social world. To my mind, Butler is particularly helpful for thinking about Dickens's view of subjectivity given her emphasis on the material body and how it might become the ground for "another kind of normative aspiration within the field of politics" (*Precarious Life* 26). For Butler, the vulnerability of the material body, and our dependence on other bodies, points to the "fundamental sociality of embodied life, the ways in which we are, from the start and by virtue of being a bodily being, already given over, beyond ourselves, implicated in lives that are not our own" (28). The idea of being "dispossessed," in other words, provides another way of thinking about social interdependence and, as I am suggesting, a newly envisioned commons—and one, importantly, that still maintains the differences among individuals. As Butler asks, in one of a series of provocative questions about the relationship between individual autonomy and sociality, "Is this not another way of imagining community, one in which we are alike only in having this condition [of vulnerability or dependence] separately and so having in common a condition that cannot be thought without difference?" (27).

While Butler's notion of dispossession, prompted as it was by the 9/11 attacks and how we might respond to violence in politically productive ways, focuses on our vulnerability and the precariousness of our lives, Dickens equally accents the pleasures in dependence and dispossession. Not surprisingly, the cataloguing and collecting of types—the means through which Dickens imagines communities of difference—is where many of the pleasures of Dickens's texts reside. In his reading of *The Pickwick Papers*, James Kincaid associates these pleasures with a "gluttonous open-heartedness": as he remarks, "[T]he very conversation is plump, full of wondrous redundancy—the redundancy of bite after bite after bite" (26). I want to extend Kincaid's emphasis on food and fat and conviviality into the textual realm and suggest that Dickens's reworkings of characteristic writing reanimate the generative possibilities of typographical culture—its quantitative pleasures—and exist in tension with the pressures of qualitative individuation—the dematerialized, deeply interior sense of character with which we are now so familiar. In doing so, they produce a vibrant culture of the commons in which equality does not translate into a reductive sameness but instead comes to life in an extensive and sprawling collective of characters whose stories are deeply connected and intricately intertwined— something the covers of *Oliver Twist*, *Bleak House*, and *Our Mutual Friend* nicely capture (see, for example, Figure 7).

Most often, Dickens figures quantity, and with it, a vision of the common people, in terms of the many and the seemingly endless forms of multiplication it generates. Williams identifies Dickens as the first urban novelist of the nineteenth century and connects the form of Dickens's novels to the streets of London and the fleeting, multiplicitous encounters that structure city life. More recently, Matthew Beaumont, in his book on nightwalking and its importance for writers ranging from Shakespeare to Poe, also links Dickens's fictional method to his experience of the city, seeing in his compulsive nighttime perambulations and his love of crowds the impetus for Dickens's creative genius. Detailing Dickens's "craving for streets," Beaumont presents an exchange between Dickens and John Forster in which Dickens, trying to write *Dombey and Son* while in Lausanne, complains of "the absence of streets and numbers and figures": "I can't express how much I want these. It seems as if they supplied something to my brain, which it cannot bear, when busy, to lose" (359). During the same stay, Dickens rues that, "I don't seem to be able to get rid of my spectres unless I can lose them in crowds" (quoted in Beaumont 360). As Beaumont concludes, "No one in the nineteenth century can have needed London quite as much as Dickens did. It was an addiction."[26] While Beaumont's emphasis is on London, given his interest in nightwalking, for our purposes Dickens's recognition of the centrality of crowds and what I am calling "the many" to his fictional method is key, and represents, as John notes, nothing short of Dickens's view of popular art, which for him was "a means of experiencing the 'pleasure of being in a crowd' in the modern world, itself 'a mysterious expression of the enjoyment of the multiplication of number', to cite Baudelaire" (25). "My figures," as Dickens notes with curiosity, "seem disposed to stagnate without crowds about them" (quoted in Beaumont 360). Crowds, the many, the common people: these are the generative materials of Dickens's craft, and like the multiplication they produce, they come from multiple sources: London and its crowds,

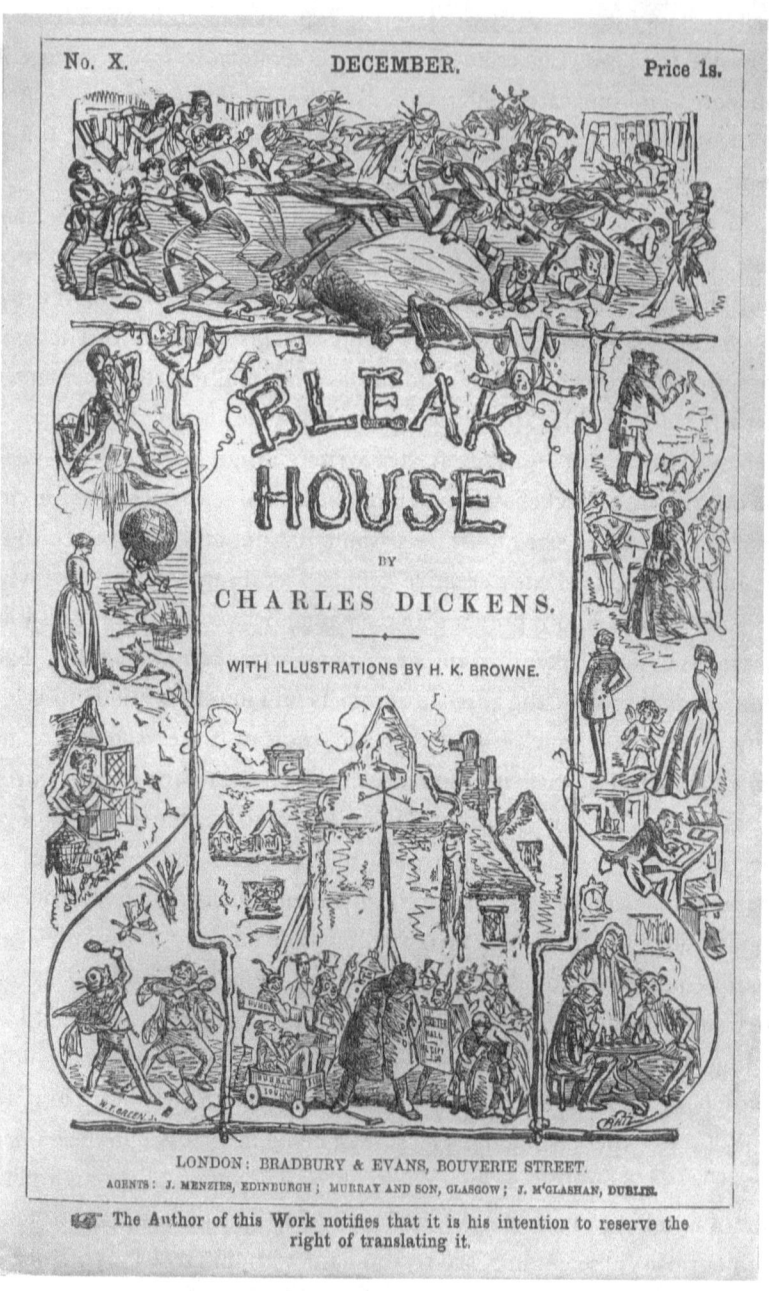

FIGURE 7. Cover of *Bleak House* by Charles Dickens, with illustrations by H. K. Browne, No. X. (London: Bradbury & Evans, 1852-53). Source: Smith College Library. Reprinted with permission.

the popular radical culture of the Regency period (more on this further on), and the form of eighteenth-century character books repurposed for a nineteenth-century urban experience and a specifically urban commons.

In *The Economy of Character*, Lynch writes, "it was in effect expected that the book of characters would go on too long" (55); Dickens echoes this sentiment when he has Boffin boast to Venus (about the character books he makes Wegg read to him), "There's plenty more; there's no end to it" (478). Books that are too long, books without end: the same could be said (practically) about most of Dickens's novels.[27] Lynch's powerful claim that eighteenth-century debates around character are truly about quantity rather than quality would seem to hold some truth well into the nineteenth century. In its eighteenth-century variant, the economy that Lynch designates the "economy of character" is all about counting; the trick is to have just the right number of "strokes or traits of character" so as to establish a character's "defining difference" (10). Too many strokes and the characterization teeters toward the grotesque and the burlesque. Too few and the ability to differentiate between characters is lost. A fine balance between legibility and variety had to be struck—and as the century progressed, the typicality associated with legibility slowly gave way to market demands for difference and distinction. Nonetheless, the very nature of character books—the largest competitors for what we retroactively term "novels"—straddles these concerns, generating as they do catalogues of varied types. And the more these "types" are differentiated, the more types get produced—hence their seeming unendingness.

Hardly the generation of a meaningless plethora, according to Lynch, this "more is better" logic enacts a Lockean epistemology by "[disengaging] differences from seeming similarities and [filling] the perceptual field with more things that the knowledge-seeking subject may single out" (53). This process of differentiation not only offers the possibility of continually refining one's perceptions but, as Lynch notes, "was made compelling by the pressures print technologies brought to bear on people's ways of discriminating sameness from similarity" (56). Difference and discrimination, via Locke, are the result of experience; the imprint or stamp of experience writes itself on one's character, thereby filling up Locke's famous "blank slate" of the mind with typefaces—in both the literal, typographical sense and the material, characterological one. His "documentary paradigm" (69), as Lynch describes it, makes minds and characters material by way of the literal processes of writing: stamps, typefaces, imprints, and brands define the construction of character.

In her account of eighteenth-century literary culture, Lynch ultimately establishes a division between the first two-thirds of the century, when quantity, or the "more and less" of character, was privileged, and the final third of the century, when novels become what we have assumed they always were: when "novels, to be good novels, had to be *about* character" (29). Dickens's *Our Mutual Friend* can be seen to uncannily mimic this division: its first three books—in which the multiple plots, mysteries, and mistaken identities come to life—revel in the quantitative pleasures of typographical character before succumbing to the pressures of qualitative individuation in its fourth and last book. Quantity comes in a number of different forms. At the level of the sentence, Dickens obsessively repeats proper names, single words, particular sentence constructions, concepts, and descriptions. Silas Wegg "declines and falls" no fewer than seven times, in the process becoming indistinguishable from the first book he reads to Boffin, "Decline-and-Fall-Off-the-Rooshan-Empire"; "Mr. Eugene Wrayburn" is repeated forty-one times over the course of the novel; characters' names are repeated in triplet, as in "Lizzie, Lizzie, Lizzie" or "Eugene, Eugene, Eugene" (two times followed by the phrase, "this is a bad business"); "a literary man—with a wooden leg" is used five times, the first three times in the space of as many pages (and, moreover, is a tag that could easily be found in any character book).[28] Repetition is also used to collapse persons into things and vice versa. Dickens echoes the title of a *Household Words* story of his, "Railway Waifs and Strays," when, describing a "grey dusty withered evening in London city," he writes "melancholy waifs and strays of house-keepers and porters sweep melancholy waifs and strays of papers and pins into the kennels, and other more melancholy waifs and strays explore them, searching and stooping and poking for anything to sell" (386).[29] In like manner, three sentences describing Bradley Headstone, all from the same paragraph, repeat the words "decent" and "mechanically" so many times that they become material things, functioning like concrete building blocks to construct Headstone's "character": "Bradley Headstone, in his decent black coat and waistcoat, and decent white shirt, and decent formal black tie, and decent pantaloons of pepper and salt, with his decent silver watch in his pocket and its decent hair-guard round his neck, looked a thoroughly decent young man of six-and-twenty"; and "He had acquired mechanically a great store of teacher's knowledge. He could do mental arithmetic mechanically, sing at sight mechanically, blow various wind instruments mechanically, even play the great church organ mechanically" (218). These sentences are then followed by references to his mind as a place of "mechanical stowage," a "mental warehouse," and a "wholesale warehouse." Lest this kind of characterization get too singularly tied to Bradley Headstone, a page later Miss Peecher gets this introduction: "A little pincushion, a little housewife, a little book, a little workbox, a little set of tables and weights and measures, and a little woman, all in one. She could write a little essay on any subject, exactly a slate long, beginning at the left-hand top of one side and ending at the right-hand bottom of the other, and the essay should be strictly according to rule" (219).[30]

These sentences and descriptions all carry weight. Whether invoking Lockean minds, characteristic writing, or people becoming things that in turn become people, they have bulk and substance, they move.[31] They pile up words; they recycle and reuse them; they give ideas heft; they add on and lengthen and accumulate meanings; they produce exactly the kind of book Boffin is looking for: "some fine bold reading, some splendid book in a gorging Lord-Mayor's Show of wollumes" (probably meaning gorgeous, but misled by association of ideas), "as'll reach right down your pint of view, and take time to go by you" (58). They thus simultaneously attend to and play with the means of production—the production of meaning, the production of character(s). After all, how can one ignore the material used to make these sentences when their very construction involves the literal piling up of signs that "mark" character just as Noddy Boffin's "altered character had never been so grossly marked" (575) by the influence of what else: character books. Even feelings in this economy take up space: overcome by Mrs. Boffin's kindness toward him, Sloppy "detached himself from that good creature that he might have room enough for his feeling, threw back his head, opened his mouth wise, and uttered a dismal howl" (333).

Mr. Lammle unwittingly hits on the overall logic of this narrative economy when he exclaims, "Now this . . . shows the accidental combinations that there are in things!" (257). Just as words pile up in the novel and produce the odd and the curious (a literary man—with a wooden leg), so too do plots and ruses—most of which equally go awry, foiled by "accidental combinations." Whether it is John Harmon's double being killed to set the novel in motion or Mr. and Mrs. Lammle each being duped into thinking the other is rich, what looks like controlled plotting continually gets tripped up by accident. The Lammles are a particularly interesting example of such accidental plotting, since Mr. Lammle gives voice to this logic exactly when nothing appears to be happening accidentally. At the moment he utters his exclamation, both he and Mrs. Lammle are actively engaged in luring Sophronia Podsnap into marrying Fascination Fledgeby; Mr. Lammle's mock surprise is itself a ruse. But this plan also collapses as Mrs. Lammle develops a fondness for Sophronia that prevents her from going through with the deception. The logic of "accidents," of characters and things coming into relation with one another in curious and surprising ways, is thus reinforced at the very moment it is disavowed. Like a "ruse of reason," the ruse of *Our Mutual Friend* reveals nothing less than the inescapability of the accidental and the contingent—themselves markers of how profoundly "open" to the world its characters are.[32] So open, in fact, that Noddy Boffin can be imprinted with the material character(s) he reads about and through which, in turn, he constructs himself.

Perhaps one way, then, to describe the difference between the body of the novel and its resolutions in Book IV is in terms of the interplay or balance between ruse and accident. If accident predominates in the early books, ruse, in the end, wins the day. In the process, the daring propositions that go along with accident are left behind. No more piling up, no more serendipity, no more characters constituted by their things and vice versa, be they books, legs, alligators, mangles, bones, or dust-heaps. Quantity and its pleasures cede to quality. The slippages that define typographical character give way to the most deflating revelation of the book:

Noddy Boffin has not been influenced by his books.[33] Instead he has merely used them pedagogically to teach Bella Wilfer—and Silas Wegg—a lesson: about things. Namely that less is better and one is best. When the Boffins and John Harmon relate the story of their scheme to test the true worth of Bella, they begin, interestingly, by piling their hands up on one another, since, as Mrs. Boffin states, "[W]e are all of us in it." Once Boffin completes the pile with his hand, Mrs. Boffin makes clear what kind of unity is thus produced: "Seems quite a family building, don't it?" (751). Piling up is no longer about adding on and endlessly accumulating meanings, but rather about assigning to things one meaning; the multiplicitous is made back into/shown to have been the singular all along: Bella proves her mettle ("the true golden gold" [753]); John becomes only John Harmon ("John Harmon now for good, and John Rokesmith for nevermore" [757]); Boffin is the same Boffin he ever was ("Please I don't believe you are a hard-hearted miser at all, and please I don't believe you ever for one single minute were!" [754]); and Mrs. Boffin is so honest that Noddy's mere feigning of miserliness was almost too much for her ("My dear, the lady thinks so high of me that she couldn't abear to see and hear me coming out as a reg'lar brown one. Couldn't abear to make-believe as I meant it!" [756]). As if to register just how plotted these resolutions are, no one is allowed to "go astray": not only must Eugene Wrayburn have hidden within him "a mine of purpose and energy" (735), but even Jenny Wren and Mr. Sloppy must be brought together, their hands joined, as Jenny's ever open potential lover—"Him who is coming to court and marry me" (788)—settles down into and becomes one with Sloppy. And as if to register just what may be lost in this move from the multiple to the singular, from quantity to quality, a burst of "him"s and "he"s precedes this settling down. No less than nine indeterminate "him"s, including two of Dickens's characteristic triplets of "him"s and six "he"s make their presence felt before being "filled" by one determinate Sloppy.

Even as Dickens's text unites its characters in manageable pairs, reducing doubleness (or more) "within" characters to simple pairings between them, it cannot, however, seem to fully let go of the utopian possibilities that the slippage between characters and things, or, more precisely, the identification of characters as things, opens up. In a negative version of this slippage, Dickens ends the novel's "Postscript" by collapsing the difference between himself and his own text, noting that when he almost lost the manuscript of *Our Mutual Friend* in the infamous railway accident that so shook him, "I can never be much nearer parting company with my readers for ever, than I was then, until there shall be written against my life, the two words with which I have this day closed this book:—THE END" (800). Character as literal material text here takes on one more meaning, as Dickens himself multiplies, his identity as *Our Mutual Friend*'s author in essence "parting company" with the Dickens who has become the book itself. The book can conceivably "die" without taking Dickens along with it. But in Dickens's construction of this relationship, significantly, it cannot: should the book be lost, so too would its author "[part] company with my readers for ever." In its last sentence, then, the novel once again revives the mutually constitutive relationship between things and characters—Dickens himself now becoming his own character—that has fueled *Our Mutual Friend*. And, as in the novel, when neither side of this relationship is slighted or, worse, canceled out, when eccentricity is allowed free play, everything seems possible, including the coexistence of life and death, the animate and the inanimate.

### Democratic Optimism

Everything seems possible—this is the power of Dickens's "subjunctive mode." But, of course, everything *isn't* possible in the current historical conjuncture. In the distance between seems and isn't lies the imperative of Dickens's politics. Again, to return to Lukács, Dickens's stated political views need to be separated from the politics of his novels, which, as I have suggested, rest in large part in the form of his nineteenth-century "character books." In Lukács's account of Balzac's *Lost Illusions*, he writes that despite being a loyalist and legitimist, Balzac "saw [the] character of the restoration with merciless clarity" (*Studies in European Realism* 48). That "character," embodied in what Lukács terms the "novel of disillusionment," captures "how the conception of life of those living in a bourgeois society—a conception which although false, is yet necessarily what it is—is shattered by the brute forces of capitalism" (47). *Lost Illusions*' hero, the poet Lucien de Rubempré, hence "not only [is] true to type" but also "provides the opportunity for unfolding all the contradictions engendered by the penetration of capitalism into literature" (52). Ultimately then, for Lukács, the "integrating principle of this novel is the social process itself and its real subject is the advance and victory of capitalism. Lucien's personal catastrophe is the typical fate of the poet and of true poetic talent in the world of fully developed capitalism" (53). In other words, there is a necessity to Lucien's fate. At the same time, however, that necessity or determination "by the totality of the socially decisive forces" is never simple nor direct. Instead "the aggregate of social determinants is expressed in an uneven, intricate, confused and contradictory pattern, in a labyrinth of personal passions and chance happenings" (53). Dickens, I want to suggest, assembles a similar "aggregate of social determinants" in his novels, and likewise employs a Lukácsian kind of type alongside his reanimation of the more literally material practice of eighteenth-century typification that I have already elaborated.

In this regard, I part ways somewhat with Williams, who also considers Lukács's model of realism in relation to Dickens and other 1848 novelists, but finds him less useful than I do. He maintains that Lukács's analysis, because it derives from Continental rather than British fiction, does not pertain to most British novels. Moreover, he finds Lukács's claim about the hero's discovery of "the objective social limits" too general, leaving no way to distinguish the nature of those limits themselves and the value placed on them by different novelists (*Writing in Society* 150–65). In contrast, I argue that it is precisely the implacably general or common nature of the objective social limits within which individual characters must function that powerfully defines Dickens's novelistic universe (as well as that of other nineteenth-century novelists, as I show throughout *The Afterlife of Enclosure*), even as the differential relations individual characters have to those common limits are also acknowledged and articulated. In other words, what a contemporary Marxist formalism attentive to the *longue durée* can illuminate within nineteenth-century realism is precisely those invisible yet nonetheless determining socioeconomic structures within which only certain actions and outcomes are possible—what Lukács, in his theory of realism, refers to as "poetic necessity" (*Studies in European Realism* 56).[34]

Time and time again, within his oeuvre, Dickens dramatizes the constraints of the current order, even as he turns with the same kind of regularity to fairy-tale endings of escape from that order. *Oliver Twist, Great Expectations, Hard Times, Bleak House, Little Dorrit*: all take aim at specific social problems from the poor laws and factory conditions to urban poverty, gender inequality, and the perils of coming of age in a "guarded and suspicious world," which, as Pip laments, makes maturity seem "hardly worth while" (392). These social problems, as we saw in Chapter 1, need to be grasped in the context of enclosure and the theft of the commons, and are all part and parcel of what Ellen Meiksins Wood refers to as both "the system of property" and "the system of propertylessness" (18), or what Karl Polanyi, characterizing enclosures, calls simply "a revolution of the rich against the poor" (35). As has often been pointed out, magical sums of money or lost origins often appear out of nowhere to mitigate these dire social problems—most often at the end of these novels. But what if we were to focus less on endings and more on middles, as Caroline Levine and others have recently argued, or, better yet, see these middles and endings in a dialectical relationship to each other?[35] What if it is the very recognition of the implacable nature of the social world as it is that drives the need for such fairy-tale endings, thereby highlighting the impossibility of those same endings for Dickens's common characters as a whole?

"They dies everywheres.... They dies in their lodgings—she knows where; I showed her—and they dies down in Tom-all-Alone's in heaps. They dies more than they lives, according to what I see" (492). The vision the illiterate Jo in *Bleak House* presents of "heaps" of people, of the many now transformed gruesomely into piles of the dead, offers the dialectical reverse of the proliferating utopian many. There is nothing serendipitous about the repetition of "they dies," as repetition equally serves the tragic and the comic. Tragedy and comedy alike compose Dickens's "character books," and neither cancels the other out, in good dialectical fashion. To reanimate the many would mean to reanimate all of the many, including especially "they" who "dies more than they lives." Necessity and logic dictate, however, that the many continue to die under the current circumstances, with Jo a case in point. The narrative makes this clear from the first time we are introduced to Tom-all-Alone's: "Jo lives—that is to say, Jo has not yet died—in a ruinous place known to the like of him by the name of Tom-all-Alone's" (256). Not yet died: Jo succumbs to disease because this is what happened, historically, to the poor and homeless in the slums of mid-nineteenth-century London. But, crucially, before he dies he passes on that disease to our heroine, Esther Summerson, who becomes one of the "many," and thus provides one definitive answer to the question shaping *Bleak House* as a whole—namely, what *is* the connection "between many people in the innumerable histories of this world, who, from opposite sides of great gulfs, have, nevertheless, been very curiously brought together!" (256). Much like the fog that opens *Bleak House*, disease, too, is a common condition in Dickens's London, whether that disease is literal as in Jo and Esther's case, or figurative, as in the depictions of the rot and decay of the aristocratic order or the inescapability of the Chancery suit. (At times disease figures a broader condition of global scope, as when the literal plague of "the East" in *Little Dorrit* morphs metaphorically into a "more lasting condition of collective, national self-incarceration of body and spirit" in London, as James Buzard observes [415]).[36] But these same diseases also affect characters differentially. Jo dies, Esther lives; Chancery "gives to monied might the means abundantly of wearying out the right" (15).

The very power of "monied might" to weary "the right" puts considerable strain on individual characters. Because a logic of necessity governs Dickens's narratives, he struggles with the place of individual actions within the large impersonal structures he narrates so powerfully: the Circumlocution Office in *Little Dorrit*; the Coodles, Doodles, and Foodles, and "all the fine gentlemen in office, down to Zoodle" (257) in *Bleak House*; the "traffic in Shares" (118) in *Our Mutual Friend*; Utilitarianism in *Hard Times*; and capital, throughout his novels.[37] Mr. Gridley, "the man from Shropshire" in *Bleak House*, palpably captures this dilemma in his repeated questioning of who is responsible for the plight of the many within these large systems: "There again!" said Mr. Gridley with no diminution of his rage. The system! I am told on all hands, it's the system. I mustn't look to individuals. It's the system." Enraged by the loss of his estate in the endless legal machinations of Chancery Court, Gridley is powerless to hold any individual accountable, recounting how he "mustn't go into court and say, 'My Lord, I beg to know this from you—is this right or wrong?' . . . My lord knows nothing of it. He sits there, to administer the system" (251). Nor can he go to Mr. Tulkinghorn and "say to him when he makes me furious by being so cool and satisfied . . . I mustn't say to him, 'I will have something out of some one for my ruin, by fair means or foul!'" For, as with all the individuals connected to Chancery, "*He* is not responsible. It's the system." Driven to violence by "the system," Gridley fears what "may happen if I am carried beyond myself at last!" and concludes, "I will accuse the individual workers of that system against me, face to face, before the great eternal bar!" (251–52). In the break between this diatribe and Gridley's vow to "shame them . . . to show myself in that court to its shame" by dying in its midst, Esther interjects to underline the desperate fierceness of his rage, commenting matter-of-factly that "[h]is passion was fearful. I could not have believed in such rage without seeing it" (252).

"It's the system." As with Jo, "the man from Shropshire" potently embodies the system's ease in wearing down and killing off "the people"; its veiled violence, in contrast to the "fearful passion" and powerless violence of Gridley's resistance, preserves an airy neutrality that leaves no room for individual responsibility, and no room for redress for its victims. Moments before Gridley dies, he admits, "I did believe that I could, and would, charge them with being the mockery they were, until I died of some bodily disorder. But I am worn out. How long I have been wearing out, I don't know; I seemed to break down in an hour" (404). A bleak vision indeed, and one which underscores that there is nothing naive about Dickens's eccentrics: the drama of Gridley's life and death enacts, broadly, the tensions within any materialist account that aims to give its due to the individual and the social, a tension or balance that continues to trouble a politics of the commons to this day.[38] The final image of kinship between Gridley and Miss Flite, narrated by Esther as Bucket prepares to apprehend Gridley, offers a striking tableau for the urban commons Dickens both envisions and eviscerates:

> The roof rang with a scream from Miss Flite, which still rings in my ears.

"Oh, no, Gridley!" she cried as he fell heavily and calmly back from before her. "Not without my blessing. After so many years!" (405)

Esther does not leave her narrative there, however. In a coda of sorts to the event of Gridley's death, Esther adds,

> The sun was down, the light had gradually stolen from the roof, and the shadow had crept upward. But to me the shadow of that pair, one living and one dead, fell heavier on Richard's departure than the darkness of the darkest night. And through Richard's farewell words I heard it echoed: "Of all my old associations, of all my old pursuits and hopes, of all the living and the dead world, this one poor soul alone comes natural to me, and I am fit for. There is a tie of many suffering years between us two, and it is the only tie I ever had on earth that Chancery has not broken!" (405–6)

Dickens's stress on "the system" can seem to leave us bereft of any sense of "democratic optimism," the term G. K. Chesterton uses to describe the "old atmosphere" his contemporaries and their critics before them have lost the ability to see in Dickens—a liability, I would add, that we too share to a great extent. But, in fact, Dickens's optimism gains its force precisely from its refusal to turn away from systemic suffering; instead Dickens remains optimistic despite the many forces allayed against the Gridleys and Oliver Twists of the world. For Chesterton, the old atmosphere of optimism is synonymous with a "confidence in common men," which Chesterton equates with nothing short of the "great glory of the Revolution." As he assesses the critical terrain in the years between Dickens's writing and his own, he notes, "[T]here has been a revolution, there has been a counter revolution, there has been no restoration" (17). The problem, he diagnoses, is that Dickens "[exaggerates] the wrong thing" (*Charles Dickens* 19). The Moderns "know what it is to feel a sadness so strange and deep that only impossible characters can express it: they do not know what it is to feel a joy so vital and violent that only impossible characters can express that. . . . They know that there is a point of depression at which one believes in Tintagiles: they do not know that there is a point of exhilaration at which one believes in Mr. Wegg" (19–20). Attuned to the "impossibilities of Maeterlink," with his fated marionettes powerless to resist the systemic forces pulling their strings, modern readers of Dickens can only perceive the "impossibilities of Dickens" as "much more impossible than they really are" (20).

From the changed perspective of our own critical moment, we can now again, I believe, imagine the "restoration" that Chesterton was hoping to bring about. In part, this restoration comes from a renewed emphasis on the common in our contemporary politics, a politics that relies less on sectarian factionalism and more on the common condition of what the Occupy movement referred to as "the 99%." This revitalized vision of the common shares much with the vision of the "common men" Chesterton sees Dickens's politics embracing and emboldening. In his reading of *Oliver Twist*, Chesterton asserts that "[Dickens's] revolt was simply and solely the eternal revolt; it was the revolt of the weak against the strong. He did not dislike this or that argument for oppression; he disliked oppression. He disliked a certain look on the face of a man when he looks down on another man" (*Appreciations* 46). Likewise, he speaks of the poor, rather than the proletariat, of the many rather than any specific class.[39] In other words, against sectarian politics, Dickens gives voice to a blunt politics, a version of what Bertolt Brecht called *plumpes Denken*— or crude thought that cuts through the chaff.[40] In contrast to other writers of his time, Chesterton notes, "Dickens attacks the modern workhouse with a sort of inspired simplicity as of a boy in a fairy tale who had wandered about, sword in hand, looking for ogres and who had found an indisputable ogre. All the other people of his time are attacking things because they are bad economics or because they are bad politics, or because they are bad science; he alone is attacking things because they are bad" (*Appreciations* 47).

But, again, the critique and the utopian optimism go hand in hand. We might then think of Dickens's stance along the lines of a more recent call to practice "Cynicism of the Intellect, Optimism of the Will," Fredric Jameson's slogan for a politics that is aware of and pushes against the "absolute limits of our current thinking" ("A New Reading of *Capital*" 13). To be sure, there is a fairy-tale aspect to Dickens's optimism that remains a source of criticism to this day: for Moretti, Dickens's narratives devolve into "family romances," the dissonance of the city "reduced" by "a biographical fairy-tale that tries, in one way or another, to establish a unity" (130); for Eagleton, Dickens's representations of the "bad"—and by extension, the "good"—are too simplistic, too black and white; and, as we have seen more generally, the realistic nature of Dickens's characters and plots overall has continually been questioned.[41]

There are important historical antecedents, however, for the turn to what has variously been referred to as the sentimental, the melodramatic, the unrealistic, or the fairy-tale nature of Dickens's politics. Significantly, Sally Ledger relates Dickens's plotlines to his ties to early nineteenth-century popular radical culture and its reliance on melodrama and satire. Regency radicalism drew on the centrality of the visual in melodrama and the "theatrical semiotics of gesture" (13) on display in response to both the Peterloo Massacre (1819) and the Queen Caroline Affair (1820). The Peterloo Massacre, in particular, in which the sixty thousand peaceful demonstrators gathered in support of parliamentary reform were attacked, appeared to be an attack on nothing less than "plebeian culture itself" (13) and was met with satirical pamphlets and caricatures that appealed to a broad readership that extended from the semiliterate to the educated. As Ledger notes, this ability to transcend the divide between high and low culture was "rarely achieved in the Victorian period other than in the writings of Charles Dickens" (16). Moreover, Dickens's connection to this form of radicalism was a personal one: Ledger opens *Dickens and the Popular Radical Imagination* with the deathbed scene of the Regency satirist and radical pamphleteer William Hone surrounded by none other than George Cruikshank and Dickens himself. (At the request of the dying Hone, Cruikshank had summoned Dickens, whose hand Hone wanted to shake.) Cobbett, too, is a central figure within Regency radicalism, and Dickens's association with these writers, as Ledger develops, counters the critical assumption that Dickens was an "essentially middle-class writer committed to middle-class values" (2). Dickens carries forward and transforms not only the visual elements of radical popular culture—its emphasis on caricature and allegorical exaggeration—but its politics as well: "A generation later Dickens would, like Hone, consistently combine the raw material of popular culture with moral and political commitment in order to produce a commercially viable literature of protest, and in this respect the two writers had a great deal in common. Similar, too, is a political temperament that drew both men to particular causes rather than to political parties or philosophies" (40). The fantasy elements that Dickens brings to this literature of protest, as John suggests in her analysis of Dickens's mass cultural appeal, are not opposed to a meaningful or "realistic" politics but fully part of it, a relationship captured in Jacqueline Rose's claim (cited by John) that "[f]antasy is not . . . antagonistic to social reality; it is its precondition or psychic glue" (5).[42]

For Ledger, the melodramatic mode Dickens inherits from his Regency heirs is especially significant if we are to understand the tension between individual agency and the larger social structures Dickens's characters inhabit. In particular, melodrama provides a narrative structure that preserves agency even as it recognizes the forces arrayed against the individual. In a provocative reading of Jo's death in *Bleak House*, Ledger shows how Dickens turns to "us," his readers, in an attempt to restore the possibility of some form of individual action in response to the devastating picture of systemic corruption and poverty the novel has so convincingly depicted: "In remarking that children like Jo are 'dying thus around us every day' . . . Dickens aligns himself with the 'us' of his readership—all those whom he believes could, like him, do something to effect change: *Bleak House* is his own contribution to that process" (208). As with melodrama more generally, *Bleak House* stops short, in Ledger's view, of blaming "'the system' tout court. . . . For a full-blooded structural critique crucially cedes the social and political agency of 'the People'. Dickens isn't ready for this in *Bleak House*" (208).

Melodrama is but one of the many genres and visual modes of representation that Dickens turns to and transforms, however, as we have seen.[43] Ledger is right, I think, in identifying Dickens's need to allow for the possibility that something can be done. And her analysis of Dickens's indebtedness to radical popular culture remains indispensable to understanding Dickens's politics. But the ability to act need not be framed in either/or terms in which agency is ceded at the expense of structural critique or vice versa. Doing so neglects or negates the utopian impulse within Dickens's novelistic universe, the sense that critique and a transformed world go hand in hand. In reaching out to his readers, in the scene of Jo's death, Dickens extends the frame of the narrative not only to affirm something good, that is, that agency is possible, but also to reinforce his vision of how "bad" things are, to echo Chesterton, that is, the sense that without fundamental change Jo and his ilk will continue to die everywhere and to die more than they live. In other words, Dickens aims to maintain both: the structural critique and the possibility for human action. The weight of both highlights the fantasy at the heart of all utopias, the value of which, as Jameson insists, rests in "something not realized and indeed unrealizable in [its] partial form" ("The Politics of Utopia" 50). This utopian impulse, for Jameson, is ultimately economic at its core because only achievable through a form of equality in which the system of rich and poor would be abolished, in which the "surplus population" that the likes of Scrooge and Malthus treat as disposable would be insupportable.

While numerous social problems form the basis of Dickens's structural critique, poverty and the fate of the poor, as in Jo's case, repeatedly stage the current state of things. The most iconic Dickensian line, "Please sir, I want some more," gains its power from the impossibility of this utopian wish being fulfilled for all the parish boys within the world of *Oliver Twist* and its Mr. Bumbles and Mrs. Sowerberry's, the latter of whose "liberality . . . to Oliver had consisted in a profuse bestowal upon him of all the dirty odds and ends which nobody else would eat" (54). For Oliver, such fulfilment is granted, but for his type, "porochial Dick," it is not (yet) possible. Yet small gestures or acts of kindness are still possible and are not to be taken lightly in such a violent, degraded world. (And the demand itself—to be properly fed—should not be taken lightly either: in an aphorism from *Minima Moralia*, Adorno observes that "[t]here is tenderness only in the coarsest demand: that no-one shall go hungry any more"[156].) As Oliver heads off to London, he passes his old orphanage and sees Dick, who beseeches him,

> "Kiss me" . . . climbing up the low gate, and flinging his little arms round Oliver's neck. "Good-b'ye, dear! God bless you!"

> The blessing was from a young child's lips, but it was the first that Oliver had ever heard invoked upon his head; and through all the struggles and sufferings of his after life, through all the troubles and changes of many weary years, he never once forgot it. (57)

Oliver, true to his word, does not forget Dick and even tries to go back and see him as his own fairy-tale narrative is coming to a close: "It is a world of disappointment—often to the hopes we most cherish and hopes that do our nature the greatest honour. Poor Dick was dead!" (440).[44]

It *is* a world of disappointment, and the ongoing presence of hunger and want, for Dickens, make all solutions within the present system partial. Dick and Jo, and the many other characters in Dickens's novels worn down and broken by inhuman structures—from the most eccentric to the most commonplace—register the partialness of the social and political solutions to date. The Coodles, Doodles, and Foodles of the world remain, as does Sir Leicester, because they do historically. But the possibility of other forms of character and community also remain, and by bringing together the commonplace and the odd, Dickens allows us to see the paucity of the commonsensical or the given; the odd upsets common sense and, in the process, shows common sense to be deeply ideological. This is the power of Dickens's world of eccentricity: in its very pleasures it allows us to see the limitations of the present, and to imagine the present otherwise. In short, Dickens's "many" help us envision what a comfort with and confidence in the common might look like, a common moreover that allows for the proliferation of difference *and* universal equality and that, against common complaints against Utopia, is more rather than less complex, experientially rich rather than uniformly dull, and pleasurable to boot. All characteristics, I would add, in short supply.

\* \* \*

At the end of his magisterial account of realism in *Mimesis*, Erich Auerbach turns to Virginia Woolf as the endpoint for the realist impulse that began with Odysseus's scar. For those of us schooled on Woolf's essays on "modern fiction," this move comes as something of a surprise. After all, in her battles with Arnold Bennett, Woolf is at pains to draw a sharp contrast between the Edwardians and the Victorians before them, and the advent of a new form of writing, now known simply as modernism. But for Auerbach the connection between classic realists such as Flaubert and Goncourt and Woolf rests with the democratic impulse they share. In its fruition in Woolf, the "elementary things which men have in common" (552) lead to a new form of "unification and simplification" (553). In its representation of the "random moment," *To the Lighthouse* makes visible how much individuals, despite their superficial differences, have in common: "It is precisely the random moment which is comparatively independent of the controversial and unstable orders over which men fight and despair; it passes unaffected by them as daily life. The more it is exploited, the more the elementary things which our lives have in common shine forth" (552).[45] A controversial claim, certainly, in its levelling of cultural difference in the name of the common. Why the inevitability of "unification and simplification" in the recognition of common bonds? How might we now, in the midst of a fully global world, imagine the common as more rather than less complex? And how might a fuller reckoning with Dickens alter Auerbach's narrative?

Dickens receives only passing notice in *Mimesis*, despite his full participation in the process of democratization Auerbach identifies with the realist project.[46] Like the French realists, Dickens brings the common people into literature and, equally and unlike the French, he brings literature to the people. Chesterton, as we have seen, defines Dickens's writing explicitly in terms of its "democratic optimism—a confidence in common men." Yet unlike Auerbach's vision of the common as the diminution of differences, Dickens's democratic optimism engenders something quite opposite: a radical vision of the proliferation of differences in a commons comfortable with and productive of the inexhaustible "many."

This "many," as we have also seen, has ties to an earlier popular radical culture as well as to Dickens's own present and the experience, in particular, of the city. Crucially, this "many" also incorporates the typical and the eccentric. To return to the reviews with which we began: less important than what side they come down on is the fact that they oscillate between the language of typicality and the language of eccentricity, something James perfectly embodies when he contends that Dickens "reconciles" us at once to the commonplace and the odd. Along this spectrum, the commonplace and the odd are weighed and valued: one critic's too odd is another's just right; as a result, Dickens's novels can be "too real to be pleasant" (*Life* 24), as his friend and biographer John Forster described *Bleak House*, or too pleasant to be real.

But missing from James's and other critics' assessments is the possibility of Dickens's characters being too real and too pleasant, a combination that Kincaid extols in his playful reading of *The Pickwick Papers* and what he sees as its celebration of fat, embodied most literally in the Fat Boy, while simultaneously expanding across the novel in its "plump" conversation, "wondrous redundancy," and "gluttonous open-heartedness" (26), and out to its "lustful reader[s]" (28), who become "fat with [Mr. Pickwick]" (32). The real in this pleasantness comes in the "trinity of flesh that defines the erotic reading of this novel: Tony Weller, Mr. Pickwick, and the Fat Boy," and the ways in which all three of them are "involved in strangely touching scenes of making contact—scenes so quiet, in fact, that we are likely not to register them or their connections consciously." In Kincaid's language such closeness comes via the "snug and cozy" (25) and the good company they engender: "The snug is most of all convivial, connecting. As Mr. Peter Magnus puts it, "Company, you see—company is—is—it's a very different thing from solitude—ain't it. . . ." As Kincaid fashions it, "Company . . . gives the child's ego, our ego, something essential, something to fatten on" (26). Company and conviviality, being friendly: these seemingly minor qualities are shown to be nothing short of essential.

These kinds of connections, as I understand them, are lateral and figure more broadly a set of common relations that Dickens attempts time and time again in his fiction to envision—without losing either the individual connectedness that Kincaid describes as "strangely touching scenes of making contact" or the larger systemic structures determining those common relations. While these might seem like slight gestures, they in fact gesture toward the utopian impulse in Dickens's world, the "subjunctive mode" through which alternative social relations are imagined. They are of the everyday and remarkable, garden variety and exceptional, and they experiment with forms of radical relationality, be it in the kiss Oliver receives from "porochial Dick," the social and political "connnexions"

*Bleak House* works to reveal,⁴⁷ or the fact that Dickens's "figures seem disposed to stagnate without crowds about them," as he himself muses. Just as the eccentric biographies that give his novels their shape are collective biographies that unsettle the very meaning of an individual life, Dickens's nineteenth-century character books imagine a transformed world where the remarkable would be common and the common remarkable. Against Henry James's assertion that "a community of eccentrics is impossible" (787), Dickens shows us that such a community is not only possible but also to be desired. Twinning critique and utopian optimism, Dickens's novels insist that the production of the commons is always a collective enterprise in the making, which would remake not only the world but "the People" in it too.

CHAPTER 3

# Eliot, Cosmopolitanism, and the Commons

WITH CHARACTERISTIC APLOMB, Terry Eagleton sets George Eliot in sharp contrast to Dickens. If in Dickens, "you cannot be virtuous and have greasy skin," in Eliot, "nobody . . . is either transcendentally good or wicked beyond redemption" (*The English Novel* 148, 163). "The worst that can happen to you in Eliot's world," Eagleton ventures, "is not spontaneous combustion or being battered to death by your vicious burglar of a lover, but 'never to be liberated from a small shivering hungry self', as she remarks of Edward Casaubon in *Middlemarch*" (163). This distinction echoes assessments of each writer by numerous other contemporary critics insofar as it positions Dickens's universe as morally less complex, and less nuanced—"flatter," in a word. But as we saw in the previous chapter, Dickens's utopianism—his abiding belief in the remarkable and the many—contains within it a rich and suggestive vision of a world in which the ordinary and the extraordinary would be hard to tell apart, and in which commonness would bring with it (or breed) multiplicity and the pleasures Kincaid associates so compellingly with girth. Certainly Eliot rarely trades in eccentricity, or in the visual radical popular culture and caricature that leads to the kind of equation Eagleton makes between greasy skin and loose values; indeed, she works in a different idiom and ethos throughout her oeuvre. Measured, judicious, at once distanced from and close to her characters, she is a relentlessly careful writer, acutely aware of the ways in which language can be slippery, obfuscating, exhilarating, hard to control.[1] Giddy from a trip to the seaside with George Henry Lewes, Eliot enthuses, "I never before longed so much to know the names of things as during this visit to Ilfracombe. The desire is part of the tendency that is now constantly growing in me to escape from all vagueness and inaccuracy into the daylight of distinct, vivid ideas "(*Letters* 2, 250–51).[2] Likewise, the desire to "escape from all vagueness and inaccuracy into the daylight of distinct, vivid ideas" entails a consonant desire to manage or control interpretation itself, whether in the form of her characters' interpretations of each other or her readers' interpretation of those self-same characters—a desire, as Elaine Freedgood positions it, that results from Eliot's recognition of the potentially limitless reach of interpretation. Significantly, though, her recognition indicates the intensity with which ideas can inhere in things, and the extent to which the range of such ideas cannot be anticipated: "[S]igns are small measurable things," she writes in *Middlemarch*, "but interpretations are illimitable, and in girls of sweet, ardent nature, every sign is apt to conjure up wonder, hope, belief, vast as a sky, and coloured by a diffuse thimbleful of matter in the shape of knowledge" (quoted in Freedgood, *The Ideas in Things* 112).

In place of a world of excess and fat, of multiplying types and teeming casts of characters, Eliot provides a materialist view of "small measurable things," of the particular rather than the abstract, that require a hermeneutics precisely because "interpretations are illimitable," not only for sweet, ardent girls but also for novelists. As a result, Eliot's thinking and her novels move by necessity from the small and measurable to the large and potentially limitless; from foreground to background, matter to knowledge and symbol to meaning—all subject to history. Or, as Jennifer Uglow stresses in her description of Eliot's Ilfracombe journal, it "combines this delight in naming particulars with a desire to place the particulars against a general background; it is the crowded banks as well as the individual plant which she admires, the whole rock-pool as well as the individual sea anemone." These connections, in turn, extend to include entire lifeworlds, "of man, of landscape and of marine life" (57–58). Less excess and multiplication than measure and relation, Eliot's experiments involve calibrating and recalibrating rather than counting and cataloguing.

Yet despite these differences in tone and idiom, Eliot shares with Dickens the sense that the common and commonness are the ground for a politics that is equally an ethics of the public good. If Dickens finds this vision in his cityscapes, Eliot remains rooted, with a few exceptions, in the rural landscape of her own upbringing—a landscape in which she witnessed firsthand the destruction of the common and the profound transformations that came in its wake. Her childhood years, in the Midlands in the early decades of the nineteenth century, coincided with the height of John Clare's career, a time, as we saw in Chapter 1, when rural life has been marked by the experience of the enclosure of common land, and described in Clare's poetry in great naturalistic detail—an experience and mode of representing a changed landscape that Eliot shares with Clare.[3] Eliot's father, Robert Evans, worked as a land agent and manager on the large landed estate of Arbury, which, during Eliot's childhood, was enclosed. Moreover, the "rate of enclosure" during this period "accelerated spectacularly," leading to "the dramatic reduction or abolition of common farming lands . . . which had allowed agricultural workers to grow their own food and supplement the income they received from the squire" (Dolin, *George Eliot* 46–47). Tim Dolin points out that Arbury also housed a coal mine and produced textiles for export still largely woven by handloom weavers. Eliot's earliest years thus came at a watershed moment, with Arbury on the cusp of the transition from hand weaving to steam-powered looms. These years were also marked by the struggles and resistance on the part of agricultural workers and weavers to preserve their way of life.

In this period of uneven development, old rural ways and forms of sociality overlapped with modern new technologies and new social formations, and highlighted the interconnectedness of country and city, making Eliot's Midlands far from isolated and idyllic. The unevenness of this development is fully on display in the introduction to *Felix Holt*, where Eliot speaks of "passing from one phase of life to another," from a village "dingy with coal-dust, noisy with the shaking of looms" to a "parish all of fields, high hedges, and deep-rutted lanes," or from a "manufacturing town, the scene of riots and trades-union meetings" to another rural region—a mere ten minutes away—"where the neighbourhood of the town was only felt in the advantages of a new market for corn, cheese, and hay, and where men with a considerable banking account were accustomed to say 'they never meddled with politics themselves'" (79–80). Eliot acknowledges that "it was easy for the traveller to conceive that town and country had no pulse in common" (80), but of course her narrative shows just how shared their pulse is, and will continue to be. In fact, as Dolin compellingly frames Eliot's time and place,

> In the Midlands it was not the advent of the railway that symbolized the advent of the modern: in 1825, the railway had hardly got going, and there were barely thirty miles of track in the whole United Kingdom. Rather, it was the radical transformation of the countryside, the transformation of the physical and social landscape, that symbolized the modern. (45)

These radical transformations predated the development of steam, "as rural populations increased in the eighteenth century and fell into grinding poverty, devastated by the loss of common lands, and subject to fluctuations in international trades." And as Dolin underscores, "One of the most traumatic effects of this was also the least visible: the loss of localism" (45).[4] In short, Eliot's rural landscape in no way limits her ability to move beyond the Midlands to the "wider public life," which, as she writes in *Felix Holt*, necessarily determines the private lives of her provincial characters (129). That wider public life, as I will argue, extends to the farthest reaches of the globe: the logic of the common inexorably carries Eliot from the local to the global and vice versa in the dialectical relationship she insists upon between the private and the public, the "small shivering hungry self" and the suffering of others, the latter refusal of which, to paraphrase Silvia Federici, forms the basis of the common.[5]

Finally, and perhaps most significantly, Eliot shares something else with Dickens—namely, the belief that "everything is politics." Dickens comically introduces this proposition in *The Pickwick Papers*: in one of the many plays on language that occur in the novel, Mr. Pickwick, in his interview with the Count, notes, "'The word politics, Sir . . . comprises, in itself, a difficult study of no inconsiderable magnitude.'" The Count, happy with this description, and "drawing out the tablets again" to record it, replies, "'ver good—fine words to begin a chapter. Chapter forty-seven. Poltics. The word poltic surprises by himself—' And down went Mr Pickwick's remark, in Count Smorltork's tablets, with such variations and additions as the Count's exuberant fancy suggested, or his imperfect knowledge of the language, occasioned" (207).

"Ver good—fine words to begin a chapter" on politics indeed. Mr. Pickwick's definition of politics and the Count's humorous mistranslation of his words perfectly capture how much politics is a matter of translation and how expansive *and* wayward its definitions can be. The exchange is a classic Dickensian moment and, in a more serious vein, it also identifies the not "inconsiderable magnitude" of politics and enacts its slipperiness as a term, the way it can move from comprising to surprising, from an object of study to a subject that takes on a life of its own—about which it becomes hard to say what *isn't* politics. In fact, Georg Lukács links a recognition like Mr. Pickwick's to the whole project of realism itself:

> An unbiased investigation of life . . . leads easily enough . . . to the discovery which had long been made by the great realists of the beginning and middle of the nineteenth century and which Gottfried Keller expressed thus: "Everything is politics." The great Swiss writer did not intend this to mean that everything was immediately tied up with politics; on the contrary, in his view—as in Balzac's and Tolstoy's—every action, thought, and emotion of human beings is inseparably bound up with the life and struggles of the community, i.e., with politics; whether the humans themselves are conscious of this, unconscious of it or even trying to escape from it, objectively their actions, thoughts and emotions nevertheless spring from and run into politics. (*Studies in European Realism* 9)

Lukács extends his claim by underlining that "the true great realists not only realized and depicted this situation—they did more than that, they set it up as a demand to be made on men," demonstrating that the separation of "the complete human personality into a public and a private sector" was "a fiction of capitalist society" (9) and hence in need of debunking.

If it seems odd to link Eliot's vision with Dickens's, connecting her political views with Lukács's might seem stranger yet. Not only is Eliot's voice radically different from Dickens's, but there is, for Eagleton, a politics to these stylistic qualities: "You can tell that George Eliot is a liberal by the shape of her sentences" (*The English Novel* 163).[6] Likewise, Lukács's Marxist politics seem a far cry from Eliot's judicious, ameliorative politics, not to mention the added fact that Eliot, even more so than Dickens, is noticeably absent from Lukács's account of nineteenth-century realism. Despite these differences, however, Eliot, like Dickens and Lukács, shares a commitment to the belief that everything truly is politics, which, in turn, necessitates experimentation with form and character in order to find the means by which to demonstrate the deep relatedness of all aspects of social life.

For Eliot, I argue, this belief finds expression in her commitment to the common and the commons, a commitment grounded in a materialist view of character that both draws on older eighteenth-century practices of character-building and refashions them in response to the pressures of a globalizing mid-nineteenth-century world and the new kinds of social bonds it brings into being. In its emphasis on the collective nature of "character," in both senses of the word, moreover, her politics of the common is irreducibly ethical and political and forestalls the critical tendency to see them as competing emphases. In *Middlemarch*, Dorothea asks, "What should I do—how should I act now?" (788), succinctly revealing the ethical and the political as inseparable, as the question of *how* to act follows from the ethical imperative of what *should* be done. Suzy Anger identifies Dorothea's question—asked as well through many of Eliot's other characters—as that which "had become the central question of modern ethics" (79). She goes on to comment that "[m]oral behavior requires what George Eliot regards as a kind of impartiality, an ability to maintain 'that sense of others' claims' [from *Mill on the Floss*] against 'clamorous selfish desires' [from *Scenes of Clerical Life*, 'Janet's Repentance']" (80). While Anger's focus is on Eliot's ethics, the "sense of other claims," as I will argue, invariably contains a politics of the common, as this passage in *Middlemarch* when Dorothea looks out her window on the following scene showcases:

> On the road there was a man with a bundle on his back and a woman carrying her baby; in the field she could see figures moving—perhaps the shepherd with his dog. Far off in the bending sky was the pearly light; and she felt the largeness of the world and the manifold wakings of men to labour and endurance. She was part of that involuntary, palpitating life, and could neither look out on it from her luxurious shelter as a mere spectator, nor hide her eyes in selfish complaining. (788)

Significantly, it is not only the capacity to sympathize with suffering and those less fortunate that constitutes "moral progress" for Eliot. One must also be able to sympathize with others' joy: "My own experience and development deepen every day my conviction that our moral progress may by measured by the degree in which we sympathize with individual suffering and individual joy" (*Letters* 2, 403). By foregrounding the materiality of Eliot's realism—that "involuntary palpitating life" that cannot be disavowed, either by distance or by turning inward—and by extension her politics, I decouple the *de rigueur* association of her writing with a predictable liberalism and suggest some of the ways in which she is more relevant to twenty-first-century readers than she has appeared to be.

### In Defense of the Common

George Eliot famously pauses in the middle of *Adam Bede* (1859) to clarify her role as a novelist and ours as readers. She distinguishes her realism from older, conventional narratives, composed by "clever [novelists]," at once refusing to produce the idealizing representations she imagines her reader demanding and establishing the terms of her own narrative, which rely on the commonplace rather than the clever and require her to "creep servilely after nature and fact" (221). Throughout the chapter, Eliot makes her case for focusing on the "great multitude" as opposed to the "rarity," the "old women scraping carrots with their work-worn hands" (224) as opposed to the "cloud-borne angels . . . and heroic warriors."[7] The homely, the commonplace, "the middle," the vulgar, the coarse: these are the stuff of realism and those "select natures" that fail to see this are akin to the "narrowest and pettiest" (229) of people.

The string of associations between the common, the vulgar, and the coarse at once reproduce and work to overturn pejorative conceptions of commonness, conceptions that Eliot persistently acknowledges and generates throughout her work. Raymond Williams comments on Eliot's own discomfort with the Dodsons and Tullivers in *The Mill on the Floss*, which in turn provokes her need to justify them as subject matter for her novel (*The Country and the City* 165–181); the narrator of *Daniel Deronda* writes of Deronda's "first sense of repulsion at the commonness of these people [the Cohens]" (579), and Lydgate's "spots of commonness" include falling prey to contemporary prejudices and self-interest (an issue I develop more fully further on). Commonness, and its ties to the vulgar and the coarse, can thus cut both ways: it is a shared condition with the potential to equalize and a shared condition that is part of the current set of prejudices, such as Deronda's class and racial distaste for "vulgar Jews" (415) and his plea to Mirah to shed the name Cohen as "inadmissible to a singer" and to understand that "[this] is one of those trifles in which we must conform to vulgar prejudice" (525).[8]

But equally the homely, the middling, and the common are the actual people inhabiting Eliot's realist texts. There is a slippage, that is to say, between the stuff of realism and its characters that makes characters akin to "nature and fact," to the "common things" Eliot's narrator in *Adam Bede* is after. No less material than the world of which they are a part, they put up material resistance to being read, by the narrator or the novel's readers, in merely self-serving ways. In perhaps the most oft-quoted line in the chapter, the narrator writes that she "[aspires] to give no more than a faithful account of men and things as they have mirrored themselves in my mind" (221). Not only are men and things equated here, but the language that Eliot uses to describe their effect on the narrator is not as straightforward as it might initially seem. Rather than referring to the way in which these things are "mirrored in [her] mind," which would grant to the mind a preeminence, they have "mirrored *themselves* in [her] mind, suggesting that they too embody a form of material agency.

The intimate reciprocity between characters and things at the center of Eliot's realism has a number of eighteenth-century antecedents, from William Cowper and William Wordsworth to *Chrysal, or the Adventures of a Guinea* and other modes of "characteristic writing."[9] I, however, want simply to note how indebted Eliot's notion of commonness is to this range of writing practices and how, in her hands, they combine to produce the specifically "materialist standards" (U. C. Knoepflmacher's term) of her realism. In her early essay "Worldliness and Other-Worldliness: The Poet Young," for example, Eliot contrasts Edward Young's apophthegmatic other-worldly appeals to Cowper's grounded "worldliness," in which "no object is too small to prompt his song" (not even a sofa), and "his song is never trivial, for he is alive to small objects, not because his mind is narrow, but because his glance is clear and his heart is large" (*Selected Essays* 209).[10] Speaking here specifically about Cowper's *The Task*, Eliot is effusive in her praise: the poem is singular in "the genuine love it breathes, at once toward inanimate and animate existence"; in "the calm gladness that springs from a delight in objects for their own sake, without self-reference—in divine sympathy with the lowliest pleasures, with the most short-lived capacity for pain"; and "the happiest lingering over [the earth's] simplest scenes with all the fond minuteness of attention that belongs to love; no pompous rhetoric about the inferiority of the 'brutes', but a warm plea on their behalf against man's inconsiderateness and cruelty, and a sense of enlarged happiness from their companionship in enjoyment" (209). The common, as Eliot interprets Cowper, is both near at hand, found as it is in small, common objects, and expansive and worldly in its capacity to prompt fellow feeling.

In like fashion, William Wordsworth's celebration of the common is integral to Eliot's vision of realism; as Dolin unequivocally states, "without Wordsworth's *Lyrical Ballads*, and his celebrated 1802 Preface to them, Eliot's realism could hardly have been imagined" (89).[11] He goes on to note the many Wordsworthian echoes in *Adam Bede*'s defense of realism and its appeal to "the faithful representing of commonplace things"; other novels, too, such as *Mill on the Floss*, recall Wordsworth (in its condemnation of "men of maxims"). There, Eliot writes,

> All people of broad, strong sense have an instinctive repugnance to the men of maxims; because such people early discern that the mysterious complexity of our life is not to be embraced by maxim, and that to lace ourselves up on formulas of that sort is to repress all the divine promptings and inspirations that spring from growing insight and sympathy. (518)

Guided as they are by "by general rules" and "thinking that these will lead them to justice by a ready-made patent method," men of maxims lack the moral judgment and insight that comes "from a life vivid and intense enough to have created a wide fellow-feeling with all that is human" (518). Significantly, Wordsworth links "the high moral vocation of the artist to the fellow feeling engendered by the imagination," an association that Eliot herself singles out as "the only effect I ardently long to produce by my writings," namely, "that those who read them should be better able to *imagine* and to *feel* the pains and the joys of those who differ from themselves in everything but the broad fact of being struggling erring human creatures" (*Letters* 3, 111).

For Eliot, fellow feeling entails an expansive closeness that can seem contradictory but in actuality defines the dialectical nature of her realism: it refuses to rest in either the close-at-hand or the distant, since to do so risks losing sight of the complex relations between "the real and concrete"—relations that she likens in *The Mill on the Floss* to a form of natural history.[12] Simultaneously acknowledging the "oppressive narrowness" of the Dodsons and the Tullivers and justifying her interest in them, Eliot advises that

> we need not shrink from this comparison of small things with great; for does not science tell us that its highest striving is after the ascertainment of a unity which shall bind the smallest things with the greatest? In natural science, I have understood, there is nothing petty to the mind that has a large vision of relations, and to which every single object suggests a vast sum of conditions. (284)

As she concludes, "It is surely the same with the observation of human life." For Eliot, fellow feeling constitutes a vision of subject-object relations in which every single subject, too, suggests a shared "vast sum of conditions." And finally, to further complicate this comparison of small and great things, this vast sum of conditions, there is the fact that the conditions themselves are always in flux, adding to the representational challenges that inhere in a "large vision of relations." In *Daniel Deronda*, Eliot's narrator defines this challenge in terms of the difference between a portrait painter and a historian: "Sir Joshua," the narrator reckons, "would have been glad to take [Gwendolen's] portrait; and he would have had an easier task than the historian at least in this, that he would not have had to represent the truth of change—only to give stability to one beautiful moment" (151). In other words, there is nothing static in the "real and concrete" for Eliot; the "truth of change" is a necessary component of natural and human life.[13]

## CHAPTER THREE

Crucially, fellow feeling as "real and concrete" is equally prompted by another vision of commonness found in characteristic writing: the idea of character type. Type in this tradition, as we saw in Dickens's indebtedness to characteristic writing, had to do with literal typefaces and the impressions characters make as well as the literal impressions necessary to inscribe characters on a page. Characters were conceived in terms of brands, stamps, letters of reference, and bodies of writing, and questions of surface legibility—assessed by such literal considerations as the number of "strokes" necessary to capture a countenance—determined what constituted character. Characteristic writing included everything from character sketches and the Fieldings novels to character books; letters; and even visual materials such as engravings, caricatures, the actor David Garrick's face, and print-shop window displays—materials and references that Eliot, like Dickens, inherits from her eighteenth-century predecessors. This model of type recognizes the profound materiality of character in a most literal sense and, as I will show, counters or at least fractures the equation of nineteenth-century British realism solely with the ideology of liberalism and the consolidation of a capitalist world economy, captured most succinctly in Eagleton's claim that "liberalism and the realist novel are spiritual twins" (*The English Novel* 164). Eliot not only directly references this tradition—the very chapter in *Middlemarch* that begins with Eliot comparing her craft to that of Henry Fielding also names *Chrysal* among Lydgate's juvenile reading—but also incorporates and amends it within her most iconic novels, novels that have been lauded historically and, as I am suggesting, erroneously, for representing an idealist concept of interiority as the essence of personality—a concept linked to the individualist politics of liberalism. In short, too often, and too automatically, critics have associated nineteenth-century conceptions of character with interiority and individualism.

But time and time again Eliot's fiction belies this definition of character. Repeatedly and emphatically, Eliot highlights the material, collective nature of character and the material, collective politics such a vision of character entails. (At the end of her career, she also turns to another older tradition of type in the form of Theophrastan character, to which I will return.) At the most obvious level, character types and commonness work by dint of their reproducibility: it is only by capturing what is typical or common, what is shared by others, that a type makes sense. When first introduced, the narrator says of Arthur Donnithorne, for example, "If you want to know more particularly how he looked, call to your remembrance some tawny-whiskered, brown-locked, clear-complexioned young Englishman whom you have met with in a foreign town, and been proud of as a fellow-countryman" (105). Likewise, the Reverend Amos Barton in "The Sad Fortunes of Amos Barton" is a man "very far from remarkable,—a man whose virtues were not heroic, and had no undetected crime within his breast . . . but was palpably and unmistakably commonplace" (*Scenes* 80).[14] A man of "insignificant stamp" (*Scenes* 81), he shares his being with "eighty out of a hundred" similarly "commonplace people" about whom the narrator asks, "Nay, is there not a pathos in their very insignificance—in our comparison of their dim and narrow existence with the glorious possibilities of that human nature which they share?" (*Scenes* 81).[15] And of course *Middlemarch* announces its concern with commonness and the "middling" in its title, a concern that pervades the novel and which Eliot explicitly theorizes in the preface and conclusion as well as throughout the novel. As with Amos Barton, the novel employs the language of unheroic or "unhistoric acts," which in turn echoes Eliot's description of *The Mill on the Floss* as a tragedy of "millers and other insignificant people" (207). "But we insignificant people with our daily words and acts," the narrator assures *Middlemarch*'s readers, "are preparing the lives of many Dorotheas, some of which may present a far sadder sacrifice than that of the Dorothea whose story we know" (838). Even as Eliot, then, acknowledges earlier in the novel how difficult it is to avoid singling out individual characters from the store of common characters when she asks, "but why always Dorothea?" (278), she ends the novel by recognizing multiple Dorotheas, some of whom may have it far worse than "our" Dorothea: "ours" in the sense that, as social beings, we—countless, nameless others—necessarily help "prepare the lives" of others, and "ours" insofar as we share a common indebtedness to one another, regardless of how presently unequal actual social arrangements might be. In the contemporary language of the commons, Michael Hardt and Antonio Negri express this indebtedness thus: "Being, after all, is just another way of saying what is ineluctably common, what refuses to be privatized or enclosed and remains constantly open to all. (There is no such thing as a private ontology.)" (*Commonwealth* 181).

Eliot's ethical commitment to the "superlatively middling" (*Scenes* 85) is nothing if not fraught, however, as the tension within this phrase might suggest. First, there is the problem of narrative voice or idiom: the sense, as Raymond Williams has argued, that Eliot's defensiveness about her own common characters and her consequent need to justify the narrative attention she gives them mark the limits of her own class position. Anxious in the company of her imagined middle-class readers, she becomes "self-conscious . . . placating and appealing to what seems a dominant image of a particular kind of reader" (The *Country and the City* 172), thereby falling into a new form of patronage. Second, throughout Eliot's oeuvre, she grapples with the issue of whether "seeing truly and feeling justly was enough to guarantee the moral effect of her stories without the help of an element of idealisation (196)," as David Lodge paraphrases Knoepflmacher. Finally, there is the sense of discomfort, in general, regarding what it means, exactly, to envision a politics premised on the "superlatively middling"—especially when this description, used to characterize Amos Barton, is followed by a further description of him as "the quintessential extract of mediocrity" (85). It is precisely in the visceral unease elicited by the celebration of mediocrity, though, that the forward-looking aspects of commonness as a radical politics are to be found.

*Adam Bede* provides perhaps the best early example of the coordinates of Eliot's politics of the common in its explicit linking of its common characters to the historical commons.[16] There she cautions that common characters, like the world, are "not just what we [as readers] like," not there to be touched up and not "entirely of [the narrator's] own choosing" (221). In short, "men and things" may teach us—readers and realist writers alike—about a kind of "material recalcitrance," which, in a different context, Jonathan Goldberg characterizes as a recognition of the ways in which "reality presses on us, resists our attempts to reduce or refuse it, chastens grandiosity or fantasies of omnipotence" (375).[17] Indeed, we might see in Eliot's version of this material recalcitrance echoes of Marx's famous maxim from *The Eighteenth Brumaire of Louis Napoleon* that "men make their own history, but not of their own free will; not under circumstances they have themselves chosen but under the given and inherited circumstances with which they are directly confronted" (*Surveys from Exile* 146). As Richard Dienst carefully parses the phrase "given and inherited," "What might sound like Marx's redundant stuttering seems on reflection to be especially well phrased. Given *and* inherited, what's taken and what's received, what remains *and* what is passed along: the phrase opens up several distinct settings in which historical circumstances confront us and are confronted, where the dispositions of agency and determination still remain to be seen" (159).

Now George Eliot is no Karl Marx, but her representations of the common types peopling *Adam Bede*—the artisan, the Methodist preacher, the dairymaid, the farmer's wife—nonetheless produce a vision of the commons that presupposes a radical transformation of day-to-day material reality almost unthinkable within the economic structure of the time. Take Mrs. Poyser, who, along with her husband, Martin Poyser, is a farming tenant on the old Squire's estate. Like characters of her ilk in other Eliot novels, she is routinely referred to in the plural, as in "the Poysers," finding her nondescript place alongside others such as the Dodsons and the Gleggs in *The Mill on the Floss*. Yet confronted with the old Squire's proposition to expand her dairy operation by taking on more dairy land from a neighboring farm in exchange for ceding some of their ploughing land to a new tenant—which we can see as a microcosm for the historical process of enclosure—Mrs. Poyser, as the title of this episode's chapter indicates, speaks up and "has her say out." Specifically, she systematically rebuts the Squire's claims regarding the common ground upon which such an exchange would be made. Throughout his appeal, the Squire couches the exchange in terms of a "mutual advantage" (390) and assumes, moreover, that the Poysers will agree with him. Mrs. Poyser, however, immediately identifies how unequal such an exchange must be: bluntly stating that she won't take on any more dairy work simply to line the Squire's pockets, she presents a sustained analysis of the dangers of specialization and identifies the division between classes inscribed in the Squire's offer. "I know there's them as is born t' own the land, and them as is born to sweat on 't", Mrs. Poyser declares, "and I know it's christened folks's duty to submit to their betters as fur as flesh and blood 'ull bear it; but I'll not make a martyr o' myself . . . for no landlord in England, not if he was King George himself" (392). Mrs. Poyser explicitly links the deference required by social relations to the economic structure undergirding them, namely private property. Lest we assume that this constitutes an idiosyncratic outburst on Mrs. Poyser's part, she and the narrator make clear she speaks for the parish; a chorus consisting of two servant girls, a waggoner, and "sour old John," not to mention a bull-dog, a terrier, a sheep-dog, and a hissing gander, confirms Mrs. Poyser's claim. Humorous as this particular collective might be, the resistance to the given it dramatizes has potentially dire consequences, for in the course of the conversation the Squire has threatened to cancel the Poysers' lease if they refuse to go along with his plan. The presumption and heat of class privilege quickly replace the liberal, polite language of mutual advantage.

Although the Poysers are ultimately spared the loss of their land and livelihood, the violence the Squire threatens—reenacting the violence of enclosure in miniature and thereby focusing and personalizing its impact—nonetheless is made good, in displaced form, in Hetty Sorrel's fate. Wooed and impregnated by the old Squire's son, Arthur, Hetty, the dairymaid on the Poysers' farm, ultimately ends up killing her baby and being sentenced to death—a sentence transmuted by Arthur's last minute-appeal into transport. Her destination, Australia, is where 80 percent of the prisoners were sent for crimes against property.[18] In short, Hetty pays the price, coded in the language of capitalism rather than the commons, for having "dreams" that "were all of luxuries" (144).

Significantly, Arthur's overriding ambition is to become a "model landlord," which he interprets as furthering the project of enclosure while simultaneously earning the respect and admiration of his laborers. In an overdetermined conversation with Mr. Irwine, in the chapter that immediately precedes Eliot's mission statement about realism, Arthur boasts that he can tame the ire roused by another tenant's enclosure of common land simply by being nice; as he assures Irwine, "I don't believe there's anything you can't prevail on people to do with kindness" (215). Needless to say, there is a terrible irony in Arthur's claim, given Hetty's tragic end. Utterly transformed and aged by his dalliance with Hetty, Arthur leaves his father's estate and only returns to his home—and to the narrative—in the epilogue, set eight years after the end of the story. He confesses to Adam Bede that he "[makes] no schemes now" (582) and, echoing what Adam had told him years ago, concludes that "[t]here's a sort of wrong that can never be made up for" (584).

This "mixed, entangled affair" (221)—a phrase Eliot uses in the novel to describe the project of realism—begins to conjure the multiple, materially and figuratively related notions of indebtedness composing *Adam Bede*'s narrative. Common types like Mrs. Poyser and Arthur are indebted to the other nameless characters making them legible types in the first place. And when character is envisioned as an exchange between common things, the supremacy of internal over external, or of mind over matter, is undercut. One particularly evocative formulation of this attempt to "dethrone"[19] the self (which I discuss more fully in the Introduction) is found in *Middlemarch* when Eliot's narrator links the most intangible of perceptions—feeling—to the concreteness of things, writing about Dorothea that

> it had been easier to imagine how she would devote herself to Mr. Casaubon, and become wise and strong in his strength and wisdom, than to conceive with that distinctness which is no longer reflection but feeling—an idea wrought back to the directness of sense, like the solidity of objects—that he had an equivalent centre of self, whence the lights and shadows must always fall with a certain difference. (211)

Such an equation, as I have argued, gives to feeling a materiality that feeling itself would seem to belie, and connects this "thingness" or solidity to an apparently immaterial psychological interiority.

By giving characters the solidity of objects, material types thus potentially enact a profound levelling of the social, phrased here as the granting of an "equivalent centre of self." Such an equivalency imaginatively places selves alongside one another in a proliferation of different reciprocal "centers," thereby envisioning a metaphorical *besideness* rather than hierarchy between selves that echoes character books' more literal mode of representing subjects as equivalent objects, as we saw in Chapter 2.[20] Crucially, though, as the narrative of enclosure at the center of *Adam Bede* demonstrates, our indebtedness to others is subtended by property relations such that any vision of equivalence remains at worst ideological, and at best, utopian within capitalism. *Adam Bede* shows us both in the twinned narratives of the verbal exchange between the Poysers and the old Squire and the sexual one between the "model landlord" and the dairymaid. Moreover, much like Eliot's desire in the Ilfracombe journal to capture a myriad set of connections ranging from individual plants to crowded banks and beyond, these exchanges, while deeply personal, also encapsulate the fundamental and far-reaching changes occurring in the countryside that need to be seen as interrelated. "As the economy develops," Raymond Williams insists, "enclosure can never really be isolated from the mainstream of land improvements, of changes in methods of production, of price-movements, and of those more general changes in property relationships which were all flowing in the same direction: an extension of cultivated land but also a concentration of ownership into the hands of a minority" (*The Country and the City* 97). Mrs. Poyser, in essence, rejects the "economics of specialization and scale" (99), in turn resisting the constellation of economic and social changes wrought by agrarian capitalism.

But the novel is not only backward looking or nostalgic, as its setting in 1799, sixty years before it was written, might suggest. Such a reading ignores the fact that Eliot's view of the past encompasses not only "emerging or fading types" (Bowlby xvi) but future types not yet realized in Eliot's own time. Type in the material sense figures a form of commonness that is always also a story about forms of indebtedness; about the fact that our debts to other selves and to the world go hand in hand. In *Adam Bede*, as well as elsewhere, Eliot sees these debts as at once metaphorical and literal (just like "character"), at once about intersubjective relations and economic structures. In this light, Dorothea's claim at the end of *Middlemarch* that she will "learn what everything costs" (812) looks less like a capitulation to the given than an acknowledgment that all relations are inescapably economic in nature—and that the "cost" of these debts has yet to be learned. Equally, it does not partake of the movement with which Andrew Miller characterizes Eliot's method: "Like the auction and the pawnshop, *Middlemarch* moves away from a narrowly materialist understanding of goods; instead of translating goods into their exchange value, however, she rewrites them as aesthetic objects" (216). In an early letter written to the Brays and Hennells in which she responds to the May 15, 1848, revolution in France and the proposed impeachment of one of its leaders, Louis Blanc, she envisions in the future "a day . . . when there will be a temple of white marble where sweet incense and anthems shall rise to the memory of every man and every woman who has had a deep *'ahnung,'* a presentiment, a yearning, or a clear vision of the time when this miserable reign of Mammon shall end" (*Letters* 1, 267).

These are not just the enthusiasms of a young Mary Ann Evans; the mature George Eliot of *Middlemarch* also underscores the utterly structural nature of "Mammon" in the current day. Filling in Lydgate's history, the narrator writes, "He was but seven-and-twenty, an age at which many men are not quite common—at which they are hopeful of achievement, resolute in avoidance, thinking that Mammon shall never put a bit in their mouths and get astride their backs, but rather that Mammon, if they have anything to do with him, shall draw their chariot" (142). To be "not quite common," as many young men are, is to hope that one can stay above the fray, that one can escape the lure and appurtenances of wealth and its snares, a belief which will be proven grievously wrong in Lydgate's case. If in Eliot's letter the realization of a genuine commonwealth takes shape as a utopian impulse, a looking back from a better future in which the present has been overcome, in *Middlemarch*, Lydgate's future makes clear that nineteenth-century Britons are still fully within the "miserable reign of Mammon."

The way out, however, is never envisioned through the recovery of a lost common; instead, anticipating what contemporary theorists such as Hardt and Negri and David Harvey emphasize with respect to the commons today, it is at once an aim and something "perpetually being produced" (Harvey, "*Commonwealth*: An Exchange" 259), given the ineluctably collective nature of social life. In "Janet's Repentance," the last story of *Scenes of Clerical Life*, set in the 1830s, the common as a literal piece of communally owned land is already an antiquated reference. The description of Paddiford Common, where the Methodist Reverend Edgar Tryan lives and preaches, pointedly draws attention to the changed nature of the common by this time: "As long as Mr. Tryan's hearers were confined to Paddiford Common—which, by the by, was hardly recognisable as a common at all, but was a dismal district where you heard the rattle of the handloom, and breathed the smoke of coal-pits—the 'canting parson' could be treated as a joke" (197). Similarly, in the much earlier 1799 setting of *Adam Bede*, another Methodist preacher, Dinah Morris, chooses to live in an equally "dismal district" described as "a bleak and barren country" (80) and "a dreary, bleak place" (133) dominated by a cotton mill, and with the lead mines of Hetton-Deeps a short walk away. In both cases, Dissent and the development of manufacturing districts characterize a newly conceived common and make it a potent site of the present economic transformations accompanying the industrial revolution. That it has direct connections with the village common, that the one is an outgrowth of or replaces the other, is made clear in the opening chapters when we are introduced to Dinah Morris preaching on the Hayslope Green, a scene that Queen Victoria was so taken with that she and Prince Albert commissioned a watercolor of it by Edward Henry Corbould titled "Dinah Morris Preaching on the Common" (see Figure 8). The common, in this context, figures something potentially new in the making, what Williams calls "active community." As he argues, "In many parts of rural Britain, a new kind of community developed as an aspect of struggle, against the dominant landowners or, as in the labourers' revolts in the time of the Swing machine-smashing and rick-burning or in the labourers' unions from Tolpuddle to Joseph Arch, against the whole class-system of rural capitalism. . . . In many thousands of cases, there is more community in the modern village, as a result of this process of new legal and democratic rights, than at any point in the recorded or imagined past" (*The Country and the City* 104).

Whether seen as process or future achievement, a politics of the commons, as Eliot envisions it, is humbling. It involves a decentering and literal objectification of self (think of Eliot's poetically declarative statement in *Middlemarch* that "I know no speck so troublesome as self" [419]), a recognition of how much we owe to others, of how much we are never simply ourselves. In its imagining of a collective being, it shares certain qualities with Eliot's vision of the chorus. In her reading of *Scenes of Clerical Life*, Barbara Hardy notes the multiple roles the chorus has: it

FIGURE 8. Edward Henry Corbould, "Dinah Morris Preaching on the Common" (1861). Source: Royal Collection Trust / © Her Majesty Queen Elizabeth II 2020. Reprinted with permission.

not only serves as background and "causal agent, making and breaking relations" but also has a formal function, moving the narrative between individual and collective views, "from the shot in the dark to the truth; from the isolated creature to the diffused and comfortable warmth of the crowd; from tension to casual humour." In its unsettling of the individual the chorus shows that "one man's tragedy is everyone else's comedy," but, "there is usually also the moment when one man's tragedy becomes everyone's tragedy" (21–22). But unlike the chorus, the commons brings into view the fact that any worthy notion of sociality must be grounded materially, not only in the common (as in the crowd, the commonplace) but in the common good. A politics of the commons, as Lydgate's fate confirms, does not permit the material realities of the world to be neglected, nor does it countenance the "spots of commonness" that lie in "the complexion of [Lydgate's] prejudices"—namely, his inability to resist or disavow the most ordinary of conceits, a noxious class ideology premised on turning a blind eye to the social conditions or makings of wealth. In this most memorable phrase of Eliot's, she reminds us of Lydgate's "not quite common" ambitions as a young man and his failure to realize them, reinforcing the woefully common attributes and characteristics of the established order and its class ideology, of the "miserable reign of Mammon." Recall Lydgate's intellectual and class "prejudice," when he first arrives in Middlemarch, that he need not "think of furniture at present; but whenever he did so, it was to be feared that neither biology nor schemes of reform would lift him above the vulgarity of feeling that there would be an incompatibility in his furniture not being of the best" (150). The fact that his disregard for the cost of the furniture—literally and figuratively—causes his downfall underscores how, as Henry Staten has ably shown, "Lydgate's class consciousness and economic unconsciousness [lie] at the centre of the account in *Middlemarch* of the 'complex web' of social relations, founding the rest of the account on the central fact of economic reality: what things cost and what one has to do to pay for them" (1001).[21] It is no accident that Dorothea declaratively states, "I hate my wealth," while Lydgate makes his name writing "a treatise on Gout, a disease," Eliot adds with a stroke of wit, "which has a good deal of wealth on its side" (834).

A politics of the commons, as, again, Lydgate's example makes clear, is also one in which a more routine politics cannot be evaded, in exactly the sense Lukács means when he defines Keller's view of politics as the idea that "every action, thought, and emotion of human beings is inseparably bound up with the life and struggles of the community, i.e. with politics." In this regard, Will Ladislaw serves as a powerful counterpoint to Lydgate, as Amanda Anderson has argued, with his commitment to a politics "responding to larger social wrongs" (71) and "his indifference to conventional forms of self-interest" (*Bleak Liberalism* 75); Staten too sees Ladislaw as the "person in the novel least under the sway of class ideology" (993) and the only person with "no vested interest in the established order" (1002), thereby amplifying Raymond Williams's claim that through him Eliot is "following a thread to the future" (quoted on 1003; The *English Novel* 93).[22] In contrast, recall Lydgate's gradual absorption into Middlemarch's local politics via the hospital debate and how his vote in the end cannot be separated from his self-interest despite his avowed intention to remain apart from "small social conditions": "For the first time," the narrator explains, "Lydgate was feeling the hampering threadlike pressure of small social conditions, and their frustrating complexity. . . . However it was, he did not distinctly say to himself on which side he would vote; and all the while he was inwardly resenting the subjection which had been forced upon him" (180). In the end Lydgate succumbs to Bulstrode's pressure and votes for the Reverend Tyke rather than Mr. Farebrother (whose name says it all). His initial indecisiveness, however, is symptomatic of the complex set of considerations that inform any notion of the common good and the multiple forms of indebtedness that it comprises: its constitution, in short, is an open question, which Dienst, in the context of the debt crisis of early twenty-first-century life, phrases thus: "It is only in the experience of the insistence of indebtedness that one can keep faith with the need to be rid of it, and the desire to construct different bonds in common" (136).

## The Commons and the World

In response to reviews of *Daniel Deronda*, Eliot took umbrage at her readers' inclination to "cut the book into scraps and talk of nothing in it but Gwendolen," claiming that she "meant everything in the book to be related to everything else there" (*Letters* 6, 290). By the latter half of the nineteenth century, the idea that everything was related to everything else had taken on an increasingly global scope. As Christopher Hitchens notes in his defense of *Daniel Deronda*, not only did Disraeli become the first Jewish prime minister the same year the novel was published, and Victoria the Empress of India, but, more generally, the "writing of the novel took place against a background of expansion and innovation—especially the opening that resulted from the digging of the Suez Canal. That is why its action can for the first time comprehend a world outside England" (10). Likewise, Goodlad identifies these "globalizing dynamics" with the existence of "actually existing cosmopolitanisms" in the nineteenth century. Against Fredric Jameson's claim that the representational and political problems attendant on a global economy are not really felt until the advent of modernism, Goodlad insists that the Victorians were already well aware of and grappling with these problems. She proposes that the period during which Eliot and other realists were writing was "noteworthy for its reinvention of empire at a time when Britain was also reinventing itself as a mass democracy" (*The Victorian Geopolitical Aesthetic* 405). In other words, the spatial disjunction Jameson identifies with modernism—between lived (metropolitan) experience and (imperial) structure—had an impact on realist practices. As a result, nineteenth-century realism needs to be understood as part of a broader "Victorian geopolitical aesthetic." In what follows, I want to suggest that Eliot's politics of the commons is inherently cosmopolitan in its "insistence on indebtedness." At the same time, however, the very dislocations accompanying an expanding, international economy often lead Eliot away from the radical premises and promises of the commons toward more partial, nationally- or class-based solutions, even as her own novels narrate the historical passing of those solutions.

Given the purview of her novels and her attention to provincial life and local affiliations, the linking of Eliot's views to cosmopolitanism is nothing if not contested. On her list of what's not in *Middlemarch*, for example, Gillian Beer includes, as the most obvious absence, *Middlemarch*. As she explains, "[T]he main thing not to be found in Middlemarch, the town, is *Middlemarch*, the book. . . . The disparities between topic and writing are striking. The town of Middlemarch is provincial, the writing of *Middlemarch* is urban, cosmopolitan even. The concerns of the people are local, of the writing polymathic" ("What's Not in *Middlemarch*" 17). This tension, Beer argues, is "supple," prompting questions about the distance between *Middlemarch*'s time of writing and its first readers and the conditions depicted in Middlemarch—"How much have things changed? How capable are they of change?"—as well as "wry comparisons" between events in the novel and current events, from bank crises to reform bills to the position of women (17–18).[23] Beer's point is well taken, but increasingly, and even in *Middlemarch*, "outsider" characters themselves either provide or yearn for an expansive, cosmopolitan view of the world—while also desiring the rootedness of provincial life. This outsider viewpoint is frequently associated with Jews, "gypsies" (Eliot's term), and other Bohemian types, such as Will Ladislaw in *Middlemarch*, the artist Klesmer in *Daniel Deronda*, and Daniel Deronda himself. Tellingly, for our purposes, "gypsies" are also linked directly to a literal common, Dunlow Common, in *The Mill on the Floss*. When Maggie Tulliver determines to run away after pushing Lucy into the mud, she reasons that "she had been so often told she was like a gypsy and 'half wild' that when she was miserable it seemed to her the only way of escaping opprobrium, and being entirely in harmony with circumstances, would be to live in a little brown tent on the commons . . . she would run straight away till she came to Dunlow Common, where there would certainly be gypsies " (112). Although Maggie's scheme is related with irony, in part because Maggie immediately reads her relationship to the gypsies in hierarchical terms—"the gypsies, she considered, would gladly receive her and pay her much respect on account of her superior knowledge" (112)— they are nonetheless figured as radically Other, living on the fringes of St. Oggs. (Maggie is thus disappointed to find them "in a lane, after all, and not on a common . . . for a mysterious illimitable common where there were sand-pits to hide in, and one was out of everybody's reach, had always made part of Maggie's picture of gypsy life" [115].)

Later incarnations of gypsy-like figures retain this radical otherness in a serious vein; they explicitly function as an "outer conscience" (Gwendolen's description of Deronda [833]), which unsettles the domestic, English center of Eliot's earlier texts.[24] Types like Arthur, described earlier as someone "whom you have met with in a foreign town, and been proud of as a fellow-countryman" (*Adam Bede* 105) are, within the expanded world of *Daniel Deronda*, nothing to be proud of. They, like Gwendolen and her gambling, are made pejoratively common by Deronda's gaze.[25] The effect is very much like that on Dorothea, when Ladislaw informs her of how outmoded Casaubon's research is.[26] Coming from elsewhere, lacking clear lines of pedigree and inheritance, without property, wandering figures like Ladislaw, Klesmer, and Deronda also build on the spatial aspect of otherness that is part of Maggie's image of "gypsydom" and that, in *Mill*, prefigures Maggie's later trip down the river and "out of everybody's reach" for a time.

But this, exactly, is the rub. The challenge the politics of a commons raises for Eliot and her twenty-first-century readers is how to imagine and represent our common, quotidian, and embodied life in relation to a seemingly abstract, often invisible, structure of wider relations, without succumbing to the fantasy of detachment, of being "out of everybody's reach" and hence free from social attachments, which has been connected, historically, to the ideal of cosmopolitanism. The concept of "actually existing cosmopolitanism" aims to uncouple this association by "scaling down," "pluralizing and particularizing" the term "cosmopolitanism." "We are connected," writes Bruce Robbins, "to all sorts of places, causally if not always consciously, including many that we have never traveled to, that we have perhaps only seen on television—including the place where the television itself was manufactured." As Eliot would likely agree, "it is frightening to think how little progress has been made in turning invisibly determining and often exploitative connections into conscious and self-critical ones, how far we remain from mastering the sorts of allegiance, ethics, and action that might go with our complex and multiple belonging" ("Introduction" 3). Or, as Goodlad phrases this project in the Victorian context, a practice is needed that "would enunciate the geohistorical as well as expressive dimensions of Victorian globality, exploring the sinuous interchange between embedding structures and embodied ethics" ("Cosmopolitanism's Actually Existing Beyond" 400).

Eliot's language of the commons enhances these contemporary discussions of "cosmopolitanisms" in its twinned emphases on the materiality of character and the materiality of the world. Equally part of the "vast sum of conditions" that define our lifeworld, the material bonds that constitute us as subjects require a rethinking not only of our relationship to others but of the construction of subjectivity itself—toward what, as we saw in Chapter 2, would constitute a form of dispossessed subjectivity. A "consent not to be a single being" by becoming part of the commons,[27] this concept of subjectivity, in Eliot's terms, involves a shedding of one's personality in the interests of joining the collective: as she describes this process of dispossession in *Romola*, in a scene where Romola inadvertently finds herself in the midst of a procession of the Cross in the streets of Florence,

> no member now was discernible as son, husband, or father. They had dropped their personality, and walked as symbols of a common vow. Each company had its colour and its badge, but the garb of all was a complete shroud, and left no expression but that of fellowship. (378)

The common and the commons, in this view, are inseparable from one another, the idea of an ethics separable from politics unthinkable. Again, this is not to say that the specific plans Eliot's characters comes up with are to be embraced.[28] Deronda's nationalistic vow at the end of *Daniel Deronda* is just one example of why. Suffice it to say that when Daniel commits to "restoring a political existence to [his] people, making them a nation again, giving them a national centre, such as the English have," the narrative substitutes an expansive view of commonwealth with a narrow, colonial, and imperial one.[29] Nor is it to ignore the fears of certain commoners, such as the industrial working class, which limit Eliot's conception especially of the intellectual commons. In the "Address to Working Men" appended to *Felix Holt: The Radical*, Eliot, in the voice of Holt, invokes an intellectual commons as "that treasure of knowledge, science, poetry, refinement of thought, feeling, and manners, great memories and the interpretation of great records, which is carried on from the minds of one generation to another." But, prefatory to this description, she writes,

> [J]ust as there are many things which we know better and feel much more strongly than the richer, softer-handed classes can know or feel them; so there are many things—many precious benefits—which we,

by the very fact of our privations, or lack of leisure and instruction, are not so likely to be aware of and take into our account. Those precious benefits form a chief part of what I may call the common estate of society: a wealth over and above buildings, machinery, produce, shipping, and so on, though closely connected with these; a wealth of a more delicate kind, that we may more unconsciously bring into danger, doing harm and not knowing that we do it. (621; appendix A)

The danger of destroying these "precious benefits" justifies the novel's conservative, gradualist politics but also jars just enough to require an explanation. "Now the security of this treasure," she adds, "demands, not only the preservation of order, but a certain patience on our part with many institutions and facts of various kinds, especially touching the accumulation of wealth, which from the light we stand in, we are more likely to discern the evil than the good of" (621). The move away from an inclusive notion of the "common estate of society" is followed directly by a reminder of the importance of "the accumulation of wealth" to any notion of the commonwealth.

In this context, it is particularly instructive to return to *Romola* for the defamiliarizing lens that fifteenth-century Florentine politics affords Eliot, as well as our understanding of her.[30] Unlike *Felix Holt*, *Romola* not only brings to the fore Eliot's politics of the commons but also dramatizes the logical outcome of that politics, which brings Eliot to the brink of advocating for revolution—something we do not see to the same degree in her other novels, but which *Romola* makes apparent. From its opening moment in the prefatory Proem, *Romola* introduces the language of the "common good." Imagining the "spirit of a Florentine citizen" who revisits his own fifteenth-century Florence to pause and consider its state of affairs, Eliot notes how he "felt the evils of his time . . . for he was a man of public spirit, and public spirit can never be wholly immoral, since its essence is care for a common good" (6). The notion of the common good is repeatedly invoked over the course of the novel, whether in the form of the common weal (as opposed to private ambition), the general lot or the general good, "common vows," and the "glow" or the "stress" of a common life.

These invocations express a faith in the public spirit and its care for a common good, yet also betray an anxiety, leaving the prospects of the common good an open question. In fact, as a whole, *Romola* stages the difficulties of a politics of the common, figured most explicitly in Savonarola's revolutionary politics but extending across the myriad familial, political, and economic relations that the novel narrates. Our resuscitated spirit, as Eliot refers to him at one point in the Proem, is equally the Florentine citizen of the past, the present British citizen reading *Romola*—with the inflection now on *our* spirit—and a future spirit yet to be redeemed, since, as the Proem ends, "little children are still the symbol of the eternal marriage between love and duty; and men still yearn for the reign of peace and righteousness—still own *that* life to be the highest which is a conscious voluntary sacrifice. For the Pope Angelico is not yet come" (8). The spirit thus figures person and thing, a prophecy foretold—the Angelic Pope who will bring in a new order—and a yearning for a more equitable world in the future. Framed by such a vision, *Romola* is best seen perhaps as less of a historical novel and more a form of speculative fiction in which Eliot experiments with the nature of the "common bonds" that might realize a common good.

In many ways, this project covers familiar critical terrain. Questions of scale, the "common deeds of a dusty life" versus a "genuine greatness of purpose," the personal as opposed to the general lot, "close relations" or distant ones, attachments or the lack thereof, all form the fabric of the novel. As in the later *Middlemarch*, the "hampering threadlike pressure of small social conditions and their complexity" that so hinder Lydgate equally vex Savonarola; likewise, Romola's intellect, her desire for a more expansive life, her bad marriage, and the conflicts she suffers share much with Eliot's earlier and later heroines. Key concerns—duty, submission, family obligations, forms of indebtedness, egoism, and the ethics of marriage and social relations more broadly—are all at play here, so much so that many of Eliot's contemporary critics deemed her story of Florentine life to be "too much in the colours of the nineteenth century," as the *Westminster Review* put it (MacCormack 348).

Crucially, too, what Knoepflmacher calls Eliot's "materialist standards" subtend the narrative: at the beginning of Book II, the narrator likens the changes in Tito and Romola's marriage to a "tree that bears a myriad of blossoms, each single bud with its fruit . . . dependent on the primary circulation of the sap": "the fortunes of Tito and Romola were dependent on certain grand political and social conditions which made an epoch in the history of Italy" (205). History writ large and "small relations" are shown to be inextricably entwined; like the single bud, the novel's characters share a common condition, their livelihoods sustained and transformed by both local and global politics. The narrator's comment here frames the arrival of the French king, and the common lot or common life of which Savonarola preaches is to be realized by the "vast multitude," not only of those in the Duomo who listen to him but, by extension, of the world's "mixed multitude" or masses. In his appeal to Romola when she first tries to leave Florence and flee her loveless marriage, Savonarola harshly criticizes her for "[carrying herself] proudly, as one who held herself not of common blood or common thoughts" (359); she is thus, Savonarola asserts, "below the life of the believer, who worships the image of the Supreme Offering, and feels the glow of a common life with the lost multitude for whom that offering was made, and beholds the history of the world as the history of a great redemption in which he is himself a fellow-worker; in his own place and among his own people!" (360). A common life with the lost multitude resides simultaneously in the ordinary, everyday and common people and relations that *Adam Bede* links directly to realism *and* in a global commons—characterized by Savonarola as "universal redemption."

In this loaded exchange in *Romola*, these close and expansive common social bonds are presented in the language of debt, the "right payment" of which is left open, even as the fact of indebtedness to others is taken as a given. As Savonarola presses Romola, "'You assert your freedom proudly, my daughter. But who is so base as the debtor that thinks himself free?'" (356). Savonarola frames this debt as "the debt of a fellow-citizen" (358), and as "the debt of a wife," who "chose the bond" of matrimony and is "breaking a pledge" (357) by leaving Tito. While the framing of this latter debt is hard to countenance (especially from a twenty-first-century perspective) given Tito's behavior toward Romola , it is important, I think, to grapple with the overarching nature of Eliot's provocation here—namely, that no one is free from social bonds and that the "good" can only be realized as a *common* good rather than through some form of individual escape. "'If your own people are wearing a yoke,'" Savonarola asks Romola, "'will you slip from under it, instead of struggling with them to lighten it? There is hunger and misery in our streets, yet you say, "I care not; I have my own sorrows, I will go away, if peradventure I can ease them"'" (358).

Even as *Romola* treads familiar terrain, however, something different is also afoot. After all, *Romola*, unlike Eliot's other novels, and, again, particularly *Felix Holt*, offers a true radical in the figure of Savonarola, and a vision of an alternative politics in Machiavelli.[31] Gary S. Wihl argues that critics have missed a crucial aspect of *Romola*'s politics by focusing almost exclusively on Eliot's reading of J. S. Mill and Matthew Arnold while writing it and thereby neglecting her intellectual interest in Machiavelli. Calling *Romola* "a truly Machiavellian novel" (250), Wihl aims to "put the novel in dialogue with two strands of political thought: cultural liberalism, which promotes a politics of disinterestedness down through the legacy of Matthew Arnold, and republican humanism, which rejects abstract rights and principles of equality in favor of moral action within the public sphere" (259). Perhaps not coincidently, within the modern political thought that comes to link the conception of republic to property (above all, in Hobbes), Michael Hardt and Antonio Negri identify in Machiavelli an alternative political path, "which poses the poor as not only the remainder left by the violent appropriation conducted by nascent powers of capital, not only prisoners of the new conditions of production and reproduction, but also a force of resistance that recognizes itself as exploited within a regime that still bears the marks of the common: a common social life, common social wealth" (*Commonwealth* 52). For our purposes, it is significant that *Romola* enacts a historical and ongoing struggle between fundamentally opposed worldviews and class positions (the Florentine poor and the pro-Medicean forces) *and*, at least for a time, advocates for the poor in the language of a common life: "[T]he inspiring consciousness breathed into [Romola] by Savonarola's influence that her lot was vitally united with the general lot had exalted even the minor details of obligation into religion. She was marching with a great army; she was feeling the stress of a common life" (552). These common bonds supplant familial ones and prompt Romola's realization vis-à-vis her marriage that "the law was sacred. Yes, but rebellion might be sacred too.... It flashed upon her mind that the problem before her was essentially the same as that which had lain before Savonarola—the problem where the sacredness of obedience ended, and where the sacredness of rebellion began" (553). This is a rare position for Eliot to lend voice to, and one quite different from *Felix Holt*'s cautionary tale regarding the preservation of Britain's cultural inheritance. It is also a position that Eliot's critics found surprising, in part because it seemed to downgrade the role of "those precious benefits" necessitating order in *Felix Holt*, such as the comforts and enrichments of Florentine art that go unremarked in *Romola* (Wihl 249).

But if we see *Romola*, as I have suggested, as historical novel cum speculative fiction centrally concerned with what a politics of the commons might look like, the very meaning and nature of the relationship between culture and politics is newly open to question and revision. For Wihl, Machiavelli and the Florentine politics specific to the period from 1494 to 1498 provide Eliot with a model of democracy and liberty radically at odds with the liberalism of Mill and Arnold. Against the stability and disinterestedness that define liberal order, and its appeal to the Arnoldian "best self," republican humanism envisions a more unstable and conflict-ridden relationship between individuals and the state. As Wihl characterizes the Machiavellian aspects of Romola, she is a "virtuous, conflicted character whose life is profoundly altered by the fragile conditions of republican liberty" (255). For him, ultimately, seeing the novel as a reworking of Machiavellian politics not only complicates our account of Eliot's own intellectual development and its influences but also speaks to the "*experience* of liberty in a liberal society" (255).

My interest lies in the possibilities this Florentine history opens up for a more utopian project on Eliot's part. For despite being set in the historical past, the novel time and time again uses this tumultuous historical moment to emphasize the open-endedness of history itself. In descriptions of the architecture of Florence, and of particular personalities, including Machiavelli himself, and in the outcome of events, the narrative makes clear that it is looking backward and that certain changes have not yet occurred and hence were not inevitable. The very instability and fragility at the heart of republican humanism, in other words, translates in *Romola* into a highly contested public sphere in which there are no best selves, no obviously right political choices, no unconflicted solutions. On the one hand, this is scarily destabilizing: the conspiracies thicken, duplicities multiply, faith is lost. On the other hand, these very insecurities reveal the stark schism between the poor and the elite; as the narrator describes Savonarola's "disturbing doctrine," he was teaching "that it was not the duty of the rich to be luxurious for the sake of the poor" (341). The Bonfire of the Vanities, moreover, broaches the possibility that the achievement of a common life with the lost multitude might entail a wholly different relationship to art and culture, one in which the selfsame "artistic legacy of Florence" that critics found missing in the novel is downgraded once its attendant class politics are made visible. At the same time, Eliot's utopianism is tempered by the constraints of historical fact, and the novel's concern for the "common lot" is finally realized only in Romola's radically transformed family, headed by three women, including Romola and her husband's mistress. In the context of Eliot's oeuvre as a whole, the revolutionary nature of this odd extended family should not be underestimated, beckoning as it does toward a future, yet to be redeemed, in which the creation of new kinship relations would be coextensive with "wide thoughts, and much feeling for the rest of the world as well as ourselves" (582).

Far from an idiosyncratic aberration, then, the struggle in *Romola* between the common lot and the privileged Medicean elite dramatizes the stakes involved in a politics of the commons, a politics that necessarily threatens class privilege and its particular forms of inheritance, cultural and otherwise. To be sure, Eliot rarely takes us to the brink of revolution as she does in *Romola*. But that does not mean that it is not the logical outcome of her politics given its sustained commitment to the commons and its increasing awareness of the global or universal aspects (in Savonarola's formulation) of the commonwealth. We might think of this commonness along the lines of what Jameson refers to in a different context as "a kind of universal plebeianization on the social and political level: and this word is meant in some strong and positive Brechtian sense as an abandonment of privilege and a new and universal equality" ("A New Reading of *Capital*" 12). In short, in this utopian future, an actually existing commonness—the key term of Eliot's realist politics—would be the desired end.

\* \* \*

If Dickens, as we saw in Chapter 2, directly draws on and brings forward a form of type associated with eighteenth-century characteristic writing, Eliot too, as we have seen, incorporates and develops notions of type taken from characteristic writing and its vision of "character" as material. As with the commons, the language of type and its insistence on the materiality of the word inherited from eighteenth-century literary practices loses some of its literalness within the nineteenth-century realist novel, without, however, losing its connection to the material nature of character types—a materialism that directly counters emerging forms of capitalist materialism and its ethos of self-interest, private gain, and vulgar materiality. No longer counting strokes per se, references to typical characters instead convey a shared conception of the self, in which selves are constituted by one another, "transferred" in the sense the narrator of *Daniel Deronda* uses when she likens Mordecai's "yearning consumptive glance" at Deronda to a "dying mother's look . . . for the sense of spiritual perpetuation in another resembles that maternal transference of self" (553). Recall too that this kind of "transference of self" is as much about sharing the joys of others as it is about shared suffering. And on the most fundamental level, it is simply about an equivalency of selves, or what Jameson calls "a new and universal equality," which, in the end, is unmoored from familial or biological identity (or an extension of it, as in Romola's case) and instead envisioned as bonds of indebtedness or dependence that encompass nothing less than the commonwealth of all.

The group of "philosophers" who meet at the Hand and Banner in *Daniel Deronda* gesture toward this notion of the commonwealth: fittingly the "company select of the select among poor men" (582) are discussing the "law of progress" (582) when they get diverted by a consideration of "the causes of social change" and the "power of ideas." Miller, a secondhand bookseller, puts forth "the power of ideas" as the "main transforming cause," to which Goodwin, the inlayer, replies, "[T]o the causes of social change, I look at it in this way—ideas are a sort of parliament, but there's a commonwealth outside, and a good deal of the commonwealth is working at change without knowing what the parliament is doing" (584). This riposte sets up the ensuing debate about nationalism, national identity, the fate of the Jewish people, and the meaning of progress. Mordecai makes his case for reviving "the soul of Judaism" and its "organic centre," but this view in no way holds sway in the debate. The "genial and rational Gideon" immediately responds by breaking down the division between Jews and Gentiles at the heart of Mordecai's vision and instead proposes a view of Judaism as "the simplest of all religions," and one that "makes no barrier, but a union, between us and the rest of the world" (593). The point here is less to determine who wins the debate than to see that, for Eliot, the question of what progress means and might look like is a genuinely open one, yet to be determined. But what is not up for debate is the need for future action, of whatever stripe, to include the claims of the commonwealth, or what, as we saw earlier in *The Mill on the Floss*, Eliot's narrator calls "that sense of others' claims" (487). For without this sense of others' claims, as Eliot's novels clarify, one's personal gains (material or otherwise) will come too easily at the expense of others or the outright exclusion of others.[32] The language of type, along with the language of indebtedness, refuses such "clamorous selfish desires" ("Janet's Repentance" 384); in their stead, the sense that any "I" is dependent on a "we" renders all forms of vulgar materiality precisely that: vulgar. "There are enough inevitable turns of fortune," Deronda tells Gwendolen in the context of her gambling, "which force us to see that our gain is another's loss:—that is one of the ugly aspects of life. One would like to reduce it as much as one could, not get amusement out of exaggerating it" (383).

"One would like to reduce it as much as one could": again, significantly, Eliot's cosmopolitanism is a conditional aim rather than a realized achievement. Reflecting on cosmopolitanism as an ideal, Bruce Robbins speculates that "if cosmopolitanism is understood as an ideal of equal concern for the well-being of everyone on the planet, then one inevitable thing to say about it is that it cannot be fully embodied or enacted, cannot be satisfactorily *lived*" ("On Amanda Anderson's *The Way We Argue Now*" 271). Its conditions of possibility, however, can be envisioned, and it is these conditions that Eliot's oeuvre delineates in the most commonplace of circumstances and characters, since these are, after all, the material conditions within which we live, and within which change will occur. Certainly the bonds of dependence these material conditions create can be tenuous in an increasingly global world, but still they cannot be denied, as Eliot's novels show over and over. Attempts to reject these bonds lead either to disaster—Tito Melema in *Romola* being but one example—or to a necessary reckoning with those bonds, as in the case of Gwendolen, whose future is left indeterminate.[33]

At base, this shared sociality or commonwealth is given form, in Eliot, through the materialist, collective nature of her characters. It is fitting, then, that she should end her writing career with a final experiment in character writing, *Impressions of Theophrastus Such*. Published in 1879, *Impressions of Theophrastus Such* plays in its very title with the materiality of words, characters, and the book itself, which offers "impressions" both *of* Theophrastus and *on* Theophrastus in his interactions with other characters. Like the notion of type in characteristic writing, the Theophrastan tradition produced character sketches that aimed to portray moral types rather than individuals. A student of Aristotle's, Theophrastus became interested, among his many other philosophical and intellectual endeavors, in the study of character and in c. 319 produced *Characters*, which became a point of origin for the genre of the character sketch. As with later character books, *Characters* contains a collection of character types, beginning with Dissemblers and moving on to other typological character traits such as Stupidity, Cowardice, Garrulity, Tactlessness, and Self-seeking Affability.[34] Although many critics have positioned nineteenth-century variants of such character sketches as "part of the novelist's apprenticeship" (Smeed 119), Eliot complicates such a trajectory in her turn to the Theophrastan tradition at the end of her novelistic career. A central misconception has helped solidify this narrative of teleological development from "character" to "sketch" to novel, namely the idea that character types gradually disappear in the novel, replaced by some version of psychological interiority or depth that belies the notion of type. Such a view of character implicitly endorses and naturalizes an individualistic view of individuals as de facto more complex, psychologically rich, and "developed," thereby reproducing a noxious developmental hierarchy in which individual interest supersedes communal concerns. This worldview continues arguments, discussed in Chapter 1, against the commons as a form of land use less "civilized" than that of private property and indicative of a lack of development in terms of both identity and culture.

In her excellent introduction to *Impressions of Theophrastus Such*, Nancy Henry works to reposition this last text of Eliot's, which has not fared well among critics.[35] She notes that, from its time of publication, it has been misunderstood: the title of it was misquoted in an advertisement in Blackwoods, where "The" was added, thereby losing the sense of the reciprocal "impressions" between Theophrastus, the world, and his readers, and the "pun on 'impressions' as printed book"(xv);[36] and the "Such" in the title has been wrongly assumed to be Theophrastus' patronym. Instead,

> what he has is a linguistic connection in "Such" to the literary tradition of characteristic writing. Rather than a "family" name, he has an ellipsis: "Such a type who . . .". The formula introduces—types—Theophrastus, but can only be completed on the completion of the book, and then only in terms of what he does, not in terms of any "first impression" of a name. Theophrastus, "Such a type who writes this book", in writing the book, has made its writing characteristic of him. (xix)

Eliot thus turns again to a more literal notion of type here in which type is enacted rather than given, a development rather than a predetermined or preordained fact, something that emerges. In this way, Eliot dramatizes in concentrated form the unfolding of type, the sense that, as Henry puts it, Theophrastus is "such a type who writes this book"—just as the characters in her novels are "such a type who," like, say, Timothy the "wiry old laborer" in *Middlemarch* "[lingered] in those times—who had his savings in a stocking foot, lived in a lone cottage, and was not to be wrought on by any oratory, having as little of the feudal spirit, and believing as little, as if he had not been totally unacquainted with the Age of Reason and the Rights of Man" (560). Or, the "blooming Englishmen of the red-whiskered type represented by Sir James Chettam" (16), who couldn't be more different from Casaubon; or who, like Maggie, when Stephen first meets her and declares, in a chapter appropriately titled "First Impressions," is "[t]oo tall . . . and a little too fiery. She is not my type of woman, you know" (397). Or, like the "very distant varieties of European type: Livonian and Spanish, Graeco-Italian and miscellaneous German, English aristocratic and English plebeian" that people the gambling tables in *Daniel Deronda*'s opening scene; or, the "beloved type" (813) that Mirah becomes for Daniel. Or, the many other types in Eliot's novels who together form and contribute to the making of a common life.

In short, types of both the literal eighteenth-century and the Lukácsian variety register Eliot's "historical knowledge" (Doody 290): "the suppressed transitions which unite all contrasts"—not in the grandeur of Rome, here, but in the "notions of a girl" (*Middlemarch* 193) like Dorothea, or Maggie, or any other common character who embodies the common in all its rich and diverse, potential equality. In the end, then, Eliot's invocation of type and the common is equal parts judiciousness and provocation: as she both reasons and prods, "[W]e need not shrink from this comparison of small things with great" (*Mill* 284). For, ultimately, we are all small, and need not shrink from that recognition—nor from the resolve that would be necessary to act on that recognition in order to realize a genuinely global commons.

CHAPTER 4

# The Typical and the Tragic in Hardy's Geopolitical Commons

THOMAS HARDY FITTINGLY OPENS his autobiography[1] with an encapsulated description of the landscape and the changes to it that will form the subject of all of his novels: "It was in a lonely and silent spot between woodland and heathland that Thomas Hardy was born," he begins, identifying aspects of a landscape—heathland and woodland—*before* the transformations wrought by enclosure. Hardy then fills in this landscape with the houses, the types of people, and the social and economic conditions that shape and are shaped by it: "The domiciles were quaint, brass-knockered, and green-shuttered then, some with green garden-doors and white balls on the posts, and mainly occupied by lifeholders of substantial footing like the Hardys themselves" (7). Change comes when "the lifeholds fell into hand, and the quaint residences with their trees, clipped hedges, orchards, white gatepost-balls, the naval officer's masts and weather-cocks, have now perished every one, and have been replaced by labourers' brick cottages and other new frame buildings, a convenient pump occupying the site of the mossy well and bucket" (7). This "falling into hand," a central process of enclosure, renders "open" villages "closed": whereas open villages are characterized by "dispersed landownership," closed villages "were usually estates or planned villages in which landownership was concentrated" (Plietzsch 96). As Birgit Plietzsch points out, Little Hintock in *The Woodlanders*, Mellstock in *Under the Greenwood Tree*, Weatherbury in *Far from the Madding Crowd*, and Talbothays and Flintcomb Ash in *Tess of the d'Urbervilles* are all closed villages; significantly the only open village is Marlott in *Tess of the d'Urbervilles*, which, "by the time the Durbeyfields lose their cottage . . . is now in the hands of an agriculturalist" (96).[2]

The "lonely and silent spot between woodland and heathland" appears at first to be an unlikely place in which to find a geopolitics, given

CHAPTER FOUR

its specificity and its localness. In contrast to the kind of commonplace cosmopolitanism of Eliot's novels explored in the previous chapter, Hardy's novels seem, on the face of it, decidedly non-cosmopolitan. As I will suggest, however, they are illustrative precisely because they bear signs of the geopolitical via figurations of the commons and its loss rather than any overtly visible, empirical evidence of it. The commons in Hardy functions specifically as a site for the profound transformations in work and identity able to capture the local, lived experience of emergent capitalist relations and capitalism's increasingly global logic. In this sense, Hardy's narratives bring the global home—but not by referencing international events or dealing in foreign affairs. Rather, this aesthetic has less to do with actual maps or the charting of global flows of commerce, people, and goods, and more to do with problems of figuration, as Fredric Jameson characterizes the challenge of how to think a system which cannot be perceived through the categories we normally use to orient ourselves in the world. As he poses the challenge, "space and demography offer the quickest short-cuts to this perceptual difficulty, provided each is used like a ladder to be kicked away after it has done its work" (*The Geopolitical Aesthetic* 2).[3] The ladder must be kicked away because the visible signs, whether spatial or demographic—red lines in insurance maps, or militarized borders, to cite Jameson's contemporary examples—are "only caricatures of the mode of production," which cannot be captured by images or "detected on the surfaces scanned by satellites" (2). For this very reason, the capacity to map the global system is a representational problem, a problem of form. Although Jameson links these "form-problems" to the specific conditions of late capitalism and a fully global world system, an analogous set of challenges confronts Hardy and nineteenth-century novelists more generally, as they navigate an earlier moment in the development of a rapidly globalizing world, a period characterized by the British historian Eric Hobsbawm as the ages of Capital (1848–75) and Empire (1875–1914), and grapple with the representational challenges of its primary mode of accumulation: the enclosure of the global commons.

In this chapter, I locate a revelatory geopolitical aesthetic in Hardy's depictions of the texture of common, everyday life and the ways in which its rhythms and modes of being are in the process of radical transformation. Moving between the typical and the tragic, the uneventful and the violent, Hardy's novels map the space and tempo of new work relations following in the wake of enclosure, and their reliance, specifically, on the structural necessity of itinerancy or the oscillation between working and wandering. But they also equally function as thought experiments in communal work relations grounded in what I call an anticipatory realism. Notably, Simon Gatrell also uses the term "anticipatory" for Hardy's vision of a global interconnectedness that, drawing on *The Woodlanders*, reaches "from the White Sea to Cape Horn" (175). But for Gatrell, it is only in *The Dynasts* that Hardy "was able to present human actions not just from the minutely realistic point of view of the later Victorian novel, but also from a perspective so remote that differences between England and abroad become irrelevant . . . a point of view from which it was possible to encompass both the White Sea and Cape Horn" (181). Linked to the common, my conception of Hardy's anticipatory realism is less about moving beyond the minute to the remote and more about seeing the remote in the minute. These dynamics are written in and on the land; as Elizabeth Miller characterizes the Wessex novels, "the land itself would be the series' through-line and its lead" ("Dendrography" 698). Land is the animating feature of Hardy's world, and he is well aware that what is happening to it and to the local inhabitants peopling his novels is hardly isolatable to Dorset but rather is part of a larger "system" of "banished people" spread across Europe and beyond, as he describes this historical process in his 1883 essay "The Dorsetshire Labourer." Hardy's realism is also, for me, anticipatory not of our own present but rather of a future yet to be realized. At one and the same time, I argue, Hardy mines the past for its archival evidence and traces of another world and for its utopianemancipatory possibilities. These traces and possibilities not only define a world in the thick of being privatized and enclosed but also resonate with the "new enclosures" of our contemporary moment, thereby offering suggestive lines of thought for theorizing the commons today.

Now it might seem especially odd to turn to Hardy for insight into our current situation, given his identification with regional writing and a nostalgia for a rural England that was disappearing in his own time.[4] But as Peter Linebaugh and others working on the commons have compellingly demonstrated, a politics of the commons helps us see this past anew and connect it directly to our present; moreover, the connection between Hardy's moment and ours is made palpable when enclosure is understood not as a punctual event around which empirical evidence accretes but rather as an "attritional catastrophe," Rob Nixon's term (explored in Chapter 1) for a seemingly non-eventful, ongoing and violent historical process like climate change. As I have argued throughout *The Afterlife of Enclosure*, treating enclosure as a form of slow violence akin to climate change not only provides a means of coming to terms with its simultaneously diffuse and catastrophic effects but also highlights the intimate connections that need to be made now between climate change and enclosure, connections I return to at the end of the chapter. Finally, the language of the commons and Hardy's particular mobilization of it offers, to my mind, a significant corrective to contemporary theorizations of work. For unlike current invocations of a postwork society, in which we will be freed from labor, or apocalyptic visions of a world in which we are made or even engineered to work continuously, without the need for any rest or respite from work at all, Hardy's revisioning of the commons neither severs life from work nor collapses them into one another.[5] Instead it provides us with a means of reframing labor by setting it in a broader, communal context in which labor is unoppressively co-extensive with life, a life that extends from the political and social to the economic and environmental spheres.

### Work and the Longue Durée of Enclosure

What, then, does Hardy know about enclosure, the commons, and work that we do not or simply cannot know given our embeddedness in the present? Raymond Williams identifies Hardy's signal contribution as his attentiveness to the inseparable and ordinary relations between life and work (*The Country and the City* 211), which, in turn, capture the deep interconnectedness of rural and urban forces in the development of nineteenth-century capitalism. For Williams, these recognitions are found primarily in actual representations of work. To be sure, work *is* visible in Hardy's Wessex in a way that it is not in many other nineteenth-century novels; there are many scenes of work in Hardy, from Tess's work milking at Talbothays dairy and the introduction of the threshing machine in *Tess of the d'Urbervilles* to Marty South cutting spars in *The Woodlanders*, Clym Yeobright cutting furze in *The Return of the Native*, and the eponymous mayor of *The Mayor of Casterbridge* cultivating and trading corn and eventually failing miserably as both corn-trader and mayor. Williams's emphasis on "life and work" has been enormously important, in large part because he made visible the (agricultural) laborers who people English fiction and, moreover, made them central to the processes of modernization and historical change. But, as I have argued elsewhere, Williams's attachment to "real lived experience" (a phrase he uses repeatedly) and authenticity risks falling prey to a reductive equation between representation and the real, in which labor is part of the picture only when it is directly represented.[6] Not insignificantly, it also limits the applicability of his analysis to more contemporary articulations of work, given the increasingly opaque nature of labor within late capitalism—a constraint that is not, I want to insist, endemic to Hardy himself.

Certainly, as Williams argues, Hardy wants to capture the realities of life and work. But for Hardy these "realities" are far less visible or transparently real than Williams's account allows. Instead, Hardy's novels are better understood as figurations of labor and life and their interrelatedness that extend beyond literal representation and whose extensiveness Hardy gestures toward when he retrospectively terms the Wessex 1912 edition of his novels "Novels of Character and Environment."[7] The language of figuration is meant to distinguish between a prosaic realism that privileges the visible and the seen and a figural or "abstract" realism that aims to capture an underlying or unseen reality; this reality represents the lived experience of Hardy's laborers and their labor, and something else: the larger, invisible structures determining that experience. This is a form of what Jameson has called cognitive mapping because it simultaneously allows us to address the difficulties with and necessity of bringing together the concrete and the abstract, lived experience and structure, and to envision an explicitly geopolitical aesthetic ("Cognitive Mapping"). But, importantly, this approach to realism also comes from Hardy. In *The Life and Work of Thomas Hardy*, in an entry from March 4, 1886, Hardy remarks about novel writing, "Novel-writing as an art cannot go backward. Having reached the analytic stage it must transcend it by going still further in the same direction. Why not by rendering as visible essences, spectres, &c. the abstract thoughts of the analytic school" (183). He then goes on to say about realism specifically,

> The human race to be shown as one great network or tissue, which quivers in every part when one point is shaken, like a spider's web if touched. Abstract realisms to be in the form of Spirits, Spectral figures, &c. The Realities to be the true realities of life, hitherto called abstractions. The old material realities to be placed behind the former, as shadowy accessories. (183)[8]

Although he does not use the language of "structure" per se, the "one great network or tissue" equally captures the need to see and show the totality of the "true realities of life" somehow, a necessity dictated by the fact, as he states elsewhere, that "the material is not the real—only the visible, the real being invisible optically." Always, then, for Hardy, the novelist (and poet) must seek the "deeper reality" (*Life* 192),[9] must make it "vividly visible" (*Life* 183).

The relation between the material and the abstract, as Ralph Pite highlights, is also a question at the heart of geography. Against readings of Hardy as a regional writer who falls prey to an isolated ruralism, Pite connects the geography of Hardy's novels to "his distinctive sense of interconnected place; one that has parallels in the geographical thinking of his day (Huxley and Geikie) and has been (mis) understood according to a slightly later geographical model (Oxford school regionalism)" (8–9).[10] Like these earlier debates about the study of geography, "modern geography runs up against similar questions about the relation between locality and region, region and nation. Geographical studies of region constantly test the relation between empirical and theoretical, struggling to describe how material and abstract interact" (9).

Hardy's understanding of the real as something other than the material speaks not only to his novelistic practice, and its importance in relation to how we theorize realism (and, in Hardy's case, regionalism), but to the move today to elevate the material or the visible over the underlying or unseen. Surface reading offers one problematic version of this approach, but it is hardly alone in its endeavor to debunk and move beyond ideology critique in the name of a crude empiricism in which things are what they appear to be. As Lauren Goodlad argues, Jameson's notion of a geopolitical aesthetic explicitly militates against the elevation of surface over depth, the visible over the invisible:

> Whatever one thinks of history as "absent cause," I believe we can affirm Jameson's conviction that the long and ongoing process of capitalist globalization is empirically real and, yet, fundamentally absent to individual perception *as the totality of that process.* This is not because of any ideological ruse that critics must demystify. It is, rather, because certain historical phenomena, however materially consequential, are (like Bourdieu's continental drift) not cognizable in the form of objects "in plain view" (Felski, "After Suspicion" 31)—not only globalization but also commodification, the turn to neoliberalism, the financialization of the world economy, the entrenchment of racism and sexism, the reduction of biodiversity, and climate change. . . . By placing artistic form in dialogue with processes that are both real and spatio-temporally complex, the notion of a geopolitical aesthetic posits a "surface" that is inextricable from its "depth." (*The Victorian Geopolitical Aesthetic* 273–74)[11]

A crude empiricism, in other words, can never approach the very phenomena realism hopes to represent.[12] "At pains to deny that realist fiction has any use for 'transparent representation,'" Harry Shaw describes realist novels in the following terms: they "create imaginative experiences that elicit the mental operations necessary to confront the world they identify as real" (131). Such a view "shifts realism's claims from fulfilling the impossible (and incoherent) task of 'direct' representation to providing a mode of grasping life in history" (131).[13]

In contrast to contemporary accounts of literature or history that privilege what is in plain view, Hardy's realism is anything but crude in its relationship to the empirical matter of everyday life. While his "abstract imaginings" (another suggestive formulation of Hardy's for the deeper reality) take a number of different forms, two key forms will interest us here: (1) Hardy's representations of the *longue durée* of enclosure and the violence it entails, and (2) his consequent figurations of identity and their relationship to private property. Against Locke's linking of the fruits of labor to private property, Hardy maps the contours of what I call an increasingly "enclosed self" produced concomitantly with the literal enclosure of the commons and gestures toward an alternative unenclosed self in the Wessex geography of his distinctly geopolitical aesthetic.[14]

## The Violence of the Everyday

Perhaps more so than any other nineteenth-century novelist, Hardy takes on the "representational, narrative, and strategic" challenges Nixon sees slow violence posing, given its "relative invisibility" (2). In the context of enclosure, specifically, *The Afterlife of Enclosure* has argued that this violence can be defined in terms of seemingly uneventful yet ultimately violent local changes, "neither spectacular, nor instantaneous," interrupted at points by discrete, identifiable "events," "its repercussions playing out across a range of temporal scales" (Nixon 2). This, in essence, describes Hardy's world and its distinctive rhythms and temporalities. (William Greenslade comments about the "Facts" notebook specifically that the "vanishing life" Hardy records there "offers itself, fugitively, as precarious, violent, oppressive and lawless" [xxv]).[15] As John Wright evocatively details in his history of the hedgerow, "slowly at first, from the thirteenth century to the close of the nineteenth, thousands of miles were planted and walls erected, enclosing common fields and common waste." Connecting slow violence and death to the land as well as those peopling the land, Wright comments that "in its various guises, common land died, slowly and painfully" (68), a fugitive marker of its death the seemingly benign hedgerow so characteristic of the modern English countryside.

In *Tess of the d'Urbervilles*, Hardy describes an utterly typical sequence of everyday events within the large movement of enclosure when he depicts the Durbeyfields' loss of their cottage after the father dies. With the need for more living space for his laborers, the tenant-farmer takes over the cottage—which was leased as a "lifeholder," that is, for a specified number of lifetimes and at an end with Tess's father's life—and the Durbeyfields become landless and therefore forced to migrate annually in search of work. When he sums up the Durbeyfields' fate, Hardy universalizes it, remarking, "Thus the Durbeyfields, once d'Urbervilles, saw descending upon them the destiny which, no doubt, when they were among the Olympians of the county, they had caused to descend many a time, and severely enough, upon the heads of such landless ones as they themselves were now. So do flux and reflux—the rhythm of change—alternate and persist in everything under the sky" (342). But at the same time, what Hardy describes is minutely historically specific, capturing in fine and largely uneventful detail the complex of changes altering the English countryside, from the observation that annual migrations have increased in the area to the fact that depopulation has occurred not only because of an increasingly landless population of laborers ever on the move but also because of the loss of artisans and other workers not directly connected to the land: "These families, who had formed the backbone of the village life in the past, who were the depositories of the village traditions, had to seek refuge in the large centres; the process, humorously designated by statisticians as 'the tendency of the rural population towards the large towns,' being really the tendency of water to flow uphill when forced by machinery" (343)—a line that Hardy first uses in "The Dorsetshire Labourer." Hardy's very move from the universal to the utterly historically specific defines his response to the problem of representing the seemingly unrepresentable without resorting to the kinds of displacements that would render the violence of enclosure invisible. In other words, the tragedy that defines Hardy's writing is the tragedy of a particular moment in which enclosure is structurally determining; Tess's tragedy is also the tragedy of Tess's world. Addressing his critics in his "Preface to the Fifth and Later Editions," Hardy notes that some accuse the novel of embodying "the views of life prevalent at the end of the nineteenth century, and not those of an earlier and simpler generation," to which Hardy replies, "an assertion which I can only hope may be well founded" (quoted in Riquelme 26). That this life also extends well beyond Dorset is explicitly made clear in the earlier "The Dorsetshire Labourer," when Hardy follows the repeated lines above regarding "the tendency of the rural populations towards the large towns" with this concluding sentence: "But the question of the Dorset cottager here merges in that of all the houseless and landless poor and the vast topic of the Rights of Man" (57).[16]

Other examples of such typical and tragic occurrences proliferate throughout Hardy's oeuvre: the very technology of his novels, the way they define and delimit space, is peripatetic—a suggestive combination of the pedestrian and the itinerant. Think of Michael Henchard wandering the countryside at the beginning of *The Mayor of Casterbridge*, as he goes to the fateful fair where he sells his wife, Susan—a not uncommon event reported and recorded multiple times in Hardy's "Facts" notebook—and wandering, again, at the end, after he has lost everything, including his home. Or of Giles Winterbourne, like the Durbeyfield family, losing his home once John South dies. Or of Jude and Sue. Attritional catastrophes, one and all. Sue's lament and Jude's response to her after she finds all her children dead embodies the crushing weight of the world and the violence it enacts on the body (not to mention the bodies of the children and Father Time):

> "We must conform!" she said mournfully. "All the ancient wrath of the Power above us has been vented upon us, his poor creatures, and we must submit. There is no choice. We must. It is no use fighting against God!"
>
> "It is only against man and senseless circumstance," said Jude.
>
> "True!" she murmured. . . . "But whoever or whatever our foe may be, I am cowed into submission. I have no more fighting strength left; no more enterprize. I am beaten, beaten! . . . 'We are made a spectacle unto the world, and to angels, and to men!' I am always saying that now." (342)

Jude corrects Sue: it is human actions in the material world—"man and senseless circumstance" (342), as Jude frames it—rather than some higher power or fate that is responsible for the violence that attends the enclosing of space and bodies. The injunction against alternative spaces or bodies or ways of being is clear: "'There is something external to us,'" Sue, in her grief cries out, "'which says, "You shan't!" First it said, "You shan't learn!" Then it said, "You shan't labour!" Now it says, "You shan't love!"'" (337). Failure to learn "the lesson of renunciation," a lesson Jude supposes he "ought to learn at this season" (207),[17] leads to catastrophe, a catastrophe shared by Hardy's wandering characters and hence hardly exceptional despite, or rather because of, the tragic nature of their respective stories.[18]

The shift from tenancy issues to general itinerancy signals how Hardy's novels move us from what seem like discrete events to common states of being—or, in other words, to less literal manifestations of enclosure and its afterlife. On the one hand, this common remainder or presence is brought to life through Hardy's use of types. On the other hand, it implies a deep reciprocity between individuals and the material world that reaches beyond the local to the geopolitical. Tess is a "pure woman," and hence one of many pure women; Michael Henchard is "The Mayor of Casterbridge," but not the only one—*and* a Man of Character, again a shared category, given its indefiniteness; Giles Winterbourne and Marty South are "woodlanders," along with many other woodlanders; and Hardy himself refers to Sue Bridehead as "a type of woman which has always had attraction for me—but the difficulty of drawing the type has kept me from attempting it till now" (*Collected Letters* 2: 100). At the most obvious level, character types and commonness, as we have seen in Dickens and Eliot, are defined by their reproducibility: a type only makes sense because it is typical or common, its qualities shared by many others, thereby making of the one the many. J. B. Bullen importantly links Hardy's types to landscape paintings and portraits and the movement in visual art toward a vision of "beauty in ugliness" (91) in which the "commonplace" has been "made a virtue" (*Expressive Eye* 94).[19] In his reading of *The Return of the Native*, for example, he argues that "through his direct and indirect allusions to the methods and techniques of Dürer, Rembrandt, and Reynolds, and to the work of the moderns—Woolner, Rossetti, and others—[Hardy] transformed his characters into symbols; his individuals become types, and even his landscape participates in the symbolic drama of the story" (*Expressive Eye* 117).

Types, as we have seen throughout *The Afterlife of Enclosure*, rely on an indebtedness to others insofar as a common type has no meaning in isolation, but they also demarcate literal forms of debt, of being in debt, of being dispossessed. Both forms gain new resonance in the context of Hardy's itinerant characters. Enduring types of the dispossessed—the pauper, the vagabond, the criminal, the rioter, to draw on the Midnight Notes Collective's description of "the physiognomy of the world proletariat" today ("Introduction to the New Enclosures" 3)—they make "vividly visible" the regime of private property and its violence against the commons.[20] Driven out of privatized and enclosed spaces, they wander and congregate on the margins, relegated to refuse. The association between such types and refuse is made manifest when Hardy names the area of the tenements in *The Mayor of Casterbridge* Mixen Lane, and describes its denizens as "those who were in distress, and in debt, and trouble of every kind" (195). His description is worth quoting at length, as it showcases the rhythm, repetitions, and word play Hardy employs to articulate these associations:

> Mixen Lane was the Adullam of all the surrounding villages. It was the hiding-place of those who were in distress, and in debt, and trouble of every kind. Farm-labourers and other peasants, who combined a little poaching with their farming, and a little brawling and bibbing with their poaching, found themselves sooner or later in Mixen Lane. Rural mechanics too idle to mechanize, rural servants too rebellious to serve, drifted or were forced into Mixen Lane.
>
> The lane and its surrounding thicket of thatched cottages stretched out like a spit into the moist and misty lowland. Much that was sad, much that was low, some things that were baneful, could be seen in Mixen Lane. Vice ran freely in and out certain of the doors in the neighbourhood; recklessness dwelt under the roof with the crooked chimney; shame in some bow-windows; theft (in times of privation) in the thatched and mud-walled houses by the sallows. Even slaughter had not been altogether unknown here. In a block of cottages up an alley there might have been erected an altar to disease in years gone by. Such was Mixen Lane in the times when Henchard and Farfrae were Mayors. (194–95)

Mixen Lane and its cast of characters are at once typically tragic and tragically typical. Far from heroic, these inhabitants are spoken of as pluralities: farm-laborers and peasants, mechanics and servants. They are the rural equivalent of Dickens's city slum dwellers. (Those who gather in Peter's Finger, Mixen Lane's inn, are labelled "waifs and strays," no less, a favorite appellation of Dickens's for lost people and lost items.) Vice, shame, and slaughter reside here, and so too does theft—with the important qualification "in times of privation." Although categorized as refuse or dung, they also refuse (to work and serve) and riot: "Rural mechanics too idle to mechanize, rural servants too rebellious to serve," they have "drifted or were forced into Mixen Lane." Drifted or forced: these seem to be the only options, and one more instance of the bringing together of the pedestrian and itinerant.

That they then become the site for a skimmington should thus not come as a surprise, given the history of this particular kind of populist uprising. A local custom going back to medieval times, a skimmington or skimmity-ride (the origin of "skimmington" most likely coming from the skimming ladles used to remove the fat from milk) was often "got up" in response to enclosures. Notably, in the period preceding the English civil war, skimmingtons were used to protest the Crown's selling of land in Dorset to courtiers intent on "enclosing and 'improving' hitherto underutilized forest land" (Underdown 210). Like the Swing Riots, in which rioters adopted the name Swing, those leading skimmingtons often took on the name Skimmington or Lady Skimmington (it was a common practice for leaders of these protests to cross-dress, hence "Lady Skimmington"). During riots in the Forest of Dean in April 1632, a local miner, John Williams, was arrested, setting off a wave of protests in which Williams adopted the name "Skimmington," while three leaders of a skimmington in Braydon took the name "Lady Skimmington" and were punished by being pilloried in women's clothing. While skimmingtons were used to protest events and actions other than enclosure (including wife beaters, adulterous women, and other perceived offenses against the community), they always involved "rituals of inversion": in the case of enclosures, the "customary world has been turned upside-down by enclosers; the protesters symbolically turn it upside-down again (dressing as women, parodying the titles and offices of their social superiors) in order to turn it right side up. The prominence of women in enclosure and grain riots is well known and is one more sign of rejection of the submissive ideal" (Underdown 213). In like fashion, men who beat their wives were, in turn, beaten by skimmity-riders bearing skimming ladles or other objects with which to whack the offender. As in *The Mayor of Casterbridge*, effigies of the offender were paraded through the village or town often accompanied by the banging of pots and pans, or "rough music," another term for a skimmington.[21] Women, too, "occasionally dressed in men's clothing and adopted male titles, such as captain, to protest enclosure and their own perceived injustices. Cross-dressing provided a battleground for the contestation between individuals, communities, and the state over the ownership of land, one's social and gendered identity, and even ownership of the title Lady Skimmington" (Langert 119).

In *The Mayor of Casterbridge*, the skimmington does double duty, punishing Lucetta and striking back against class privilege. Jopp is "animated by resentment at Lucetta's haughtiness, as he thought it" (194) to open the letters that reveal Lucetta's past relationship with Henchard, which are then shared with those gathered at Peter's Finger. The laying low of those above is highlighted when the group plans to proceed with the skimmington the very night of the Royal Personage's visit to Casterbridge (a fictionalized account of Prince Albert's visit in 1849). The "Peter's party" sees "how ripe the great jocular plot really was": "as a wind-up to the Royal visit the hit will be all the more pat by reason of [Farfrae and Lucetta's] elevation to-day" (206). For Jopp, however, "it was not a joke, but a retaliation" (206). Other reversals and ironies coalesce around the skimmity-ride, making it hard to disentangle the social grievances from the sexual ones and vice versa, a common confusion in Hardy's novels. Having stumbled upon Peter's Finger the night the letters are opened and learning with amusement what a skimmington is, the sailor Richard Newson (who so fatefully purchases Henchard's wife in the opening scene of the novel), without knowing who is being targeted, helps fund it. Henchard, snubbed by Farfrae and Lucetta when they refuse to include him in the official delegation, makes a spectacle of himself at the arrival of the royal carriage and is physically rebuffed by Farfrae (an insult Henchard likens to being "shaken at the collar by him as a vagabond in the face of the whole town" [207]). Once the Mayor, Henchard has been brought low, pushed out, and put in his place by the new Mayor. Meeting Jopp shortly afterward, Jopp sees in him a kindred soul, both having been snubbed: "'Why, I've had one too, so we are both under the same cold shade'" (206). Both snubs, moreover, relate to the loss of work: Lucetta refuses to put in a good word for Jopp with Farfrae when he is looking for a business partner, and Henchard, of course, has been supplanted by Farfrae, and with his business ruined ends up living in Jopp's cottage for a time. Economic grievances, the loss of one's livelihood, the presence of poverty and slums—at one point, Mixen Lane is referred to as "a back slum of the town, the *pis aller* of Casterbridge domiciliation" (140)—find expression in Hardy's types, be it the passionate "man of character" Henchard, those domiciled in Mixen Lane, or the range of "characters" making up the "rough music" of the "Facts" notebook.

Just as with Eliot, types in Hardy thus function as provocations, but whereas Eliot presses us to see ourselves in her common characters, to accept our own commonness, Hardy uses them as forms of popular protest to invert expectations: he claims for his types the very qualities conventional morality deems them to be lacking. Laborers and mechanics are types that refuse their position as refuse, and Tess is a pure woman but only in some alternative future world, certainly not her own. Sue, too, is a type before her time, as are Clym and Jude: more like a page than a picture, Clym's "features," for example, are "attractive in the light of symbols, as sounds intrinsically common become attractive in language, and as shapes intrinsically simple become interesting in writing"; in Clym's face "could be seen the typical countenance of the future" (167). And Jude was "the sort of man who was born to ache a good deal before the fall of the curtain upon his unnecessary life should signify that all was well with him again" (17).[22]

The provocation, therefore, is to imagine a world in which types such as Tess and Sue could survive, and one in which the Farfraes of the world were not ascendant and everything was not increasingly up for sale to the highest bidder, a situation literalized when Farfrae buys up Henchard's auctioned furniture and Henchard exclaims, "My furniture too! Surely he'll buy my body and soul likewise!" (172). Getting in his rub, Jopp retorts, "There's no saying he won't, if you be willing to sell" (172). Commonality is also to be seen, as Hardy explains in his rebuttal to Gosse's review of *Jude the Obscure*, in "the contrast between the ideal life a man [or woman, in Sue's and Tess's case] wished to lead, & the squalid real life he was fated to lead." After saying that this contrast comes in *Jude* when Arabella throws the pizzle at Jude, he concludes, "But I must have lamentably failed, as I feel I have, if this requires explanation & is not self evident. The idea was meant to run all through the novel. It is, in fact to be discovered in *every* body's life—though it lies less on the surface perhaps than it does in my poor puppet's" (*Collected Letters* 2: 93).

"Squalid real life" does not stop at the borders of Wessex. The conditions of possibility for "doing well," for a revivified common (both open questions, as Clym in *The Return of the Native* shows when he asks, simply, "Mother, what is doing well?" [175]), are inseparable from the larger work of the world. As I have argued throughout this book, the common inevitably leads to the commons, now figured as fully global. Early on in *The Woodlanders* (1887), for example, Giles and Marty are walking together in the woods outside Marty's cottage, when the narrator famously notes that

> hardly anything could be more isolated or more self-contained than the lives of these two walking here in the lonely hour before day, when grey shades, material and mental, are so very grey. And yet, looked at in a certain way, their lonely courses formed no detached design at all, but were part of the pattern in the great web of human doings then weaving in both hemispheres, from the White Sea to Cape Horn. (21–22)

How then to see the world in that which could not be more isolated and more self-contained? Not, Hardy's fiction implies, by compiling facts and evidence of the hemispheres—which not only remain out of reach for most of Hardy's characters but also do not actually provide what is needed, as Angel Clare's trip to Brazil suggests. In other words, a conventional view of cosmopolitanism is not the answer.

Far more figurative than these kinds of facts, Hardy's geopolitical aesthetic is to be found in his attentiveness to the texture of the common and its particular dynamics: repetition, typification, (mis)recognition, the non-event.[23] These dynamics define the closed nature of Hardy's world; they register the afterlife of enclosure and the myriad ways in which common space, common property, and common selves are being enclosed—the sense, as a colleague describing her experience of reading Hardy put it, that there isn't enough air in the room. Or, I would add, that there are simply not enough characters in Hardy's novels to go around as a result of the environment in which they must circulate and survive (to which I will return further on). Unlike the surfeit of characters who crowd the pages of Dickens's novels, Hardy's aesthetic is one of scarcity, of the same scenarios being replayed by the same small set of characters, as if he is continually reworking the limited space available in order to show how there is no way out under the current circumstances. For Hardy, this economy of scarcity ultimately affords a better vantage point from which to see the multitude. Asking what the "great world" was to Mrs. Yeobright in *The Return of the Native*, the narrator replies, "A multitude whose tendencies could be perceived, though not its essences." For her, "communities were seen . . . as from a distance; she saw them as we see the throngs which cover the canvases of Sallaert, Van Alsloot, and others of that school—vast masses of beings, jostling, zigzagging, and processioning in definite directions, but whose features are indistinguishable by the very comprehensiveness of the view" (188). In short, "the very comprehensiveness of the view" limits what one can see. In place of the "canvases" of Sallaert and others, Hardy's preferred paintings feature solitary figures in isolated landscapes. But the challenge is the same—namely, how to represent the multitude.

These figures and dynamics are signature Hardy, but they are also, importantly, based on local facts. Thus the problem, for Hardy, is not with facts per se; instead what matters is the nature and purview of them.[24] Hardy, with help from his first wife Emma Hardy, carefully and almost obsessively compiled and documented the changes in his rural environs in his remarkable "Facts" notebook, a collection of stories and news articles from the *Dorset County Chronicle*, as well as other miscellaneous local histories and memoirs, reviews, and biographies.[25] Providing Hardy with a treasure trove of material, much of which would find its way into his later novels, this "Facts" notebook is akin to the eccentric biographies that inspired Dickens's aesthetic and gave it its form. In this spirit, Michael Millgate says of Hardy's notebook entries from the period that they "further testify to an active and outgoing appetite for whatever was lively, local and curious—from the 'beheading' of a woman in a twopenny sideshow at Shroton Fair to the springtime singing of thrushes and blackbirds, 'with such modulation that you seem to see their little tongues curl inside their bills in their emphasis'"(172).[26] It is worth noting, as well, that although the notebook and the eccentric biographies obviously produce very different aesthetics, both forms of "biography" significantly elevate the collective over the individual.

Subtitled "from Newspapers, Histories, Biographies, & other chronicles (mainly Local)," the "Facts" notebook opens with an entry from the *Spectator* from July 21, 1883, which contains a review of James Edwin Thorold Rogers's *History of Agriculture and Prices in England, 1259–1793*.[27] Setting the stage for the entries to follow,[28] Hardy clips from the review descriptions of local life and customs, changes in land leases and their effects on the rural class structure, and information about sixteenth-century enclosures:

> The landlord leases land more & more frequently to capitalist farmers—the class of yeoman rise—Farmer dependent on his hay & straw for his winter keep. Cattle & sheep were fattened in summer & killed at its close, their flesh being salted for winter use—"Summer is y-cumin in," meant much more in those days than it does in ours on this account. Sheep farming takes the place of agriculture—vast enclosures are made from the common field, wh was the chief cause of Ket's rebellion in 1549—"the 15th cent. & the early years of the 16th were the golden age of husbandman, the artisan, & the labourer." It was not till after the Dissolution of monasteries that the roads went out of repair. (3)

As this opening entry demonstrates, Hardy's interests range from the specificity of language—"summer is y-cumin in"—and its connection to social and agricultural practices to large structural changes such as the "vast enclosures" of the sixteenth century. Attentive to detail and scope, Hardy moves between micro and macro levels of observation and analysis, linking small- and large-scale events. The fattening and killing of sheep relates to the shift from agriculture to sheep farming, which in turn relates to the enclosing of common fields, Ket's rebellion, and the increase in the yeoman class as more leases are given to capitalist farmers, providing a thumbnail sketch of all the players and relations affected by enclosure—including the sheep![29]

Greenslade's introduction to *Thomas Hardy's "Facts" Notebook* is invaluable for its wealth of information about the shape and contents of the notebook, how it was put together, and what it says about Hardy's interests and aesthetic. For our purposes, the entries from the *Dorset County Chronicle* (*DCC*) are particularly illuminating. These entries all come from the years 1826–30, and provide a vivid picture of the economic distress of the countryside during this period and the changes in rural life, *and* the shape these changes will take in Hardy's narratives. A series of entries reflect the suffering and privation experienced as a result of poor economic times, and are worth quoting at length:

> 50a: Great distress & poverty in the country at this period (1826)—Suicides: horse stealing: highway robbery frequent. Talk of grant of pub. money necessary."
>
> Source: *DCC*, 24 August 1826 (76)

> 50b: Fall of Townsman. "Somersetshire". At Frome—several persons—formerly considerable business-clothiers, & ranked among most respect$^{le}$ tradesmen of town—subsisting on parish allowance, wh. they obtain by breaking stones on the road. We are sorry that no hopes yet present them$^s$ of improve$^t$ in the commerce of this once active & thriving town . . .
>
> Source: *DCC*, 31 August 1826 (76–77)

> 53b: Frome: does not recover from the depression like the towns in the north. 400 weavers and shearmen are at work on t.p. roads . . . paid by fund . . . Population of this once flourishing town consists about 13,000, 8000 of whom dep$^t$ on cloth manufacture.
>
> Source: *DCC*, 21 September 1826 (81)

> 54g: Gone down—Hindon market (Wilts—old clock) Some years ago an important one—now on Thursday exhibited 42 pigs 2 baskets of butter 3 butchers stalls. The rates on small houses are more than the rent!
>
> Source: *DCC*, October 1826, p.1, col. 4 (83)

> 117g: Weyhill Fair—By 12 o'c only 40 waggons had passed through

Andover gate—in former, abundant years, 400 horses have passed it by same hour.

Source: "Weyhill Sheep Fair," *DCC*, 15 October 1829, p. 2., col. 5 (175)

The theme of economic depression and increasing precarity is constant throughout. A long entry on paupers from 1829 describes a man and his wife applying for relief at the Worcester house of Industry, whose passes for relief turn out to be forgeries. The story mentions that the "system of forged passes is carried on largely," and ends on a Brechtian note:

> Near Basingstoke lately one of these <u>passing</u> strangers addressed some labr$^s$ turnip hoeing, wondering how they c$^d$ be constant to work, when they might get a pass, & travel at pleasure. "We see all sights" sd he. "live well, go where we like, own no master, & get handsomely paid." Such at a time of gen$^l$ depression among honest men is the flourishing state of beggary! (173)

Summing up these conditions, Terry Eagleton writes that the "rural England of Hardy's day was not a place of maypoles and Morris dancers but of poverty, falling profits, unemployment, uncertain harvests, cutthroat overseas competition, trade-union militancy, and loss of traditional skills, and the steady hemorrhaging of the population to the industrial towns" ("Buried" 92). Moreover, as Eagleton concludes, and the "Facts" notebook makes clear, "[a]lthough Hardy experiments with pastoral forms and traditional rustic scenarios, he is keenly aware of the sweated labor, social isolation, and economic instability of agricultural England" ("Buried" 92).

Hardy is also keenly aware of local responses to these conditions. Notebook entries record resistance in the form of rick burning and the destruction of threshing machines:

> [192b]: <u>Incendiarism</u>—ricks—farm-buildings &c—Vigilant watch kept on most farms—scarcely a farmer employing a machine to whom a notice has not been sent—several farmers have removed their threshing machines from their premises.
>
> Source: "Outrages in the Country," *DCC*, 18 November 1830, p. 2, col. 5 (284)

192d: <u>Incendiarism</u> at its climax—corn ricks & machines destroyed—special constables sworn. At Salisbury the yeoman were called out Rewards of £200 on the conviction of any incendiary—60 rioters taken at Basingstoke. 25th.
Source: *DCC*, 25 November 1830 (285)

192f: <u>Some incendiaries killed</u> by military firing on them: sentences from one month to transpn for life.
Source: *DCC*, 2 December 1830 (285)

[193]c: <u>The disturbances</u>—assemblages in neighb$^d$ of Shftesb$^y$—proceeded to Stower Provost: destroyed some machines: thence to the residence of the clergyman from whom they demanded, with threats, a considerable reduction of tithes: 5 of the ring leaders captured by party of armed yeoman: brought to county gaol on following morning. One of the prisoners is a farmer named Dore, in respect$^{ble}$ circs . . . In aftern$^n$ a mob collected, & openly burnt a threshing machine . . . another . . . another . . . Barn burnt at Bere - incendiary . . . [& other details] Old D.D. D. Dec. 9.30—Many labourers out of employ—distress great—
Source: *DCC*, 9 December 1830, p. 4. cols. 1–2 (287)

The first of these entries, Greenslade notes, refers for the first time to the protests taking place in Dorset in the autumn of 1830. "Captain Swing" arrived in Dorset as farmers and landowners reduced wages and increasingly used threshing machines rather than human labor to thresh their grains, the introduction of which Hardy represents famously in *Tess of the d'Urbervilles*. In November 1830 protesters sent letters to local farmers and landowners, much as had happened earlier in Kent, with demands for increased wages and money (as well as food and beer). Rioters also demanded that threshing machines stop being used, as the *DCC* clipping mentions. These events are interleaved with a range of other clippings that speak to the texture of a lived history. Alongside the entries on incendiarism are entries on dancing at the Portland Fair, where "floor gave way; all precipitated into the cellar" (November 11, 1830); a stolen silver plate, "found concealed in a hayrick" (November 18, 1830); resurrectionists in whose house "many teeth found ... graves empty" (November 18, 1830); and a young woman who "returns to her g.m$^{rs}$ cottage late: breaks key in trying to unlock door: stays out all night" (December 2, 1830)—the breaking of a key a bad omen that finds its way into *Far from the Madding Crowd* (284–86). In short, the meaning of what constitutes the history of a particular place is expanded by the choices Hardy and Emma make as to what to include as "facts" in the notebook. In essence they curate the everyday.

These entries and the notebook as a whole, as Greenslade argues, were "less an innocent text than one which authenticated and enlarged on, from public sources, what he had long ago heard from the private testimony of his family." The notebook thus served to "[equip] Hardy with the documentary authority he needed to address an educated metropolitan readership" (Greenslade xviii). Hardy's turn to these kinds of "facts" coincided with his return to Dorset; it also represented an "orderly falling back upon [Hardy's] oldest, deepest, and surest creative resources" (Millgate 230). Millgate describes Hardy revisiting his childhood haunts and speaking with people in the neighborhood of Bockhampton, reminiscences found in notes of his from 1883 and 1884. In particular, he mentions a "Still life scene" that Hardy observed: "Pond by T. Lock's. Pond wrinkled, a cow having just come out: the slow waves *bend* the inverted reflections of the other cows without breaking them. The rich reds & duns are as full coloured in the reflection as in the reality." Millgate notes the "meticulousness of the perception," a familiar Hardy trait, which is here "enhanced by a pervasive sense of context, as if the status of these particular cows as local and typical, hence regionally immemorial, made them peculiarly available to the Hardyan imagination" (230–31). In its typicality, the local landscape and local life do not remain local. Referring to the "Facts" notebook specifically, Millgate writes that "Hardy's reinvigorated interest in regional materials" is "not just for their own familiar sakes but as offering distinctive particularizations of general themes and universal phenomena" (231), particularizations which, I contend, are ultimately also deeply historical precisely because of their particularity. The particular history that Hardy authenticates, as these entries show, is the history of enclosure and the incendiary resistance to it seen up close and personal, which, in turn, is also a history of the new technologies and ways of being that come in the wake of enclosure. Universal phenomena in this history, as the Midnight Notes Collective identify, include "the basic device of 'original accumulation,' which created a population of workers 'free' from any means of reproduction and thus compelled (in time) to work for a wage" ("Introduction to the New Enclosures" 1); "ending communal control of the means of subsistence" (3); "seizing land for debt" (4); and making "mobile and migrant labor the dominant form of labor" (4).[30]

The "facts" Hardy and Emma gather in the notebook also make some of the most unlikely events in Hardy's novels seem less sensational. About the form of many of the entries, Greenslade notes, for example, that "a reader familiar with Hardy can hardly miss the recognizable pattern of many of the entries, a baldly ironic reversal, often producing sensational outcomes, marked by the grotesque or the macabre" (xix). Episodes from the novels mirror these plot twists and outcomes, with many incidents finding their inspiration in specific events. Multiple entries, for example, describe the sale of wives: an entry from 1827 titled "Selling wife" relates the story of a laborer near Frome who sold his wife to a shoemaker for £5 and then "delivered her in a halter in the public street. She seemed very willing. Bells rang" (113); likewise, an entry in 1829 contains a wife sale at Stamford that also includes delivering the wife in a halter to her purchaser, after which the trio "retired to a p.house to quaff the heavy wet" (172), the latter being part of the price of the sale. The declining fortunes of Weyhill fair (noted above in entry 117g) bring together these wife sales and economic decline, with the opening scene in which Henchard sells Susan occurring at this fair. There are also numerous entries on wedding ceremonies and marriages that go awry: a woman about to be married in 1829 receives a letter from her husband-to-be on her wedding day announcing that he won't be marrying her because he has married another woman on the same day, a clipping that ends with the unwittingly humorous bracketed clause: "[Probably had wavered between the two]"; another story involves a landlady who eloped with a man staying at her inn and then asks for forgiveness from her husband, "since it was the only crime she had ever been guilty of." The husband agrees and "the prisoner (in custody for stealing landlady's wearing apparel) was discharged" (178). Suicides, one of which involves blood dripping from the ceiling, offer suggestive details for Alec d'Urbervilles's fate at the end of *Tess of the d'Urbervilles* (xxvii); a fatal encounter between a wagon and horse in 1830 provides grist for the death of the Durbeyfields' horse, Prince (237); and numerous scenarios in which snap weddings occur and people marry strangers, some of whom die suddenly, others of whom make nice replacements for the intended bride or groom, are imaginatively reworked in numerous Hardy novels. Less specific to the novels themselves, the notebook also provides a view of Dorset in which burglars, thieves, and convicts roam the countryside, and news of executions and prisoners sentenced to transportation is not uncommon, characters and events that could easily find their way into a Dickens novel.

How then are we to assess these facts in relation to the novels and vice versa? On the one hand, they show how there is nothing incidental about Hardy's descriptions of the land and the different landscapes and foodscapes (to borrow the phrase Jessica Martell uses to discuss the import of the Dorset dairy in *Tess of the d'Urbervilles* and the network of relations it traces) that make up Wessex.[31] But even more to the point: they testify to the specificity of the economic and social changes Hardy aims to represent—namely, the profound transformations that mark the slow but violent processes of enclosure and that find form in Hardy's depictions of the shift from an unenclosed to an enclosed world.

In *The Return of the Native*, enclosure comes to the fore in the fate of two groups of trees:

> At length Clym reached the margin of a fir and beech plantation that had been enclosed from heathland in the year of his birth. Here the trees, laden heavily with their new and humid leaves, were now suffering more damage than during the highest winds of winter, when the boughs are specially disencumbered to do battle with the storm. The wet young beeches were undergoing amputations, bruises, cripplings, and harsh lacerations, from which the wasting sap would bleed for many a day to come, and which would leave scars visible till the day of their burning. Each stem was wrenched at the root, where it moved like a bone in its socket, and at every onset of the

gale convulsive sounds came from the branches, as if pain were felt. In a neighbouring brake a finch was trying to sing; but the wind blew under his feathers till they stood on end, twisted round his little tail, and made him give up his song.

Yet a few yards to Yeobright's left, on the open heath, how ineffectively gnashed the storm! Those gusts which tore the trees merely waved the furze and heather in a light caress. Egdon was made for such times as these. (206–7)

Seamlessly mixing the arboreal and the human, the trees on the enclosed plantation suffer under the storm in terms that equally apply to people: "amputations," "bruises," "cripplings and harsh lacerations" sound more like the effects of human warfare than the damage a tree might undergo. The image of each "wrenched" stem moving "like a bone in a socket" directly ties the fate of the trees to that of human bodies, both of which, the association implies, have the same capacity to convulse and to feel pain.[32] The scale and duration of effects ranges from large to small, long to short term: days of bleeding sap and scars that will remain "visible till the day of their burning" are one sign of the damage, the tiny finch blown about by the winds and left unable to sing another. In stark contrast, the open heath weathers the storm with ease, its furze and heather "waved" in a "light caress." At home in its environment, the heath is perfectly adapted: "Egdon was made for such times as these."

This dramatization of the before and after of enclosure is not merely an interlude but rather is a central narrative of the novel. It is no accident that *The Return of the Native* begins thus: "A Saturday afternoon in November was approaching the time of twilight, and the vast tract of unenclosed heath know as Egdon Heath embrowned itself moment by moment" (9).[33] This "vast tract of unenclosed heath," it becomes clear, is the entire subject of the novel's opening chapter, the self-same "Face on which Time makes but little Impression" that forms the chapter's title. In fact, early reviewers identified Egdon Heath as one of the novel's main dramatis personae.[34] But of course while Time alone may make little impression on the unenclosed heath, the act of enclosing it will: "Every night [the heath's] Titanic form seemed to await something; but it had waited thus, unmoved, during so many centuries, through the crises of so many things, that it could only be imagined to await one last crisis: the final overthrow" (10). The chapter moves back and forth from the present to the future, imagining what will become of the heath and singing its praises now. Tinged with twilight, the heath in its present form is "a thing majestic without severity, impressive without showiness, emphatic in its admonitions, grand in its simplicity" (10); "It was *at present* a place perfectly accordant with man's nature—neither ghastly, hateful, nor ugly: neither commonplace, unmeaning, nor tame; but, like man, slighted and enduring; and withal singularly colossal and mysterious in its swarthy monotony" (11, emphasis added). Sublime rather than charming, sombre and subdued, it "[tells"] its true tale" in the "transitional point of its nightly roll into darkness": it was then that "the sombre stretch of rounds and hollows seemed to rise and meet the evening gloom in pure sympathy, the heath exhaling darkness as rapidly as the heavens precipitated it" (9–10).[35] Along with these characterizations, the chapter also works overtime to convince us of the heath's timelessness: "The great inviolate place had an ancient permanence which the sea cannot claim" (12). As the narrator queries, "Who can say of a particular sea that it is old? Distilled by the sun, kneaded by the moon, it is renewed in a year, in a day, or in an hour. The sea changed, the fields changed, the rivers, the villages, and the people changed, yet Egdon remained . . . even the trifling irregularities remained as the very finger-touches of the last geological change" (12). This sense of permanence, the knowledge that "everything around and underneath had been from prehistoric times as unaltered as the stars overhead," provides "ballast to the mind adrift on change, and harassed by the irrepressible New" (12).

Yet the "final overthrow" looms nonetheless. The "enemy" of Egdon Heath is nothing short of "civilisation" (12), one image of which are the blasted lacerated trees on the enclosed plantation land. The extent of the enemy is also made clear in the history of the "real" heath (as opposed to the "fictional" heath), as Hardy referred to it in the preface to the 1895 edition of the novel and the postscript to the 1912 edition: as Tony Slade remarks in an editorial note, the area in which *The Return of the Native* is set is "today so altered—mainly by afforestation—since Hardy's time that it can no longer be easily viewed as if it were the actual location of the fictional events described in the novel" (*Return* 399). Despite the narrator's sanguine vision, in the opening chapter, that places like "haggard Egdon" may become the "new Vale of Tempe" (10), with the northern climes of Iceland and Scheveningen replacing "the vineyards and myrtle-gardens of South Europe" for those of "the more thinking among mankind" (11),[36] the narrative unfolds a different story: a character as much as an environment, the heath, like its inhabitants, is on the brink of extinction, and one of the stories it has to tell, like that of the novel itself, involves the loss of such "unenclosed" spaces and the reciprocity they afford between human and landscape.

Time and time again, for both his characters and their environment, the demands of the "irrepressible New" win out. As the narrator says of the reddleman Diggory Venn, "He was one of a class rapidly becoming extinct in Wessex, filling at present in the rural world the place which, during the last century, the dodo occupied in the world of animals" (13). (The same could be said for Michael Henchard, Giles Winterbourne, Tess Durbeyfield, and Marty South.) An enduring sign of the past, like the heath, Venn is "a curious, interesting, and nearly perished link between obsolete forms of life and those which generally prevail" (14). Integral to these obsolete forms of life is the right to subsistence, a right that Hardy's heroes and heroines are continually deprived of. Hardy makes a point of mentioning this right, when he includes the following information about Egdon Heath: "This obscure, obsolete, superseded country figures in Domesday. Its condition is recorded therein as that of heathy, furzy, briary wilderness—'Bruaria.'" This is followed by an additional note: "'Turbaria Bruaria'—the right of cutting heath-turf—occurs in charters relating to the district" (11). The right to subsistence, to, in this case, cut heath-turf, is at the heart of the Forest Charter, the charter of rights that, as we saw in Chapter 1, guarantees the right to commoning. Even as the opening chapter of *The Return of the Native* presents the heath as seemingly unchangeable, then, it complicates its own claims by acknowledging the social nature of its landscape. After all, the charter is what keeps the heath the "untameable, Ishmaelite thing" that it is and "always had been" (12). Managed and regulated by common rights, the heath is a social rather than a natural creation or entity; signs of its disappearance are equally a result of social, political, and historical forces, encapsulated here in "civilization" and "the irrepressible New." There is nothing natural about either the heath's existence or its extinction, contra claims about private property as an inevitable and hence naturalized historical development with regard to property relations. "Property rights," Derek Wall underscores, "establish relationships between people and things. They are also social and shape relationships between different groups of people. Property rights determine who gets what and who is excluded in terms of access to resources" (5). Hardy uses descriptions of landscape to dramatize these shifting relationships. Far from expressing a wistful nostalgia for a sylvan past, these relationships are shown to be intimately tied to property rights. With hindsight, we can also appreciate the prescience in his characterization of this process as a land war, with its amputations and cripplings, given the centrality of land today in the attacks on common resources, surviving commons, and the earthly commons, all pressing issues at the heart of environmental battles about how best to respond to global warming and climate change.

This same marking (and the literal scarring) of an unfolding history, of an attentiveness to "obsolete forms of life" present in the landscape, shapes the opening of *The Woodlanders*. We hear in the first sentence of the "extensive woodlands, interspersed with apple-orchards" (5), which over the course of the narrative will be subject to the processes of enclosure. Likewise, Hardy's first novel, *Under the Greenwood Tree*, opens with this description of the woods and its dwellers:

> To dwellers in a wood almost every species of tree has its voice as well as its feature. At the passing of the breeze the fir-trees sob and moan no less distinctly than they rock; the holly whistles as it battles with itself; the ash hisses amid its quiverings; the beech rustles while its flat boughs rise and fall. And winter, which modifies the note of such trees as shed their leaves, does not destroy its individuality. (7)

For some, like Fitzpiers, coming from elsewhere, woods are profoundly inhospitable. For others, like Tess, they offer what initially seems like respite but turns out to be something else altogether: "[I]t was [after dark], when out in the woods, that she seemed least solitary. She knew how to hit to a hair's-breadth that moment of evening when the light and the darkness are so evenly balanced that the constraint of day and the suspense of night neutralize each other, leaving absolute mental liberty." Drawn to the woods, "she had no fear of the shadows; her sole idea seemed to be to shun mankind—or rather that cold accretion called the world, which, so terrible in the mass, is so unformidable, even pitiable, in its units." (104) The woods, ultimately, are not a retreat from the world: "her sole idea" only "*seemed* to be to shun mankind." Instead, they provide a different optic on the world. Like Nixon's language of a kind of violence that is incremental and accretive, "that cold accretion called the world . . . so terrible in its mass" can here be seen as something "unformidable" and "even pitiable, in its units." Allowing "absolute mental liberty," the woods permit a view of the world unencumbered by concerns or fears for the self, a view that recalls Eliot's assertion in *Middlemarch* that "I know no speck so troublesome as self" (419), and that Gillian Beer refers to, more generally, as "a leveled insight" on Eliot's part.[37] More recently, in a reading of *Under the Greenwood Tree*, Elizabeth Miller has referred to this insight in terms of an "ecological realism," or dendrography ("tree-writing") in which "Hardy represents the human characters in the same register as the trees, in species terms, producing the effect of an environmental realism rather than the effect of realist individuation" (706).[38] For Hardy, interactions between human and landscape afford one version of this kind of levelling, which, again, is not a turning away from the world but a way of seeing it more clearly, of bringing it back, as it were, into the orbit of the everyday, its "units" thereby manageable in a way they otherwise are not. The direness of the current order rests in the loss of such environments *figured* in woodlands and heaths and the enclosing of the self that accompanies this loss. Hardy's common characters show us just how these forms of enclosure work on identity and how they might also be thwarted—but not through any sort of return to the past. For ultimately Clym Yeobright's story is a cautionary tale about the impossibility of the "return of the native," and Tess's a calling into question of "accepted social law" and her sense of "feeling herself in antagonism" where, in fact, "she was quite in accord," having broken "no law known to the environment in which she fancied herself such an anomaly" (105).

## Letters, Character, and the Law

If the literal loss of the commons denudes environments of their ability to sustain "mental liberty," it is the scarcity of words and characters and plots that register this loss in Hardy's humanscapes. Hardy's characters are doomed to repetitions that operate relentlessly to foreclose new openings, and his novels seem to be at a loss for words for existing and emerging sexual and social relations. Often there are simply not enough names to go around. The pain attendant on such paucity is viscerally felt in Jude and Sue's case, where the trio of injunctions against learning, laboring, and loving closes down all possibility of escape or movement beyond these strictures. In their second attempt at marriage, for example, Sue grows "painfully apprehensive" as she reads the "four-square undertaking . . . into which her own and Jude's names were inserted" (281). This form of notice requires Jude and Sue to fit themselves into a series of categories—name, rank, married status, occupation, and so on—that turn a "very volatile essence, their love for each other" into something solid and square, something to be "made permanent." Sue is particularly struck by the marriage certificate's request for the "Names and Surnames of the Parties," musing that "they were to be parties now, not lovers" (281). Not only are the categories felt to be crippling and "sordid" ("It spoils the sentiment, doesn't it! . . . It seems making a more sordid business of it even than signing the contract in a vestry" (281), reflects Sue), but the words that will have to be said in the marriage ceremony can in no way differentiate between the "parties" saying them: "I am going to vow to you in the same words I vowed in to my other husband," Sue bemoans, "and you to me in the same as you used to your other wife; regardless of the deterrent lesson we were taught by those experiments!" (283). These words and the bonds of marriage, more generally, are felt as physical, material constrictions, so much so that Sue desperately appeals to Jude to kiss her, "as a lover, incorporeally," because "[i]t won't be ever like this any more, will it?" Wishing they "hadn't begun the business," but feeling like they "must go on," Sue finds the morning of the wedding "unpleasantly like that other morning." Again, though, echoing the need to "go on," she tells Jude, "Let us go on now" (283). Of course, they don't "go on," but instead leave the church "stealthily and guiltily, as if they had committed a misdemeanour" (284). As Jude sums up this episode: "We are making a mess of it, it strikes me" (285), and so they are, but without fully understanding the extent of their transgression and the mess it puts them in. As Penny Boumelha describes the catch-22 they find themselves in, "Jude and Sue escape none of the oppressions of marriage, but they incur over and above these the penalties reserved for transgressors against it. There is no form for the relationship to take except those named and determined by the very form they seek to transcend: unless it is marriage, it is adultery or fornication" (150).

The impasse that results from this paucity of forms takes various guises in *The Return of the Native*, *The Mayor of Casterbridge*, and *The Woodlanders*. Repeated marriages, repeated names, and frustrating doublings of many sorts vex all of Hardy's common characters. In *The Return of the Native*, Thomasin and Wildeve name their child Eustacia Clementine, leading Clym to remonstrate, "What a mockery! . . . That this unhappy marriage of mine [to Eustacia Vye] should be perpetuated in that child's name!" (324); there are two Elizabeth-Janes in *The Mayor of Casterbridge*, one Henchard's child, the other Newson's, not to mention two mayors, as well as two Henchards and two Lucettas, thanks to the skimmington effigies ("'Tis me!'" Lucetta exclaims when she sees her effigy [213]); and *The Woodlanders*, like all of Hardy's Wessex plots, cycles through combinations of relationships in which small groups of characters are shuffled and reshuffled among themselves—all thereby functioning essentially as experiments in living within a limited set of possibilities. Winterborne, Fitzpiers, and Grace Melbury combine in different constellations; Sue, Jude, Phillotson, and Arabella marry, remarry, and separate but can never really escape each other's orbits (so much so that Jude ends up giving Sue away to Phillotson because there seems to be no one else who can even act as a witness); and the main cast of *The Mayor of Casterbridge* tries just about every possible pairing, each pairing attempting to make out of a threesome or foursome a couple.[39]

While on the face of it these repetitions are improbable at best (an oft-repeated complaint of Hardy's contemporary reviewers), they are not without their own logic. Whereas, in Dickens, as we saw, the one *as* the many led to a proliferation of difference, Hardy, in a sense, shows us the reverse: the many reduced to the one in the oppressive figure of the couple *and* the resistance to such deformations. The enforcement of two or more as the one in Hardy is equated to forms of possessiveness in which selves become objects to be owned. Sue is disturbed by the notion of having to be "given away" in marriage; Wildeve speaks of Eustacia "rightly [belonging] to [him]" (275); and Fitzpiers, weighing the benefits and disadvantages of marrying Grace Melbury, is described in the following terms:

> Fitzpiers kept himself continually near her dominating any rebellious impulse, and shaping her will into passive concurrence with all his desires. Apart from his lover-like anxiety to possess her, the few golden hundreds of the timber-dealer, ready to hand, formed a warm background to Grace's lovely face, and went some way to remove his uneasiness at the prospect of endangering his professional and social chances by an alliance with the family of a simple countryman. (171)

The gendered nature of this logic is apparent: Hardy's women suffer at the hands of men who desire to possess them or to treat them like property, as Henchard does when he literally sells his wife to open *The Mayor of Casterbridge*. But the suffering is also more generalized than this, betokening a stultifying possessiveness in which the endless proliferation of the same offers no way out for either men or women. Looking toward a future when the world catches up to her and Jude, "in fifty, ay, twenty years," Sue optimistically opines that the couple being married in the church from which she and Jude flee "'will see weltering humanity still more vividly than we do now, as "Shapes like our own selves hideously multiplied," and will be afraid to reproduce them'" (287). As with land and private property, the desire to possess another constitutes a violent act of enclosure, this time entailing the enclosure of bodies or selves such that human social bonds "of a forced kind snuff out cordiality and spontaneousness," in Jude's language. Sue is convinced that "more are like us than we think!" and "that there was nothing queer or exceptional in it:

that all were so" (286–87). The enclosure of bodies and selves functions to pervert sociality across a range of registers including but not limited to marriage. For Jude and Sue, it closes down where they can go or live, as more and more places become off limits: "'We must sail under sealed orders, that nobody may trace us.... We mustn't go to Alfredston, or to Melchester or to Shaston, or to Christminster. Apart from those we may go anywhere'" (308). The extent of this prohibition is brought home by the fact that virtually all of the places named together make up the social world of the novel as a whole; indeed, aside from Alfredston, they reiterate the titles to all the preceding books organizing the different parts and locations of the novel. In other words, social space in toto is shown to be constricted and constricting, bringing together the enclosure of bodies and space.

But the ambit and restlessness of the circulation of common bodies also figure a commonness in which forms of self-enclosure are shown to be impossible, in which the "all" who "were so" of whom Sue speaks finds expression. Tellingly, in the same chapter in *The Woodlanders* in which Marty and Giles's isolation is emphasized we also learn that Marty has cut off her hair to sell to Felice Charmond, conjuring an aleatory, mobile self—at once materially there and elsewhere. Marty's hair literally circulates, "shared" as it is by Felice, underscoring how "selves" in Hardy's world are as materially shared as the material world in which they exist. The physical sharing of hair incarnates an idea Hardy wrote about in a later journal entry (March–April 1890) in which he muses, "Mankind, in fact, may be and possibly will be viewed as members of one corporeal frame" (*Life and Work* 235). Significantly, seeing the pain or suffering of others "reacting on ourselves" will be the means through which we feel ourselves "part of one body" (235). Without invoking the specific language of the commons, Hardy nonetheless envisions a form of what Silvia Federici has called a "common subject" (discussed in Chapter 3). As Federici argues, "[N]o common is possible unless we refuse to base our life and our reproduction on the suffering of others, unless we refuse to see ourselves as separate from them."

While hair is the form of transport in Marty's case, the more typical Hardyan device through which selves get circulated is physical letters, which (drawing on eighteenth-century conventions) are themselves literally and figuratively "characters." *The Return of the Native* makes this connection explicit: when Diggory Venn meets Wildeve to give him a letter from Eustacia, Venn says, "'[H]ere we are—we three.'" Wildeve queries, "'We three?' ... looking around quickly," to which Venn responds, "'Yes; you, and I and she. This is she,'" as he holds up Eustacia's letter and parcel (151). This letter is but one of many throughout Hardy's oeuvre. To stay with the example of Marty's hair for a moment: I approached *The Woodlanders* with the aim of following the letter Marty writes to Fitzpiers, in which she reveals that Felice's hair is indeed hers. This letter, like all crucial Hardy letters, is pocketed, in this case by Fitzpiers, and only read by him once he has fled England for the continent and Felice. But a search of the novel reveals no fewer than nineteen letters (excluding numerous other kinds of writing, including a note written on the wall outside Giles's house), all of which circulate key pieces of information among the novel's characters, including the knowledge that Grace Melbury will *not* be able to get a divorce from Fitzpiers easily, and therefore be freed to follow her reawakening desire for the woodlander Giles Winterborne. (Faces, too, become pages to be read for what they have recorded, as we saw earlier with Clym in *The Return of the Native*.)

While some of these letters certainly have more dramatic consequences than others, most of them share the quality of being "pocketed" or enclosed in one sense or another. If we move beyond *The Woodlanders*, the examples proliferate: there are at least four letters in *Tess of the d'Urbervilles* that are either not sent at all—two from Tess revealing the depths of her deprivation to Angel while he is away in Brazil—or are "mis-placed," as in the case of Tess's letter to Angel the night before their wedding, or sent by others—Izz Huett's and Marian's letter to Angel warning him that Tess is "sore put" by Alec d'Urberville and that "a woman should not be try'd beyond her Strength, and continual dropping will wear away a Stone—ay, more—a Diamond" (450). Additionally, Tess's mother, Mrs. Durbeyfield, sends Angel two letters, neither of which adequately apprises him of the dire situation Tess is in at the time of their writing. In short, Angel receives or is the intended recipient of a lot of mail, the contents of which, nevertheless, never quite reach him, either literally or figuratively. And last but not least, one final example from another novel, which aptly illustrates the perverse effects and prevalence of such misbegotten missives: in *The Mayor of Casterbridge*, after Susan Henchard dies, Michael Henchard decides to tell Elizabeth-Jane that he is her father; he does so, and although she is shocked, she takes in the news relatively well. Going upstairs to find the papers to prove his paternity, Henchard finds a letter left by Susan with instructions that it not be opened until Elizabeth-Jane's wedding. Of course, given that it is a Hardy novel, we can see the writing on the wall. Henchard opens the letter and learns that he is not in fact Elizabeth-Jane's father. Susan narrates how their daughter died and how she named the new child of hers and Newson's the same name! This letter has the distinction of being opened too early *and* too late. Henchard, Hardy writes,

> regarded the paper as if it were a window-pane through which he saw for miles. His lip twitched, and he seemed to compress his frame, as if to bear better. His usual habit was not to consider whether destiny were hard upon him or not—the shape of his ideas in cases of affliction being simply a moody, "I am to suffer, I perceive." This much scourging, then, is it for me. But now through his passionate head there stormed this thought—that the blasting disclosure was what he had deserved. (96)

Blame or no blame, after this Henchard becomes increasingly hostile toward Elizabeth-Jane without her knowing why, thereby setting him up for more pain and suffering.

The perverse but perfect timing of Hardy's letters tempt a Lacanian reading. As Lacan states, in his reading of Poe's "The Purloined Letter," "The letter always arrives at its destination." Now, on first reading, the opposite might seem to be true, since as we have seen, Hardyan letters continually miss their mark, are misplaced or improperly sealed, are left unsent or read too late, are delivered but unread, "pocketed" or opened at all the wrong times. But as Žižek points out in his analysis of this Lacanian concept, objections to Lacan's claim in the end only prove its truth all the more. Take Henchard, for example. Is it that the letter is too early or too late? Or that it actually reaches Henchard just in time, that is, once he recognizes himself as its addressee: "the blasting disclosure was what he had deserved." Žižek, following Lacan, reads this sort of recognition variously as the return of the repressed (*Enjoy Your Symptom* 12), "the remainder left over after we have lost our symbolic support" (7), and "the stain spoiling the picture" (8). As he explains, "the letter arrives at its destination when we are no longer 'fillers' of the empty places in another's fantasy structure, i.e., when the other finally 'opens his eyes' and realizes that the real letter is not the message we are supposed to carry but our being itself, the object in us that resists symbolization" (7).[40] Importantly, too, Žižek argues that the letter's arrival always feels absurdly contingent: Why now? What if? What if it had happened in another way, at another time, or not at all? "'Fate' in psychoanalysis," he avers, "always asserts itself through such contingent encounters" (11).

That "fate" asserts itself through contingent encounters: this piece of Žižekian Lacanianism is central to Hardy's novelistic universe (so much so that one can imagine lifting it straight out of the novels) and helps to unsettle simplistic readings of Hardy's fatalism by tying fate directly to a psychically complex and, as I am suggesting, historically specific vision of the self, a self that Hardy understands to be in a radically contingent relation to the world. At the same time, however, I want to resist the temptation to turn Hardy into Lacan *avant la lettre*, thereby conceiving his project as an anticipatory one about desire and the Other, and instead argue for a Hardy who writes his own version of the eccentric biography (of the "pure woman," or "man of character," to recall the typicality Hardy assigns his protagonists) prompted by the challenge of how to represent the transformations in identity that accompany the transformations in land and notions of property brought about by enclosure. Note how in each of the instances above—and there are many more as well—letters radically compromise the wholeness of a character's identity. When Marty South, for example, learns that she and her father won't lose their house if she refuses to give her hair up to Felice Charmond (their landlord), she reassures herself, "Thank Heaven, then . . . what belongs to me I keep" (15). Again and again, though, Hardy's novels sever identity from ownership: thought experiments in communal, global relations, they deny the fantasy of self-enclosure or self-possession even as they recognize the logic of enclosure as the current way of the world. Marty

South gives up her hair (to her landlord, no less)—she has to; Henchard's progeny cannot finally be his own; Tess's first letter to Angel on the night before their wedding is simultaneously delivered and unreadable given Angel's response the next day to the contents of the letter: "O Tess . . . You were one person and now you are another. My God—how can forgiveness meet such a grotesque—prestidigitation as that!" (298).

Grotesque magic indeed—but not in the sense Angel means: for Hardy, the self *is* always elsewhere, a part of the world, impossible to conceive apart from the world. Simultaneously dystopian and driven by a utopian impulse—an impulse that Jameson, as we have seen, identifies with the attempt to "imagine the life of a different mode of production . . . of a different economic system" (8–9)—Hardy's response to the slow violence of enclosure and its work regimen offers an alternative vision of his realism. Countering readings of Hardy as a pessimist, Terry Eagleton grants that "he did not believe that the universe was spontaneously on our side, but this *is* known as realism, not pessimism. Those who come a cropper in his fiction tend to do so because they fail to adapt to circumstance or are trapped between aspiration and frustration, not because they are victims of a malevolent universe" ("Buried in the Life" 92). Hardy too weighs in on this debate when he objects to his contemporary critics brandishing the term "pessimistic" ("as if that were a very wicked adjective") synonymous with a critique of his work, and suggests that it "shows a curious muddle-mindedness":

> Existence is either ordered in a certain way, or it is not so ordered, and conjectures which harmonize best with experience are removed above all comparison with other conjectures which do not so harmonize. So that to say one view is worse than other views without proving it erroneous implies the possibility of a false view being better or more expedient than a true view; and no pragmatic proppings can make that *idolum specus* ["phantasm of the cave"] stand on its feet, for it postulates a prescience denied to humanity. (*Tess of the d'Urbervilles* 401)

To attempt to represent how existence is ordered, another set of terms for the "deeper reality" that contradicts the equation of the material with the real, can never be an attitudinal choice, just as Hardy's characters cannot choose simply to step outside the world as it is ordered. The novelistic universe Hardy constructs to try and tell the truth of that world makes such a choice impossible.

In a conversation in *The Return of the Native* when Clym is anxious to tell Eustacia about his plans for a local school, Eustacia frankly states, "I have not much love for my fellow-creatures. Sometimes I quite hate them," to which Clym replies, "Still I think that if you were to hear my scheme you might take an interest in it. There is no use in hating people—if you hate anything, you should hate what produced them." In characteristic fashion, Eustacia then responds, "Do you mean Nature? I hate her already. But I shall be glad to hear your scheme at any time" (185). Eustacia both gets it right and doesn't get it: on the one hand, Nature in the broadest sense of Hardy's notion of "Environment," which includes the natural world but also the social one, is what produces people; on the other hand, Eustacia's "Nature" is essentially Egdon heath, the smallness of the village, and her hatred of provincial life.[41] Of course, the former view of environment is not unique to Hardy, but rather a recognizable position, very much in keeping with the basic tenets of Marxist theory and Marx's famous line, in the preface to *A Contribution to the Critique of Political Economy*, that "the mode of production of material life determines the social, political and intellectual life process in general. It is not the consciousness of men that determines their being, but, on the contrary, their social being that determines their consciousness" (Tucker, *Marx-Engels* 4).

Yet the language of the commons, so common in Hardy's own day, and once again on the table, shows us something else as well: that "the universe" is not "out there" and mappable in any conventionally realistic or empirical way, but rather is evidenced only figurally for Hardy, in his attentiveness to "space, representability and allegory," the very theoretical tools Jameson employs in his analysis of the contemporary world system. By attending to the most quotidian aspects of the changes in how we occupy space, while aware that those changes are part of "the great web of human doing then weaving in both hemispheres, from the White Sea to Cape Horn," Hardy's realism reinvigorates the local-global dialectic in the name of an embedded and embodied local. In doing so, it thus anticipates our present need to rethink our relationship to a global earthly commons in the face of environmental threat. That the local has now come back to the fore in the most global of crises is an irony that would not be lost on the so-called regional writer Thomas Hardy.

## Hardy and the Environment

Just as the contemporary Occupy movement permits the common and the commune to "[enter] vividly into the figurability of the present" (2), to recall Kristin Ross's formulation cited in the Introduction, climate change brings into view anew the space of the local and its significance within the local-global dialectic. Changes—often minute or invisible—in ecosystems can have massive global consequences. Communities are now aware in new ways of the local impacts of global phenomena and of the need to address their own contributions to these global phenomena. More so than ever, the most pressing questions involve relations between humans and landscapes.

In his essay on *The Woodlanders*, William A. Cohen poses this relationship in terms of what he calls Hardy's "tactile ecology" or "tactile imagination" (1), an ecology that has less to do with descriptions of the natural world than with "a reorientation of ideas about what constitutes nature and how we understand the human" (2). Crucially, "[concerns] with affect and environment are not just anticipated or interpreted by Hardy, but are in many ways exceeded by the conception of the human, through the tactile, that he undertakes" (2–3). Ultimately, for Cohen, Hardy's tactile ecology embodies a "reciprocal relationship between human and non-human agency" (15), in which the trees in *The Woodlanders* (or the natural world more generally) are granted a kind of agency, and touch provides new ways of knowing. To the apple tree that roots Giles Winterborne to the spot when Grace Melbury sees him in the marketplace, for example, Cohen grants "a form of tactile perception: it knows but that with which it comes into proximate contact, and that mode of knowledge is shared with the most tree-like people in the book" (14). While Cohen also acknowledges that the trees are cultivated and hence the "product of human labour and intention," his emphasis rests on reconceiving the nonhuman as having agency. His analysis also relies on a "proximate contact" between "ideas and things" that, in the end, I think, belies the geopolitical reach of Hardy's view of the world and his vision of sociality, an approach better captured in the notion of a "political ecology of enclosure" that positions the economy and the environment in a mutually constitutive relationship.[42] As I have aimed to show, it is on the human, social end of the spectrum that Hardy's novelistic world is most revelatory for our own present and future. For not only do we need to resituate ourselves in relation to an imperiled earthly commons, we need to reinvent ourselves *as selves* in the manufactured landscapes of our own making. To my mind, this is an integral aspect of what Geoff Mann and Joel Wainwright refer to as "the planetary crisis" today: as they insist, "the planetary crisis is, among other things, a crisis of the imagination, a crisis of ideology, the result of an inability to conceive any alternative to walls, guns, and finance as tools to address the problems that loom on the horizon" (197). But as with many accounts of climate change and environmental crises, they give scant attention to the kind of subject necessary to move beyond this crisis.

We have seen how literal, physical letters in Hardy's fiction circulate the self across the material world. Selves, in essence, are "thinned" by losing their centeredness and gaining their eccentricity.[43] In short, in Hardy's world "selves" are profoundly reciprocal: they are as material as the material world in which they exist. (The language of possession, in contrast, refuses such reciprocity: it is always a one-way street in which one belongs to another, is owned by another, is a discrete individual). This materiality doesn't guarantee success or happiness—more often than not it brings disaster—but conversely no possibility of happiness exists without a recognition of this deep reciprocity.[44]

Even this formulation though gives too much weight to subjects. Hardy ends the opening scene of *The Mayor of Casterbridge* with Henchard looking out of the fair tent noting the "peacefulness of inferior nature" in contrast to the "wilful hostilities of mankind" (11). He refuses this desired resting place, however, adding the following coda: "In presence of this scene after the other there was a natural instinct to abjure man as the blot on an otherwise kindly universe; till it was remembered that all terrestrial conditions were intermittent, and that mankind might some night be innocently sleeping when these quiet objects were raging loud"

(11). "Inferior nature" can be as "wilful" and as hostile as humans; in this revision of subject-object relations, objects do not gain agency, as Cohen would have it, so much as subjects lose their centrality, now no less exalted than "quiet objects." Similarly, in *Jude the Obscure*, the narrator speaks of the "scorn of Nature for man's finer emotions, and her lack of interest in his aspirations" (177). So in Hardy it is not so much subjects being punished for being subjects—but rather for thinking of themselves as something other than objects in a world filled with other objects. As Adorno articulates this self-same relation between subject and object, "The subject's real impotence has its echo in its mental omnipotence. The ego principle imitates its negation. It is not true that the object is a subject, as idealism has been drilling into us for thousands of years, but it is true that the subject is an object" (*Negative Dialectics* 179). Without emphasizing objects specifically, Gillian Beer characterizes this recognition in the following way: "Instead of man disjunct from all other aspects of the material order, or at the pinnacle of hierarchy, he must now find a place in a world of 'horizontality,' as it comes home to Clym in *The Return of the Native*. 'It gave him a sense of bare equality with, and no superiority to, a single living thing under the sun'" (*Darwin's Plots* 232–33). Unlike John Stuart Mill's equation of individuality with singularity, and of democratization with mediocrity, this modeling of character leads to the recognition of an individual's profound entanglements in a global commons. In place of individual genius, there is Darwinian profusion in a conjoined world, famously captured in Darwin's image of the "tangled bank" and his notion that the "elaborately constructed forms" it contains, "so different from each other, and dependent upon each other in so complex a manner, have all been produced by laws acting around us" (219). In a more recent formulation, Richard Powers, in *The Overstory*, a novel centered around trees and our relationship to them, writes that "There are no individuals in a forest, no separable events. The bird and the branch it sits on are a joint thing" (218).

But Hardy also broadens these Darwinian formulations by applying them to subjectivity. His world not only links diversification and complex dependence, it also envisions a wayward, unenclosed self, a notion of character as radical as the Darwinian environment. At the end of *The*

CHAPTER FOUR

*Woodlanders*, Marty whispers to Giles Winterborne in his grave, "'Now, my own love . . . you are mine, and on'y mine; for she [Grace] has forgot 'ee at last, although for her you died'" (367); at the end of *The Mayor of Casterbridge*, the novel's final "letter," Henchard's will, wills away Henchard: "'That Elizabeth-Jane Farfrae be not told of my death . . . & that nobody is wished to see my dead body . . . & that no flours be planted on my grave. & that no man remember me. To this I put my name'" (254). Selves, like letters, always miss one another, are never one with themselves; the letter, like the self, "killeth," as the epigraph to *Jude the Obscure* announces. To be fully on the side of objects is to make the self literally eccentric. Whereas the eccentric collective biographies of Dickens, as we saw in Chapter 2, realize this beside-ness formally in their cataloguing of characters, the letters in Hardy's fiction can only gesture toward it, circulating as literal reminders of how dispersed and piecemeal the self is.

\* \* \*

In an aphorism on technology in *Minima Moralia*, Adorno shows how an object as seemingly insignificant and unimposing as a door has the capacity to subject individuals to "the implacable, as it were ahistorical demands of objects": "Technology is making gestures precise and brutal, and with them men. It expels from movements all hesitation, deliberation, civility" (40). As Adorno continues, car doors and refrigerator doors must be slammed, while other doors "snap shut by themselves, imposing on those entering the bad manners of not looking behind them, not shielding the interior of the house which receives them." For Adorno, the consequences of these transformations in the most mundane, quotidian of objects are profound, leading to nothing short of what he calls the "withering of experience":

> The new human type cannot be properly understood without awareness of what he is continuously exposed to from the world of things about him, even in his most secret innervations. . . . Not least to blame for the withering of experience is the fact that things, under the law of pure functionality, assume a form that limits contact with them to mere operation, and tolerates no surplus, either of freedom

of contact or in autonomy of things, which would survive as the core of experience, because it is not consumed by the moment of action. (*Minima Moralia* 40)

As I have argued, Hardy witnessed the beginnings of these technological changes, which in turn led, as Adorno remarks, to the creation of a "new human type," the contours and aspects of which Hardy represents figurally in the newly emerging relations to the land and environment and the oppressive social strictures premised on the logic of privatization, a logic that gathers everything in its wake, from property and interests to sexual relations and the writing of fiction itself. As with Adorno, Hardy locates these transformations in the everyday and common, which are given concrete form in many minute and local particularities: we see them in the "amputation" and "crippling" of trees on enclosed land in the face of a violent windstorm in *The Return of the Native*, in the loss of the Durbeyfields' cottage in *Tess of the d'Urbervilles*, and in the convenient, but lifeless, pump that replaces the mossy well and bucket of Hardy's childhood home in his autobiography. Again, as in Adorno's account, the recording of this "vanishing life" need not be reduced to a nostalgic or regressive turning away from modernity, a pessimistic response to change; to attempt to tell the truth about a new order of existence, to recall Hardy's words, and to identify a logic in that order, can hardly be equated to pessimism, or any other attitudinal "ism."[45] This is, in effect, the essence of a dialectical imagination: it is never about taking sides in relation to historical developments, but rather about analyzing the reasons and conditions for their emergence and the logic behind them.

In the roughly fifty years between the time Hardy published his last novel, *Jude the Obscure*, and Adorno published *Minima Moralia*, the emerging changes Hardy powerfully delineated in his novels came to pass. What Adorno's language helps bring into view is a relation to the world, whether urban or rural, metropolis or provincial town, in which pure functionality increasingly supersedes all other possible relations, a development that Hardy could see in the making but obviously not see through to its full unfolding in the twentieth century, or in our own moment. But like Adorno, Hardy uses the object world and the natural world to shape and give expression to the reduction of both by "mere operation" in which "no surplus, either of freedom of contact or in autonomy of things" is tolerated. This limiting of contact, as well as its obverse, essentially defines Hardy's novelistic universe, and is in no way confined to a rural world, or a "vanishing life." Like the processes of enclosure, in other words, there is a *longue durée* to this "new human type" which is no less violent for being slow in the making. The violence of this new everyday is perhaps most painfully evoked in *Jude the Obscure*, in which Jude and Sue can neither live within the letter of the law nor escape it. There truly is no atmosphere in which to breathe. Boumelha powerfully articulates the oppressive, well-nigh physical force of convention that encloses any alternative form of relationship once Sue finally has sex with Jude: "Once she has children, she is forced to live with Jude the economic life of the couple, and gradually to reduce her opposition to marriage to formalism by pretending to marry Jude and adopting his name" (148). Boumelha's stress on "the economic life of the couple" makes clear how typification functions negatively to reproduce "the couple" and how intimately tied to the economic the social pressures Hardy represents are: in essence they define and deform individuals.[46] Sue's and Jude's relationship thus dramatizes the violence that lurks beneath the seemingly benign order of the day and how that order makes any and all alternatives to it appear to be impossible. As Boumelha describes this violence, Sue and Jude

> show . . . the unimaginable nature of female-male relations as they would exist outside the economic and ideological pressures which wrench the relationship back into pre-determined forms of marriage, just as Hardy's novel is wrenched back finally into pre-existing fictional forms; but it is part of the strength of *Jude* that it makes visible the violence of those wrenchings, and gives a sense of the energy which cannot be wholly contained within those forms. (150)

In a letter to Edmund Gosse in which Hardy essentially defends Sue against negative reviews of the novel which portray her as "perverted or depraved," Hardy explicitly addresses the sexual pressures that "pre-determined forms of marriage" exert, an aspect of the relations between Sue and Jude that he admits he "cd not dwell upon":

that, though she has children, her intimacies with Jude have never been more than occasional, even while they were living together (I mention that they occupy separate rooms, except towards the end), & one of her reasons for fearing the marriage ceremony is that she fears it wd be breaking faith with Jude to withhold herself at pleasure, or altogether, after it; though while uncontracted she feels at liberty to yield herself as seldom as she chooses. This has tended to keep his passion as hot at the end as at the beginning, & helps to break his heart. He has never really possessed her as freely as he desired. (*Collected Letters* 2: 100)

Tellingly, Hardy associates the pressures of this form of social and sexual expectation with Jude's desire or need to possess Sue, once again foregrounding the intimate and violent ties between possession and identity that Hardy both recognizes and attempts to unsettle.

The violence of these wrenchings, as I understand them, extends across Hardy's oeuvre and realistically portrays the implacable force of convention in all its guises and the ways in which it shapes everything in its image, much like Marx's description in *The Communist Manifesto* of capitalism and its capacity to "[compel] all nations, on pain of extinction, to adopt the bourgeois mode of production" and to "[compel] them to introduce what it calls civilisation into their midst, i.e., to become bourgeois themselves. In one word, it creates a world after its own image" (40).

Moreover, the connections between these social and ideological "wrenchings" and enclosure go even deeper. Peter Linebaugh points out that the first English translation of *The Communist Manifesto* opened with the following language: "A frightful hobgoblin stalks throughout Europe. We are haunted by a ghost, the ghost of Communism." He writes about this translation:

> The translator was Helen MacFarlane, a Lancashire Chartist, whose choice of words derived from the forest commons—"Hob" was the name of a country laborer, "goblin" a mischievous sprite. Thus communism manifested itself in the *Manifesto* in the discourse of the agrarian commons, the substrate of language revealing the imprint

> of the clouted shoon in the sixteenth century who fought to have all things common. The trajectory from the commons to communism can be cast as the passage from past to future. For Marx personally it corresponded to his intellectual progress. The criminalization of the woodland commons of the Moselle Valley peasantry provided him with his first experience with economic questions and led him directly to the critique of political economy. (144–45)

For Hardy, as for Marx, the woodland commons was the ground for thinking about a retreating past and an alternative future. In Hardy's vision of this future, new characters, new language, new air is needed, glimpses of which are offered in a new common collective. Sue imagines a future in which her and Jude's descendants will refuse to reproduce the welter of present humanity ("our own selves hideously multiplied"), and Jude envisages a time when "the mean exclusiveness" that "the beggarly question of parentage" reveals will no longer constitute the status quo. Then, not only will "all the little ones of our time" be seen "collectively" as "the children of us adults of the time," and hence "entitled to our general care," but the present order of things and the values it promotes—from "class-feeling" to "patriotism" and "save-your-soul-ism" (274–75)—will of necessity be upended. With the hindsight afforded by the unfolding of Hardy's account in the twentieth century and the present, the accusation that Hardy was too pessimistic could not seem more misplaced. But, equally, without a recognition of Hardy's utopian hopes for and visions of a new geopolitical commons, the possibilities for an alternative collective future envisioned by Hardy but far from realized in our own time would also be lost.

# Afterword
## Old and New Enclosures

IF NINETEENTH-CENTURY NOVELS, as I have argued, are thought experiments for their writers, they are also occasions for thought experiments of our own. At a time when we seem to be at a loss when it comes to producing new narratives, and new forms of realism, with the capacity to both compellingly generate contemporary figurations of enclosure *and* imagine utopian responses to it, this book's gambit is that earlier nineteenth-century attempts to do just this open up potential avenues for thinking through this challenge anew. Less blueprints than visions, the classic realist novels that form the backbone of *The Afterlife of Enclosure* recall for us the intimate and expansive connections between the common and the ordinary—the commonplace world that, in the end, we all reside in, with greater or lesser ease—and the commons, the shared resources, the work and spaces that determine our being. From within the belly of the beast, as it were, at a moment when the regime of private property and ideologies of individualism and self-interest were being consolidated, these novels nonetheless produced ideas of the collective and of a collective future with the power to unsettle the capitalist order of things and to inspire alternative ways forward. In short, the *longue durée* of enclosure and the drive to validate and naturalize privatization tout court—whether in the literal form of private property or the values accompanying it, which Weber called the "spirit of capitalism"—has gone hand-in-hand with a *longue durée* of resistance to enclosure, a fierce and ongoing resistance that can get lost in "evental" histories and histories that focus on the victors. To be sure, historians of enclosure and the commons, such as Peter Linebaugh and J. M. Neeson, have brought this history of resistance to the fore and argued for its ongoing endurance today. What has gone less remarked upon and what this book has shown is that nineteenth-century realism played a part in this "bottom-up history," and that its role is particularly significant now, given the dearth of forms and narratives with the capacity not only to represent our current moment but also to inspire resistance to it—in essence, to evoke a *desirable* common future and engender a desire *for* that future.

Although the landscape has changed immeasurably since Dickens, Eliot, and Hardy were trying to come to terms with its altered state in their lifetimes, there are striking similarities between then and now—whether in the ubiquity of indebtedness, both literal and figurative, defining local and global populations; in the presence of homelessness and famine in the midst of plenty; or in the increasingly stark contrast between the rich and the poor that makes Oliver Twist's modest plea for "more" as resonant now as it was in 1837. Likewise, the move from tenancy to itinerancy continues apace with mass migrations, economic instability, and corporate and state seizures of land for resource extraction and pipelines—all part of what David Harvey calls "accumulation by dispossession."[1] These seizures of land, along with a whole host of other means of dispossession, including the granting of easements on public lands, global trade agreements, and the "privatization of every aspect of life, and the transformation of every activity and value into a commodity" (Klein 82), constitute the new enclosures. They are also part of a centuries-long process to eradicate Indigenous peoples and their cultures.[2] As the Midnight Notes Collective underscores, the 1980s saw "the largest Enclosure of the worldly Common in history" ("Introduction to the New Enclosures" 1), a trend that, as Harvey and others have shown, continues under twenty-first-century neoliberalism.

Connections between the old enclosures and the new enclosures of today do not only highlight the devastating impact of the destruction of communal land and common right, however. Just as nineteenth-century representations of enclosure and its afterlife show, the explanatory power of viewing the transformations ushered in by industrial capitalism and modernity through the lens of the commons is dialectical in nature: while surveying the damage without shying away from the losses that come with the destruction of the commons—and, with it, subsistence rights—my view of this history also points forward toward a renewed or reinvented global commons grounded in an actually existing or genuinely common life and commonwealth. Moreover, a politics of the commons brings to the fore—in ways that other Marxist or materialist analyses do not—the centrality of land within global capitalism.

In *The Magna Carta Manifesto*, Linebaugh compares the old and new struggles against enclosure, represented respectively by Gerrard Winstanley and the Diggers' defense of the English forest commons in 1649 and the Zapatista's Forest People's Manifesto of 1985, and identifies three tendencies that unite these movements, all of which are tied to the land: (1) the destruction of the planetary woodlands in the interest of commercial profit; (2) the substitution of petroleum products as "the base commodity of human reproduction and world economic development"; and (3) the expropriation of Indigenous peoples—"commoners all"—across the globe. The lesson Linebaugh draws from this, a lesson that the everyday lives of common characters within nineteenth-century realism dramatize and enact, is that "political and legal rights can exist only on an economic foundation" (6). Whether in the figure of Mrs. Poyser in Eliot's *Adam Bede* resisting her landlord's plans to enclose the land, the depictions of the homeless poor in Dickens, or the precarity of Hardy's lease-holders and the preponderance of itinerancy in his novels, we see how the commons can be realized only with a fundamental restructuring of the economic foundation of everyday reality itself. What is needed today then and what this book has sought to reveal within nineteenth-century realism is a "political ecology of enclosure," in which the economy and the environment are understood as mutually constitutive. From this vantage point, appeals to "green capitalism," or other programs that imagine the twinning of a growth economy with a green politics, can be seen for what they are: class fantasies in which profit and the protection of the environment are compatible rather than contradictory, ensuring that those at the top need not change their lifestyles in any substantial, material way. But even more to the point, these solutions ensure that class relations remain unaltered and that a genuinely global commons is not possible.

With its insistence on the dialectical relationship between everyday reality and the economic underpinnings of that reality, nineteenth-century realism exposes this view for the fantasy it is. Realist writers look back with a clear eye and see in the disappearance of the agrarian commons a series of profound transformations, both in the land and in the myriad social and political relations attendant on the land. They see the loss for what it is. But rather than creating nostalgic narratives about irrevocable loss, or attempting to resurrect a bygone era, they turn to the future and conjure new relations that neither forego nor forget the premises or promise of the commons and its communal relations. Instead they reinvent a commons for a world defined increasingly by its global reach.[3] Unlike many contemporary invocations of the global, in other words, they retain the notion of the commons, even as they recognize the necessity of reimagining it under changed circumstances.

Ultimately, and despite the centrality to contemporary capitalism of that thing called land that a politics of the commons evokes, we must recall Silvia Federici's insistence that "commons are not things but social relations" (*Re-enchanting the World* 94). Moreover, commoning, she insists, can be found all around us. In the midst of a dominant culture intent on establishing the inevitability and morality of individual self-interest, people nonetheless continue to form common bonds, to work in collective, self-sustaining communities, and to resist the systematic logic of enclosure, which relentlessly works to turn "a collective interest into an individualized one" (Blomley 316). Under that same seemingly overwhelming pressure, of the transformation of collective life into individual life, the writers in this study imagined ways that collective life sustained itself, reinvented itself, and endured. Without a doubt, such an imaginative task still stands before us today.

# Notes

### Introduction

1. See, for example, Hensley, *Forms of Empire*; Davis, *Late Victorian Holocausts*; Bigelow; and Bhandar. As Hensley forcefully writes, "[T]he Victorian state's structurally unfinishable war against uprising natives, antagonistic regimes, and other enemies of universal principles is best understood not as one topic within the broader field of Victorian studies, but as the general fact subtending the entirety of domestic life and therefore cultural production in the period" (6).

2. In a representative critique of classic realism from a poststructuralist position, Catherine Belsey distinguishes "between those forms [of representation] which tend to efface their own textuality, their existence as discourse, and those which explicitly draw attention to it. Realism offers itself as transparent" (51).

3. As Bowlby concludes, "as speaking, conversing animals . . . we are already 'in' realism, living a life that includes ongoing attempts to represent it 'like' it is to others and to ourselves; thinking about 'real' realism can help us to reflect on this predicament" (xviii).

4. Goodlad's book argues for a Victorian geopolitical aesthetic that "[creates] memorable formal experiments that do not simply reproduce or reify material realities but, rather, capture their dynamism across time and space" (66); Armstrong's book "reads for a democratic imagination in the nineteenth-century novel," in which "'democratic' . . . collocates a number of meanings that on their own would be insufficient—egalitarian, radical, a life in common, comprehending an inclusive human species being" (6, 7); and Kornbluh advances a "political formalism" that emphasizes the "world-making" nature of realist form and its capacity to model "futures possible," because "we can build with it" (33, 32).

5. Christopher Prendergast's *The Order of Mimesis* is representative of such critiques of realism in its declaration that "the authoritarian gesture of mimesis is to imprison us in a world which, by virtue of its familiarity, is closed to analysis and criticism" (6). See also Terry Eagleton, *Literary Theory*, and Colin McCabe, whose influential 1974 essay "Realism and the Cinema" asserts that "the classic realist text cannot deal with the real as contradictory" and that "the real is not articulated—it is" in realism (39). As Harry E. Shaw quips about such approaches, "[I]t is difficult to cast realism as either a stupid or manipulative genre without making its readers seem chumps" (33). See also Amanda Anderson, who argues in

*Bleak Liberalism* that reductive analyses of realism have also produced reductive analyses of liberalism, and Goodlad, *The Victorian Geopolitical Aesthetic*, esp. 1–38.

6. In her analysis of the "democratic imagination" of the nineteenth-century novel, Isobel Armstrong employs a similar strategy, stating that a "democratic imagination emerges through praxis in novels, through the capacity to *image* states and conditions, not through discursive definition" (18). Moreover, a writer's stated political affiliations and his or her "novel politics" should be kept separate, since "the fiction often belies what is said outside it" (19).

7. The notion of "extending relationships" comes from Raymond Williams, who, in the context of defining a new realism for the contemporary novel, insists that the "truly creative effort of our time is the struggle for relationships, of a whole kind, and it is possible to see this as both personal and social: the practical learning of *extending* relationships" (*The Long Revolution* 314). Kristin Ross argues that the Paris Commune, for Marx, involved this very kind of "practical learning," extending as it did "from the city to the French countryside, and to the countryside and the world outside Europe" (89).

8. Writing about the relationship between enclosures and their effects on communities, Williams cautions that "community must not always been seen in retrospect." Historically, "a new kind of community," which he calls "active community," came into being as a result of local struggles against enclosure and laborers' demands for economic and political rights (The *Country and the City* 104).

9. For a history of the Occupy movement that teases out the particular resonances of the tent (and its associations with camping and national parks) as "both medium and message" for the right to occupy, see Young. As she argues, "These forms of public nature became vehicles to assert voice, access, and a sense of commonwealth and shared future" (291).

10. For recent work on modern technologies, new forms of transport and new media, and the development of an urban industrial culture in the Victorian period, see, for example, Daly; Menke; Grossman; Michie and Thomas; Colligan and Linley.

11. Weber clarifies that this is hardly a peaceful process: "[T]he spirit of capitalism . . . had to fight its way to supremacy against a whole world of hostile forces" (56). Lukács is less concerned with the "spirit" of capitalism, per se, and more focused on how commodity relations "yield a model of all the objective forms of bourgeois society together with all the subjective forms corresponding to them" (*History and Class Consciousness* 83).

12. Brett Christophers points out that in Britain the commons themselves were not communally owned: "What were 'common' were instead the *rights* to land, specifically to access and to take or use part of a piece of land or its produce. And those that enjoyed and exercised these rights were 'commoners'" (80).

13. Constitutive violence, as Slavoj Žižek insists, is to be distinguished from "constituted" violence: whereas "democracy can more or less eliminate constituted

violence, it still has to rely continuously on constitutive violence" (*In Defense of Lost Causes* 413).

14. Williams notes that the root word for common is "*communis* ... which has been derived, alternatively, from *com-*, L - together and *munis*, L - under obligation, and from *com-* and *unus*, L - one" (*Keywords* 70). He also begins his entry by noting that "several of its particular meanings are inseparable from a still active social history," a history that, I am suggesting, is given life in nineteenth-century realism and that brings together the two senses of the common in *munis* and *unus*, as both an obligation *to* others and a recognition of the world as a unified whole or totality.

15. Tellingly, the various terms for representing such a project are themselves riven with ambivalence. Like *common, cosmopolitanism,* as Tanya Agathoceleous and Jason R. Rudy explain, "ranges in connotation from the pejorative to the progressive and in denotation from a phenomenon to an ideal. This constitutive ambivalence helps to explain the controversy that has attended the term, both then and now" (389). The same can be said for the *multitude*, with its connections to "the rabble," the "many," and, more recently, the new subjectivities and figures of resistance within contemporary capitalism, as Michael Hardt and Antonio Negri theorize it. See Hardt and Negri, *Empire* 42–66; *Multitude*, and *Commonwealth* (*passim*).

16. Bate too suggests that the specific history of Helpston added to Clare's intimate and personal experience of enclosure: "An unusually high proportion of Helpston villagers held common rights. An unusually large area of the parish consisted of heathland and 'wastes' from which the commoners could gather fuel. And the open fields survived until an unusually late date. For all these reasons, the effect of enclosure was felt especially strongly in Helpston and by Clare" (49).

17. The social historian Lynn Lees makes a similar point in her study of the English Poor Laws, commenting that historians such as Alan MacFarlane and others have tended to construct this history in relation to English individualism, rather than stressing "the collective ties that bound citizens together, while dividing them along lines of culture and class" (10). Turning our attention to these collective ties allows us to understand not only how the poor laws and their implementation remained fundamentally local and thus involved face-to-face negotiation and contestation between rich and poor over questions of need, social obligation, and "social citizenship," but also how connected they were to notions of the collective, providing "daily occasions for the reexamination of social duties and social rights by both the haves and have-nots" (10–11).

18. E. M. Forster introduces the distinction between flat and round characters in his influential *Aspects of the Novel*. As I discuss in Chapter 2, his description of flat characters is more nuanced than generally acknowledged. At the same time, Forster concedes, "we must admit that flat people are not in themselves as big achievements as round ones" (72–73). While all of Dickens's characters are flat in

Forster's estimation, all of Austen's are round and "ready for an extended life" (75).

19. This relationship of nonidentity between subject and object is not limited to classic realist texts. As I have argued elsewhere, Oscar Wilde's materialist aesthetic works to unsettle utilitarian or instrumental forms of use with the aim of opening up space for a more intimate set of relations with objects. See *Working Fictions*, 181–203.

20. The building of character has most often been associated with an antimaterialist, liberal view of character in which improvement is synonymous with individual moral and spiritual growth. In her book *Victorian Literature and the Victorian State*, Goodlad invokes this term in its liberal guise as a project of mid-Victorian education reform. In contrast, types foreground the literalness of character-building and their indebtedness to the materialist emphases of eighteenth-century typographical culture. See *Victorian Literature*, 32–85.

21. Federici links this neglect of social reproduction to Hardt and Negri's focus on immaterial labor and information and argues that this is true not only for them but for analyses of the commons in general. As she elaborates, these accounts are "mostly concerned with the formal preconditions for the existence of commons and less with the material requirements for the construction of a commons-based economy enabling us to resist dependence on wage labor and subordination to capitalist relations" ("Feminism"). See also Bartolovich, who criticizes the vagueness of Hardt and Negri's theory when it comes to thinking about how the multitude would be organized ("Organizing" 88).

22. For Isabelle Stengers, the history of capitalist development and the history of climate change are the "two histories" of the present between which we are "suspended" (17). They both "speak of a world become 'global'" and they both "have in common . . . the necessity of resisting what is leading us straight to the wall" (19).

## Chapter 1: The Persistence of the Commons, The Persistence of Enclosure

1. Davis uses the term "urban climacteric" to capture the speed and scale of urbanization and industrialization. As a way to gauge the magnitude of the transformations taking place, he compares the growth of megacities and desakotas today—where "cities will account for virtually all future world population growth, which is expected to peak at about 10 billion in 2050"—to Victorian Europe:

> The scale and velocity of Third World urbanization . . . utterly dwarfs that of Victorian Europe. London in 1910 was seven times larger than it had been in 1800, but Dhaka, Kinshasa, and Lagos today are approximately *forty* times larger than they were in 1950. China—urbanizing "at a speed unprecedented in human history"—added more city-dwellers in the 1980s than did all of Europe (including Russia) in the entire nineteenth century!" (*Planet of Slums* 2)

NOTES TO CHAPTER 1

Despite the difference in scale, Charles Dickens, as well as other nineteenth-century writers, nonetheless anticipated the profound effects of urbanization and how urban life would alter not only human beings and human character but also the very atmosphere (in both senses of the word) in which humans live, as I discuss in Chapter 2.

2. As Michael Turner characterizes the extent of this transformation,

> Parliamentary Enclosure was possibly the largest single aggregate landscape change induced by man in an equivalent period of time, producing scattered farmsteads where once nucleated villages proliferated, walls, hedgerows and then a mosaic of geometrically shaped fields and ordered landownership patterns where once existed the relatively disorderly open fields with their complicated ownership patterns and equally complex tenurial or occupational farming patterns. (33)

He goes on to note, as well, that the process of enclosure varied in time and space.

3. J. M. Neeson importantly complicates how we should think about resistance in relation to enclosure, pointing out that "counting signatures and riots is a wretchedly inadequate guide to the level of hatred in villages after enclosure." Noting that "the deep hostility generated by enclosure was as corrosive of social relations as signing a petition or pulling down fences," Neeson foregrounds "the sense of loss, the sense of *robbery* [that] could last forever as the bitter inheritance of the rural poor" (291). Throughout her work, Neeson reminds us of the incalculable effects of injustice, of the silences within the archives, that are a crucial aspect of the enclosure movement's history.

4. As Hardy goes on to show, were one to spend some actual time with Hodge and enter his home, the caricature would "cease to exist," for Hodge would have "disintegrated into a number of dissimilar fellow-creatures, men of many minds, infinite in difference; some happy, many serene, a few depressed; some clever, even to genius, some stupid, some wanton, some austere ... and each of whom walks in his own way the road to dusty death" (40). The dissolving of Hodge the figure into multiple, differentiated individuals, as Hardy narrates, mirrors the work of realist fiction as it enters the homes of its common characters and disabuses its readers of reflexive judgments regarding these characters.

In like fashion, George Eliot in *The Mill on the Floss* anticipates her readers' sense of the "oppressive narrowness" of "old-fashioned family life on the banks of the Floss" in order to draw them in and make them care about the "sordid life" of the Tullivers and Dodsons: "I share with you this sense of oppressive narrowness," Eliot assures her readers, "but it is necessary that we should feel it, if we care to understand how it acted on the lives of Tom and Maggie.... In natural science, I have understood, there is nothing petty to the mind that has a large vision of relations, and to which every single object suggests a vast sum of conditions. It is surely the same with the observation of human life" (283).

5. Also responding to this quote by Marx, Silvia Federici lists the number of uprisings in the precapitalist world in the period from the 1530s to the 1670s to

combat the stereotype of passive rural folk: "In France, one thousand "emotions" (uprisings) occurred . . . England, Italy and Spain present a similar picture, indicating that the pre-capitalist world of the village, which Marx dismissed under the rubric of "rural idiocy," could produce as high a level of struggle as any the industrial proletariat has waged" (*Caliban and the Witch* 82).

6. Likewise, recent work on climate change identifies the inextricable connections between enclosure, the development of industrial capitalism, and global warming. In *Climate Leviathan: A Political Theory of our Planetary Future*, for example, Geoff Mann and Joel Wainwright write that the "historical coincidence of the emergence of global capitalism and the transformation of our planet's atmosphere is no accident. The sharp rise in carbon emissions . . . begins in the late eighteenth century, when capitalist social relations transformed much of the world" (99). As they and others argue, "any substantial attempt to come to grips with climate change *must* contend with capitalism" (99), an argument that I will take up more fully further on.

7. Peter Linebaugh describes Cobbett as "the liveliest, most prolific English language journalist writing between Daniel Defoe and Alexander Cockburn" and notes that as someone writing in "the midst of the second most fundamental development of English capitalism, the beginning of the factory system in the early nineteenth century, he was in a good position to understand the primary principle of English capitalism, namely, the removal of people from the land or from their means of subsistence" (*The Magna Carta Manifesto* 49).

8. More substantially, Cobbett and Dickens also share a political allegiance to popular radical culture, an association that will be further developed in Chapter 2.

9. Moreover, the vantage point from which enclosure is viewed determines whether this "traditional integument of custom and of right" is visible. The persistence of customary rights is only seen when we consider the perspective of the villager rather than government surveys or accounts such as Arthur Young's *Annals of Agriculture*: then, Thompson explains, "one finds a dense cluster of claims and usages, which stretch from the common to the marketplace and which, taken together, made up the economic and cultural universe of the poor" (239).

10. This history is also visibly present, as Williams argues, in the outsized scale of landowners' estates that are now tourist destinations in the English countryside: "The extraordinary phase of extension, rebuilding and enlarging, which occurred in the eighteenth century, represents a spectacular increase in the rate of exploitation: a good deal of it, of course the profit of trade and of colonial exploitation; much of it, however, the higher surplus value of a new and more efficient mode of production." Asking us to see these "great houses" in contrast to the farms of laborers, Williams writes, "Think it through as labour and see how long and systematic the exploitation and seizure must have been, to rear that many houses, on that scale" (105). The grand vistas of these houses with their tree-lined avenues, manicured grounds and elaborate facades—all physical

manifestations of exploitation—constitute nothing short of "a visible stamping of power, of displayed wealth and command: a social disproportion which was meant to impress and overawe" and which presented "a uniform exposition, at every turn, of an established and commanding class power" (*The Country and the City* 106).

11. Wood adumbrates the need for the state to, on the one hand, "keep alive a propertyless population which has no other means of survival when work is unavailable, maintaining a 'reserve army' of workers through the inevitable cyclical declines in the demand for labour," and, on the other hand, "ensure that escape routes are closed and that means of survival other than wage labour for capital are not so readily available as to liberate the propertyless from the compulsion to sell their labour power when they are needed by capital" (18). The English Poor Laws serve just this role for the state, "controlling the mobility of labour, while preserving capital's freedom of movement" (19), an issue to which I will return further on.

12. The nature of the connection between enclosure and the "Swing" riots is a point of contention among historians. Eric Hobsbawm and George Rudé, in their calculation of the number of incidents, note that there were, in the 1830 laborer's movement, "only three cases of rioting over enclosure, two of them in Oxfordshire" (195). In contrast, Neeson faults Hobsbawm and Rudé for their reliance on a limited historical record gleaned from "the pens of those reporters to the Board of Agriculture who supported enclosure and were necessarily hostile to common right" (8). Specifically, this record "discounted the large volume of anti-enclosure opinion," lacked an awareness of "the frequency of anti-enclosure protest," and "gave little weight to the apostasy of Arthur Young and others who began seriously to question the treatment of commoners from the 1790s onwards." A closer scrutiny of common right, as Neeson argues, will not only illuminate the "economic value to commoners of common right" but also show common right to be "a part of the structure of social relations in common-field villages" (8–9).

13. Marx registers something of this dynamic between the eventual and non-eventual when he quotes the politician Samuel Laing about the condition of agricultural workers:

> This state of affairs [the oppression and displacement of labourers by enclosure] continued quietly until "the Swing Riots, in 1830, revealed to us" (i.e. the ruling classes) "by the light of blazing corn-stacks, that misery and black mutinous discontent smouldered quite as fiercely under the surface of agricultural as of manufacturing England." (*Capital I* 830)

14. Ellen Rosenman similarly notes that while "the reliance of radical politics on a static myth of national identity [tied to the land and the commons] was a form of nostalgia . . . opposition to the Enclosure Acts was not only nostalgic." As she clarifies, "Although the preoccupation with rural life seems anachronistic

in the face of urbanization and industrialization, it is a reminder that agriculture was still a significant part of the nineteenth-century economy and that industrial capitalism was not the self-evident future of England." The continuing presence of the "rural ideal" within working-class politics, moreover, highlights how class based visions of the nation are at this time, as "novels, journals, and parliamentary reports focused on urbanization and industrialization" can be seen in this light to "reflect a class-specific version of the nation rather than providing a transparent account of the truth."

15. Linebaugh specifies that "[w]e can uncover in history the five principles of Magna Carta's commons, namely, anti-enclosure, reparation, subsistence, neighborhood, and travel" (*The Magna Carta Manifesto* 245), a set of principles whose relevance has hardly faded over time.

16. The notion of *terra nullius* equally forms the basis for the larger projects of imperialism and colonialism. In the Canadian context, for example, in relation to Indigenous claims to the land, Emma Battell Lowman and Adam J. Barker argue that "both in the past and present," given the actual presence of Indigenous peoples on the land, "settler colonizers have to work hard to erase or deny Indigenous presence and authority on the land. Terra nullius . . . is a narrative and practice of erasure, but it also a way of rooting and justifying settler colonial societies on the land" (60). For accounts of British imperial-colonial discourse and the myth of *terra nullius* in Australia, the United States, New Zealand, and Canada, see Banner.

17. About property more generally and the Victorian ethos, Richard D. Altick asserts that "transcending the issue of laissez faire was one principle upon which landowning Tory and industrialist Whig, Benthamite and business-oriented Evangelical found no difficulty in agreeing: property was sacred" (133). Noting that property determined social worth and citizenship, Altick adds that "even more deep-seated than the equation of property with political responsibility was the tendency of landowners and industrialists to look upon their workers as chattels; they treated them often with a proprietary air that would have been more suitable under feudalistic conditions than in the shadow of factory chimneys." As a result, "legislation and court decisions tended also to favor property rights over human ones" (134).

18. Locke recognizes that the invention of money complicates the issue of use since money can be "stored" or hoarded whereas the actual produce from one's property cannot. As John Dunn comments, "The invention of money greatly amplifies the inequality of possessions made possible by the 'different degrees of Industry' which men display (II 48). It makes it possible, in Locke's judgment, for a man *fairly* to 'possess more than he can use the product of'" (45–46). See also C. B. Macpherson, who, in contrast to Dunn, sees in Locke's theory of property an intentional justification for the "specifically capitalist appropriation of land and money" (208).

19. Jonathan Crary notes that Locke's rationalist philosophy of private, individual interests also entailed the theft of sleep: "Sleep became devalued in the

privileging of consciousness and volition, of notions of utility, objectivity, and self-interested agency. For Locke, sleep was a regrettable if unavoidable interruption of God's intended priorities for human beings: to be industrious and rational" (12). Crary traces the erosion of sleep to our present moment and the 24/7 regime of late capitalism, an analysis I will return to in Chapter 4.

20. In *Silent Theft: The Private Plunder of Our Common Wealth*, David Bollier cites the following statistics about land ownership: "By 1876, it was estimated, 2,250 people owned half the agricultural land in England and Wales, and 0.6 percent of the population owned 98.5% of it" (46). So much for there still being enough.

21. Bollier refers to Locke's reference to the common good and an abundance of common resources in the midst of his argument for private property—often called the "Lockean proviso"—as an "unresolved tension" that is "mostly treated as a symbolic, throwaway gesture. . . . Whatever one makes of this proviso, Locke's singular intent was to justify private property, not assure the longevity of the commons" (106).

22. Malthus's overall aim is to counter William Godwin's claims regarding "the perfectibility of the mass of mankind" (20) by showing that Godwin's ideal society would be insupportable. After listing all the beneficial effects of Godwin's radical vision of equality, ranging from the elimination of poverty and war to improved living conditions and the sharing of labor, Malthus concludes that "with these extraordinary encouragements to population . . . the numbers would necessarily increase faster than in any society that has ever yet been known" (65–66). See also Gallagher, *The Body Economic*, for an account of the debate between Malthus and Godwin, and the larger radical circle, including Samuel Taylor Coleridge and Robert Southey.

23. To be sure, debate over how the poor law was administered exists among historians. K.D.M. Snell reappraises claims regarding in-door versus out-door poor relief in the wake of the 1834 Poor Law and argues that relief remained primarily out-door relief. He notes, however, that "the *threat* of the workhouse loomed large in working-class consciousness, and yet in-door relief was usually a minority experience" (17). Snell's analysis in no way diminishes the number of paupers or the propertyless; it aims, rather, to show how individual parishes continued to oversee poor relief as part of his overall argument that the parish remains the primary site of "belonging" well into the early twentieth century. See Snell, esp. 207–338.

24. In *Hunger Movements in Early Victorian Literature: Want, Riots, Migration*, Lesa Scholl develops the connections between propertylessness and the forced mobility of the poor in her focus on "dual physical and social hunger as the catalyst of protest." She argues that the poor were "effectively exiled in a domestic diaspora, evidenced, for example, in the itinerant workers leaving their regions of origin in order to find employment" (87–88). For Scholl, Dickens's *Oliver Twist* perfectly illustrates this form of exile and the associations "between

poverty, mobility, and crime . . . at the fore of the nineteenth-century social and political consciousness" (89).

25. Brundage recounts a scandal at the Andover Union in Hampshire in 1845 that arose when it was discovered that paupers there were so underfed that they took to gnawing the bones they were assigned to crush (87–88).

26. Against this claim, Wall shows how the subsistence rights of usufruct and estover that govern commoning are meant, as their Latin derivations suggest, to promote sustainability. *Usufruct*, from the Latin phrase *usus et fructus*, means "use and enjoyment of fruits," while *estover* derives from *est opus*, meaning "it is necessary." Both rights thus establish and regulate "an appropriate use of property so that it can be enjoyed" (8). Wall also points out that Marx links usufructuries to sustainability, when he writes in a chapter on rent and the ownership of land,

> From the standpoint of a higher socio-economic formation, the private property of particular individuals in the earth will appear just as absurd as the private property of one man in other men. Even an entire society, a nation, or all simultaneously existing societies taken together, are not the owners of the earth. They are simply its possessors, its beneficiaries, and have to bequeath it in an improved state to succeeding generations as *boni patres familias* [good heads of the household]. (*Capital* III 911)

27. In a direct response to Hardin's claims, the economist Elinor Ostrom clarifies that the real target of his critique is specifically the unmanaged commons. Her work focuses on the range of institutions and forms of self-governance with the capacity to manage or "govern" the commons. See especially *Governing the Commons*, 1–28.

28. In his account of Clare's escape from High Beach and subsequent journey home by foot in 1841 (a three-day journey covering eighty miles), Iain Sinclair refers to the years Clare spent in the asylum as "four years enclosed in the forest" (*Edge of the Orison* 120).

29. In "The Village Minstrel," Clare speaks through the fictional figure of Lubin, "a peasant from his birth," who despite "untimely toil . . .'e'n as now/ Ambitious prospects fired his little soul,/ And fancy soared and sung, 'bove poverty's control" (*"I AM"* 31).

30. Patrick Bresnihan connects Clare's pleasure in roaming to his desire for learning, seeing in both a joy in "the open-endedness of the activity: not done for any reason other than to open up new associations and meanings" (76).

31. In *Green Writing*, James C. McKusick envisions one possible path from Clare's present to our future in Clare's notion of "circling round the same place": "If the human 'tribe' is embarked on a rectilinear path of conquest over nature, Clare will follow a different course, circling round the same place until it truly becomes a home to him. Any place, no matter how desolate, known intimately enough, can become a miniature analogue of the Earth itself." For him, Clare's poetry "allows us an awkward but authentic vision of what kinds of dwelling

may be possible for humankind in a post-industrial landscape" (94). McKusick places Clare alongside other Romantic poets, including Coleridge, Wordsworth, Blake, and Mary Shelley, and connects their respective ecological visions to the environmental movement today. In a similar vein, the connections between Romantic ecology and contemporary ecocriticism are developed in Coupe, *The Green Studies Reader*.

32. Scholars such as Bate, Barrell, Thompson, and Sinclair, among others, all of whom I have relied on here, provide invaluable accounts of Clare's life and poetry. See also Haughton et al.; Storey; and Brownlow. For a creative response that, like Sinclair's *Edge of the Orison*, loosely follows Clare's path after he has escaped from the Essex asylum, see Collis.

33. Reminiscent of Clare's representation of nature, but reflecting on a completely different time and place, for example, Elizabeth Gaskell's *Ruth* opens with a description of the changed landscape of "an assize-town in one of the eastern counties" that evinces how the landscape is as "classed" as the social relations that leave Ruth an unmarried mother. After detailing the development of the town from one of "picturesque grandeur" (1) in the time of the Tudors to "the flat, mean, unrelieved style of George the Third" (3), the narrator introduces us to Ruth and the scene she sees out the window of the dressmaker's where she has been forced to work. "Poor old larch!," the narrator laments, "the time had been when it had stood in a pleasant lawn, with the tender grass creeping caressingly up to its very trunk; but now the lawn was divided into yards and squalid back premises, and the larch was pent up and girded about with flagstones" (5). These historical details are important, the narrator takes pains to inform us, because the "traditions of those bygone times, even to the smallest social particular, enable one to understand more clearly the circumstances which contributed to the formation of character" (2).

34. This kind of recognition can be found in a range of fiction beyond the realist novels I will analyze. In *The Victorian Geopolitical Aesthetic*, for example, Lauren Goodlad addresses this issue in Wilkie Collins's sensation novel, *The Woman in White*, noting how Collins's novel exemplifies "the spatial deracination" that has occurred over the course of the eighteenth and early nineteenth centuries and which comes to the fore as Walter Hartright searches for Laura's identity: "Such scenes dramatize the modern devastation of space, old as well as new" (113). A consequence of this devastation, which Clare's poetry captures so beautifully, involves not only the evacuation of historical experience but a concomitant transformation of identity itself, with the human counterpart of this deracinated, devastated space being the infamous Count Fosco. Walter observes the "civilized desolation" and "depressing influence" of a new-minted "English country town" (*Woman* 503; quoted in Goodlad 113).

35. In relation to both Clare's time and our own, Federici specifically defines the destruction of women's economic power and role in agricultural production as central aspects of capitalist development. In an interview, she notes how "the

World Bank has tried to convince us that land is a dead asset when used for sustenance and shelter, and it becomes productive only when it is brought to a bank as collateral to gain credit. Behind this view," she underscores, "is an arrogant philosophy that sees only money as creative of wealth, and believes capitalism and industry can recreate nature" (Haiven). She also cautions that "it is a mistake for left movements to underestimate, practically and analytically, the importance of agricultural work in today's political economy and, consequently, the transformative capacity of the struggles that farmers are making on this terrain"—a mistake capitalists are not making, she adds, given the priority within World Bank restructuring programs to "the reorganization of agricultural relations" (Haiven). As we will see in Chapter 3, George Eliot's *Adam Bede* dramatizes this process of reorganization in its representation of the old Squire's plans to enclose neighboring land and shift the Poysers' agricultural work solely to dairy production. Tellingly, Mrs. Poyser is at the center of the battle with the old Squire.

36. Malm references John Nef, who, in *The Rise of the British Coal Industry*, points out that mining rights in Great Britain were unique insofar as "the rights of the landowner to all minerals, except gold and silver" were "made absolute" (*Rise* 266). These rights, as Malm highlights, aided "truly revolutionary transformations on the supply side" (325) of the developing fossil economy.

37. For a reading that directly connects nineteenth- and twenty-first-century responses to environmental change, see Allen MacDuffie, "Charles Darwin and the Victorian Pre-History of Climate Denial." MacDuffie links Victorian responses to Darwin to what Naomi Klein has called the "soft denialism" of climate change today.

### Chapter 2: Dickensian Types and a Culture of the Commons

1. One of the few times Dickens directly writes about enclosure is in his much-maligned *A Child's History of England*, where he mentions Ket's Rebellion in his chapter on Edward VI. The rebellion was named after Robert Ket, a yeoman farmer who became a target of local peasants in Norfolk protesting against the enclosure of common land in 1549. Convinced by the peasants' arguments against enclosure, Ket became a leader of the rebellion, and was ultimately hanged for treason. Dickens's treatment of the rebellion is short and unremarkable. See *A Child's History*, 306–7.

2. Within analyses of these novels there are, however, less literal references to enclosure that address how Dickens constructs his fictional landscapes in terms of the opposition between open and enclosed spaces. See, for example, Connor, J. Hillis Miller, and Sicher.

3. In his powerful account of the African Americanization of Victorian literature, Daniel Hack enumerates how Dickens's *Bleak House* was repurposed in just such a way in its own day when it was published in *Frederick Douglass' Paper*. Despite the novel's construction of a national community premised on the

exclusion of black people, slaves, and people of color across the globe, Douglass appropriates it for the antislavery cause and those "dark others" who have been "abjected from the text" of *Bleak House* (33).

4. For a comprehensive study of *Our Mutual Friend*'s publishing history that attempts to "show how and why" the novel is the "very richest of Dickens's works" (8), see Grass.

5. Dallas differentiates between the "weak part of [*Our Mutual Friend*]," which is "to be found in what may be called 'The Social Chorus'" (the name Dickens gives to Chapter 17 in Book III) and which includes Twemlow, as well as the Veneerings, Lady Tippins, and the Lammles, and the "gallery of portraits... which might set up half a dozen novelists for life" (6), including Bella Wilfer, Boffin and Mrs. Boffin, Riderhood, Lizzie Hexam, and Jenny Wren, among others. Hence the division between the "dead weight of 'the Social Chorus'" and the main players in Dallas's account does not fall along the assumed line between eccentric and more realistic characters, even as certain eccentricities are singled out for their lack of life as "species of knick-knacks."

6. Dickens famously draws on multiple sources for his writing; his mode of caricature, in particular, is indebted to the tradition of radical popular culture, as Sally Ledger and others argue and as I will discuss further on. Unlike these other sources, however, eighteenth-century eccentric biographies have not been addressed in any significant way within Dickens criticism to date.

7. In addition to Merryweather's book, the following character books were found in Dickens's library after his death: the *Annual Register*, James Caulfield's *Characters*, R. S. Kirby's *Wonderful and Eccentric Museum*, and Henry Wilson's *Characters*. See Friedman 47.

8. Two of the guests who arrive at the Jolly Sandboys in *The Old Curiosity Shop* include

> the proprietor of a giant, and a little lady without legs or arms... the other, a silent gentleman who earned his living by showing tricks upon the cards, and who had rather deranged the natural expression of his countenance by putting small leaden lozenges into his eyes and bringing them out at his mouth, which was one of his professional accomplishments. (150)

The "little lady without legs or arms" is Sarah Biffen, a "regular" in character books, as well as in Dickens's novels, as are all manner of giants, so-called grotesques, and people with unusual "professional accomplishments," as I develop further on.

9. The issue of terminology is always vexed, a matter of nuance rather than definitive difference. Obviously, all of these terms are representations, and should remind us of Fredric Jameson's insistence that "all conceptuality is figurative." Addressing yet another term for the collective in vogue today, namely the "multitude," Jameson writes, "Surely all of those collective words— *the people, the multitude, the nation, the masses*, and so forth—these are all representations—so is general will—and I think all of them are attempts to model

something that's not representable" (*Jameson on Jameson* 230). The same can be said for my use of the common, whose heuristic value, as I will argue, rests in its ability to imagine a political past and future contained within the very language of nineteenth-century realism and the hopes it engendered in its appeal to the common, to what Dickens called "the great ocean of humanity."

10. Williams frames this distinction in the following way: "One can say that much of the narrative mode of the emergent novel-form was predominantly *indicative*. It was, or offered to be an account of what had happened and what was happening. If one takes 'indicative' as that description, then one can—the term is obviously not fully satisfactory—talk of an element of Dickens's writing which is *subjunctive*, which is clearly 'what if' or 'would that' or 'let us suppose that'" (160–61).

11. We might think of the space Dickens's remarkable characters and world hold open in terms similar to those Suzanne Césaire uses to describe surrealism: less an ideology than a state of mind, as Robin D. G. Kelley notes, it was, for Césaire, a "permanent readiness for the Marvelous" (Kelley 8).

12. As Alan Ryan points out in his study of Mill, and of the connection, specifically, between Dickens's portrayal of the Gradgrind children in *Hard Times* and Mill's education under the tutelage of his father, James Mill, what is more interesting than this likely apocryphal connection is "the extent to which Mill, Carlyle and Dickens shared the belief that the age was hostile to imagination, or 'Fancy,' and the extent to which they did *not* share a common diagnosis of that situation." In terms of utilitarianism, in particular, J. S. Mill distinguished between the theory and his father's temperament, and therefore found Dickens's critique of it "silly" (24).

13. Julia F. Saville also links Mill's thinking on eccentricity with Dickens's, in the context of her reading of the eccentric characters in *David Copperfield*. But for Saville, Dickens's "gallery of eccentrics" remain within Mill's vision of a "reforming individualism": "eccentricity disrupts the status quo only to guarantee a new social order that may be more morally decent but is not necessarily more politically or economically just than its predecessor" (791). Whereas Saville limits her analysis to the political *content* of Dickens's eccentrics, and judges it to be one with a developing mid-Victorian nationalism and construction of Englishness as eccentricity, I argue that the radical political content of Dickens's novels is to be found in their *form* as eccentric biographies and the materialist vision of character that form embodies and mobilizes.

14. Other titles include Robert Malcolm, *Curiosities of Biography*; Henry Wilson and James Caulfield, *The Book of Wonderful Characters*; Paul Pindar, *Remarkable Biography; or, The Peculiarities and Eccentricities of the Human Character Displayed*; *The Historic Gallery of Portraits and Paintings, and Biographical Review*; and G. H. Wilson, *The Eccentric Mirror: Reflecting a Faithful and Interesting Delineation of Male and Female Characters*.

There are also some much later versions of these books. From England, books include Edith Sitwell, *The English Eccentrics* (1933); and E. J. Dingwall, *Some*

*Human Oddities: Studies in the Queer, the Uncanny and the Fanatical* (1947) and *Very Peculiar People: Portrait Studies in the Queer, the Abnormal and the Uncanny* (1950).

15. See especially Stocking.

16. The construction of the self through repetition: this formulation can be seen as a point of contact between Victorian object relations and more recent theorizations of subjectivity, such as Judith Butler's. In her 1999 preface to *Gender Trouble*, for example, Butler describes the performativity of gender as "not a singular act, but a repetition and a ritual, which achieves its effect through its naturalization in the context of a body, understood, in part, as a culturally sustained temporal duration." Character books, in a sense, disrupt this process of naturalization, making visible (and visual) the repetitive, ritualistic performance of the self. See Butler, *Gender Trouble*, xv. Saville, too, comments on the performative aspect of eccentricity, noting that "the oddity of the most striking eccentrics in Dickens's novels is ironically less that 'originality' for which Mill will subsequently yearn than the capacity to masquerade, the power to don and remove masks that does not *depend* on some original essence but rather brings that essence into being" (785).

17. Vrettos focuses on Dickens's "habit-obsessed characters" as exemplary sites for exploring the "wider nineteenth-century philosophical debate about the psychology and sociology of habit" and the concerns that coalesced around the impact an increasingly mechanized industrial culture would have on individuals (401). Within this context, Vrettos argues, Dickens's eccentric characters are less quirky anomalies than part of a significant conversation among "philosophers of habit" trying to come to terms with "the troubling convergence of individual and cultural routines" (420).

18. Other notable misers in Dickens less directly tied to character books include Arthur Gride in *Nicholas Nickleby*, Anthony Chuzzlewit in *Martin Chuzzlewit*, and, of course, Ebenezer Scrooge in *A Christmas Carol*.

19. Elaine Freedgood uses the concept of a "subject/object ratio" in her analysis of it-narratives to capture how these narratives, which feature everyday objects as their narrators (from pins and shillings to dolls, umbrellas, and books), depict the "boundary between people and things" as "remarkably permeable"—at a historical moment generally characterized within contemporary scholarship, by "the triumphal instantiation of commodity culture, and the attendant harsh (and final) separation of people and things" ("What Objects Know" 89). A wealth of criticism now exists on it- and object-narratives, and the status of objects, more broadly, within both eighteenth-century and Victorian culture. For readings of it-narratives in the eighteenth century, see Blackwell, *The Secret Life of Things*; Lamb, *The Things Things Say*; Festa; and Lupton. On Victorian objects and commodity culture, see Price; Plotz, *Portable Property*; Miller, *Novels Behind Glass*; Gagnier; and Richards. For a reading of Dickens's engagement with commodity culture in *Household Words*, see Waters.

20. Lynch goes on to argue that these books essentially lose their cultural purchase over the course of the century, something I try to complicate by locating

different articulations of material character—not necessarily limited to the form of character books—in a range of classic realist novels and later nineteenth-century writers.

21. Quoted in Gregory, "Eccentric Lives," 80.

22. New collections were offered as well as republications of older works. Frederick Fairholt, the author of *Eccentric and Remarkable Characters* (1849), did express concern that his collection's sales suffered because of the public's familiarity with his characters, many of whom had already been catalogued by Kirby or Caulfield. See Gregory, "Eccentric Biography" 345.

23. Judith Butler also envisions being "beside oneself" with feelings other than grief. As she writes with respect to the history of the feminist and lesbian/gay movement and its invocation of ecstasy in the 1960s, 1970s, and first half of the 1980s, "maybe [ecstasy] is with us all along. To be ec-static means, literally, to be outside oneself, and thus can have several meanings: to be transported beyond oneself by a passion, but also to be *beside oneself* with rage or grief. I think that if I can still address a 'we,' or include myself within its terms, I am speaking to those of us who are living in certain ways *beside ourselves*, whether in sexual passion, or emotional grief, or political rage" (24).

24. Alex Woloch, for example, deals extensively with Dickens's minor characters with no mention of this source material. Sambudha Sen notes, as well, that the radical populist tradition goes missing in Woloch's account: when we position an early sketch from Boz ("A Parliamentary Sketch") in relation to "the whole sequence of caricaturized figures who appear in Dickens's fiction, from Bumble to Tite Barnacle," Sen asserts, they appear "not as products of Dickens's unique comic genius or as figures, flattened by the dynamic character systems that Woloch describes, but rather as displacements within a certain form of entertainment-oriented fictionalizing, of a strand of radical satire oriented toward building around its irreverent representations of those who wielded political power a community of the excluded" (33–34). As I will suggest, we need to consider eighteenth-century types and Dickens's connections to popular radical culture together in order to see not only the "community of the excluded" but also the materialist basis on which that community is envisioned both negatively *and* positively.

25. The common trajectory of this development involves a break after *Bleak House*, which, as Dickens's contemporaries noted, was the first of his "dark" books, having lost Dickens's characteristic humor.

26. Jesse Oak Taylor identifies the city as Dickens's "one true subject," so much so that "all Dickens's characters are minor by comparison" (32). Given this emphasis on the city, he contends that the "central work of Dickens's novels thus becomes understanding the principles and processes of aggregation, of situating character, interaction, and individuality within networks whose scale seems to render individual agency irrelevant." For him, this effort is "not simply related to the problem of understanding anthropogenic climate change; it is the same

problem, albeit at a different scale" (32–33).

27. Recent work on nineteenth-century serialization also emphasizes how long-form serial narratives more generally resist closure by extending the experience of reading over months or years. Linda Hughes and Michael Lund argue that the effect of such long reading times meant that the "interpretation of the literature went on during the expansive middle of serial works." Serials could thus "become entwined with readers' own sense of lived experience and passing time" (8). A special issue of *Romanticism and Victorianism on the Net* titled "Television for Victorianists" extends the analysis of serial narrative form to contemporary serial TV programs such as *The Sopranos* and *The Wire*. For Goodlad, a key point of contact between nineteenth- and twenty-first-century serial forms is that both provide "serialized narratives of capitalist globalization" that "not only proffer naturalistic pictures of 'real life,' but also capture the real-life experience of inhabiting long-evolving structures that challenge our limited capacity to grasp and communicate ongoing histories" ("Afterword"). As I will argue, Dickens's narratives are particularly concerned with representing long-evolving structures without ceding our capacity to understand or change them.

28. There is also Jenny Wren's repetition of Lammle's name a record five times in the space of two sentences: "'Lammle, Lammle, Lammle?' Miss Jenny repeated as she panted from stair to stair, 'where have I hear that name? Lammle, Lammle?'" (703). And if we go beyond *Our Mutual Friend*, there are many more examples, from the incantatory repetition of "fog" in *Bleak House*'s opening passage to the repetition of "stares" and "staring" in the opening pages of *Little Dorrit*. Setting the scene in a burning Marseilles, *Little Dorrit* records, "Every thing in Marseilles, and about Marseilles, had stared at the fervid sky, and been stared at in return, until a staring habit had become universal there. Strangers were stared out of countenance by staring white houses, staring white walls, staring white streets, staring tracts of arid road, staring hills from which verdure was burnt away" (15).

29. In the *Household Words* story, "waifs and strays" are the numerous items left and forgotten by railway passengers on trains. As Dickens says of the warehouses used to store these items, "A visit to this depository would repay a philosopher. He might readily guess at the owners from the articles—they are so perfectly characteristic" ("Railway Waifs" 319). Dickens also refers to the items in old Harmon's dust-heaps as waifs and strays (*Our Mutual Friend* 759).

30. In the tension between enough and too much, Dickens certainly can veer toward the latter, as when he writes of "all the jobbers who job in all the jobberies jobbed" (211) and meaning, material or otherwise, is all but lost.

31. In his study on the anticipatory cinematic aspects of novels such as *Bleak House*, Grahame Smith refers to the "element of process" in Dickens's writing, "the ways in which his language seems to track, dissolve, pan, cut—in short, to anticipate those qualities which are so characteristic of film's continuous movement through time." He goes on to characterize Dickens's

work in relation to early film technology by noting that "Noël Burch points to an interesting difference in how film pioneers named their apparatus: Edison and Dickson called their project the Vitascope—that is, 'the vision of life'— while for Lumière it was the Cinématographe, 'writing in movement.' Dickens's work encompasses both. (164).

32. The language of contingency might also provide another frame for understanding the gender division that Catherine Gallagher locates in the differential ability of men and women to "suspend" value (*The Body Economic* 115–17). When Bella seeks to link her fate to Lizzie's, she describes herself as "the willed-away girl who was to have been married to the unfortunate gentleman, if he had been pleased to approve of me. So I was dragged into the subject without my consent, and you were dragged into it without your consent, and there is very little to choose between us" (515). The notion of being "willed-away" defines a state of absolute determination: Bella and Lizzie are essentially "dragged into" determinate subject positions that deny them the reciprocal subject-object relations that thwart commodification. As a result, the differences between them are nullified: "there is very little to choose between us." While their ultimate ability to "choose" that which they were "dragged into" might not seem all that compelling to twenty-first-century readers, it nonetheless suggests a resistance on the narrative's part to reductive forms of determinism and commodification.

33. For an account of the anxieties and uncertainties surrounding novel reading and the kinds of influence it might wield over an increasingly mass readership, see Brantlinger, *The Reading Lesson*.

34. Lukács develops this concept in his analysis of Balzac's *Lost Illusions*. Key here is the relationship between chance (or accidents within a narrative's plot) and necessity: "[T]he necessity which nullifies chance consists of an intricate network of causal connections . . . only the aggregate necessity of an entire trend of developments constitutes a *poetic* necessity." About Balzac in particular, he writes, "By means of a broad and deep conception of his characters, a broad and deep portrayal of society and of the subtle and multiple interconnections between his characters and the social basis and setting of their actions, Balzac creates a wide space within which hundreds of accidents may intersect each other and yet in their aggregate produce fateful necessities" (*Studies in European Realism* 56–57). The same, I suggest, can be said about Dickens.

35. In Levine's focus on the multiplicity of forms within any novel, "closure is too spatializing a term for narrative endings." As she argues about the end of Gaskell's *North and South*, "[W]hat the novel imagines in its conclusion is really not an enclosure at all, but a *beginning*. . . . The ending's political force depends not on resolution and finality, but on repetitions that will extend past the time represented in the text. To call this closure and containment is to overlook the future implied by the text, a deliberately uncontained temporal process" (41). For a series of readings that take up the challenge of the "middle" in Victorian

literature, see also Levine and Ortiz-Robles, *Narrative Middles: Navigating the Nineteenth-Century British Novel*.

36. For readings of *Little Dorrit* as more global in scope than *Bleak House*, in general, see Buzard and also Amanda Anderson. As Anderson comments about Arthur Clennam, "[T]he vague sense of guilt haunting this commercial traveler from the east, and his forceful resigning of all connection with Clennam and Co. upon his return to England, suggest a wider sensitivity to the violence of British global capitalism and imperial concerns, and to the vast economic imbalances generated thereby" (*The Powers of Distance* 73).

37. Anna Kornbluh highlights a particularly resonant passage in *Great Expectations*, in which Pip and Herbert Pocket bring capitalism to the fore as they stare at a fire and muse on just how difficult it is "to realize capital" (*Realizing Capital* 1).

38. In her critique of Michael Hardt and Antonio Negri's notion of the commons, for example, Crystal Bartolovich notes how their vision of the commons fails to take account of the impediments within the social that limit individual action, including commodification and the ideological structures that make resistance to the social politically challenging. See "Organizing the (Un)Common." Virginia Woolf's claim that "we remodel our psychological geography when we read Dickens" is instructive here in its stress on psychological change as a necessary corollary to social change; and, in somewhat different language, Juliet John identifies Dickens's imagination as dialectical, and notes that "the seeming paradoxes and contradictions that pervade Dickens's logic are also the result of his persistent and conscious attempts to think outside established categories, to think creatively, or to project 'the potential for living otherwise'" (31), borrowing a phrase from Lauren Berlant.

39. Franco Moretti criticizes Dickens for just this, condemning his vision as a "petty bourgeois utopia" in which there is no longer the "devouring ambition to 'make it' at whatever cost . . . but only the modest hope for a decent and laborious life, open to the best elements of the proletariat —where 'best' indicates, again, a total lack of ambition." As a result, for Moretti, "social mobility is granted only to the meek" (132).

40. Terry Eagleton characterizes *plumpes Denken* as "non-elegant thinking," or "putting the complex into the simple" ("The Critic as Clown" 628).

41. With respect to Moretti, specifically, his dismissal of Dickens's brand of utopianism betrays a broader anti-utopian stance within Moretti's thinking as a whole. See Lesjak, "All or Nothing."

42. Audrey Jaffe also emphasizes the inseparability of realism and fantasy, and argues that "realism . . . is not fantasy's alternative, as the usual generic distinctions would have it, but rather its fulfillment" (5).

43. More than this, Dickens actively plays with our expectations regarding melodrama. In *Oliver Twist*, for example, he walks us, melodramatically, through the key features of "murderous melodramas," narrating how they "present the

tragic and the comic scenes in as regular alternation as the layers of red and white in a side of streaky, well-cured bacon. The hero sinks upon his straw bed, weighed down by fetters and misfortunes; and, in the next scene, his faithful but unconscious squire regales the audience with a comic song" (134). This elaborate setup is presented merely in order to tell us what, as a narrator, Dickens will *not* be doing in his telling of Oliver Twist's "history"—namely taking time to digress rather than "[proceeding] straight through this history with all convenient despatch" (135), even as he does just that. Neither "well-cured bacon" nor straight history, *Oliver Twist* makes visible its own conceits; in the process, it refuses to become one with itself, to claim for itself any sort of realistic transparency.

44. In the context of his history *The Matchgirl and the Heiress*, Seth Koven notes, "Children of the possessing classes get childhood; the poor in general and poor orphans in particular do not" (22), a class distinction that *Oliver Twist* powerfully dramatizes in the dialectical tension between individuals (like Oliver) and types (like Dick). Types here put pressure on individual subjects, thereby unsettling what has often been denigrated as Dickens's sentimental individualism.

45. Rita Felski similarly links the concept of the everyday to the secular and the democratic: "Secular because it conveys the sense of a world leached of transcendence . . . Democratic because it recognizes the paramount shared reality of a mundane, material embeddedness in the world. Everyone, from the most famous to the most humble, eats, sleeps, yawns, defecates; no one escapes the reach of the quotidian." As with Auerbach, for Felski "everyday life . . . does not only describe the lives of ordinary people, but recognises that every life contains an element of the ordinary" ("The Invention of Everyday Life" 16).

46. Bruce Robbins suggests that Auerbach neglects moments of what he calls "abridged, transient utopia" because of the providential nature of his narrative: "[P]rovidential history," he writes, "devalues and suppresses premature or untimely manifestations of that which it reserves for the end. There exist resources of political precedent that cannot be perceived at all if they cannot be neatly placed in an upward trajectory. Inattentive to the contingency of history, this vision squanders its available energies" (*The Servant's Hand* 33). He goes on to say these energies "are often to be recovered only by searching out a logic, like Foucault or the Annales historians, in what appear to be trivial, unbearably repetitive patterns of everyday life, in the sub-historical constants usually canceled out in favor of more momentous variables" (33).

47. These are connections that extend far beyond the urban landscape of London, encompassing nothing short of anthropogenic climate change, as Jesse Oak Taylor has argued.

**Chapter 3: Eliot, Cosmopolitanism, and the Commons**

1. A. S. Byatt reminds us though that Eliot's range is more varied than many accounts that emphasize her judiciousness allow for. Writing about the major essays Eliot wrote between 1854 and 1857 for the *Westminster Review*, Byatt clarifies

that these essays "were written for money, but they were also written with a new intellectual authority, freedom and sense of excitement. It is usual for critics of George Eliot to look for the weighty, the sibylline and the scrupulously just. But these essays are also at times savagely ironic, often very funny, and have a speed and sharpness that is less frequently remarked on" (Eliot, *Selected Essays* xii).

2. Jennifer Uglow ties Eliot's enthusiasm in the journal directly to her desire to write fiction and, more precisely, to "an awareness of *how* she wants to write," noting that, for Eliot, the holiday "brought her to the brink of 'a new era in my life, for it was then I began to write fiction'" (57).

3. Hugh Witemeyer writes of Eliot's "penchant for topographical specificity in landscape" and of the "ecological dimension" of her descriptions of landscape. Commenting specifically on a passage in her Ilfracombe journal, in which she likens humans to epizoons and compares the shells of mollusks to houses on a hillside that "look so tiny against the huge limbs of Mother Earth" that "one cannot help thinking of man as a parasitic animal—an epizoon making his abode on the skin of the planetary organism," he speculates that "[i]t is difficult to know whether these words came originally from George Eliot or from Lewes, since they appear almost verbatim in *Sea-Side Studies*. But the ideas were in any case shared. Man, the figure in the landscape, becomes a mollusk or epizoon when viewed from a biological perspective" (134).

4. Dolin lists some very material ways in which Eliot and her contemporaries experienced how "local concerns are never *just* local, but are mediated by national or global conditions" (46), including the fact that Eliot's friends, the Brays, lost their ribbon business due to changes in the American cotton market, and that, more generally, local time and local dialects were replaced by standard time and standard English, respectively. Here too can be seen the homogenizing effects of modernity that we saw character books trying to offset in their production of difference and eccentricity.

5. In *Adventures in Realism*, Matthew Beaumont also highlights the dialectical nature of Eliot's realism. Eliot's "formal games" in the opening passages of *Adam Bede* exemplify for him the necessarily experimental nature of realism, given its attempt to navigate the historical changes—industrial and agrarian—taking place in the nineteenth century. As a result, "the concept of realism that Eliot operates is a distinctly dialectical one . . . in addition to a democratic one. It is a dynamic force field rather than some static phenomenon" (6). Overall, Beaumont aims to counter simplistic views of realism that assume that "all realism is a species of *trompe l'oeil*, an act of representation that, in replicating empirical reality as exactly as possible, dreams of attaining a complete correspondence to it" (4).

6. Eagleton, for example, notes that "whereas Dickens's prose is declamatory and impressionistic, Eliot's sentences unroll like undulating hills, full of wry asides and scrupulously qualifying sub-clauses" (163).

7. Amy King notes that many theories of realism tend to stress the narrative momentum that spurs readers on toward the endings of novels. Pauses such as

Eliot's here in *Adam Bede*, as well as narrative description more broadly, suggest an alternate form of "readerly interest generated by lingering in narrative moments of protracted description: descriptive *pause* as opposed to plot," which, in turn, "works against the headlong thrust toward closure" ("Dilatory Description" 163). Eliot's "pause" works explicitly to generate a new kind of "readerly interest" in the common. See also Gallagher, "Formalism and Time."

8. For a sense of the range of associations "vulgarity" carries within the Victorian period, see Bernstein and Michie, *Victorian Vulgarity*. For a reading of Eliot's use of vulgarity specifically, see Joseph Litvak's essay "Vulgarity, Stupidity, and Worldliness in *Middlemarch*," in which he argues that "vulgarity, in *Middlemarch*, is nothing less than the ontological condition of characterhood as such. The near-synonymy of "vulgarity" and "commonness" underscores vulgarity's status as the fate that, precisely, every inhabitant of this fictional world has *in common*" (171). For Litvak, the refusal of seemingly vulgar desires, not the desires themselves, is the real problem, as "Lydgate's tragedy" indicates: "his tragedy is that he never sees *with* his infatuations," but instead tries to subordinate them to his "science" (181).

9. Written by the Irish writer Charles Johnstone, *Chrysal* (1760) is one of many eighteenth-century narratives told from the perspective of inanimate, everyday objects. For more on these narratives, now referred to as it- or object-narratives, see Chapter 2.

10. *The Task* opens with Lady Austen's prompt to Cowper, contained in the advertisement for the poem, to write in blank verse about a sofa. "I sing the Sofa" (11), the poem begins, before Cowper confesses to being unsuited to staying put on it: "The Sofa suits/The gouty limb, 'tis true; but gouty limb,/Though on a Sofa, may I never feel" (14). From here, Cowper is off on his walks through the countryside, describing in the kind of detail Eliot so admired the rural sounds and sights he encounters: "For I have loved the rural walk through lanes/Of grassy swarth, close cropped by nibbling sheep/And skirted thick with intertexture firm/ of thorny boughs: have loved the rural walk/O'er hills, through valleys, and by river's brink/E'er since a truant boy I passed my bounds/To enjoy a ramble on the banks of Thames" (14).

11. In his analysis of *The Prelude*, E. P. Thompson notes how Wordsworth "[reverses] the customary assumptions of the polite culture" when he writes in Book XII of conversing with common wayfarers and seeing in them "the depths of human souls, /Souls that appear to have no depth at all/To vulgar eyes" (11). He goes on to say, "Criticism, in recent years, has fastened upon so many other matters that it is possible for readers of this great poem to come from it unaware that it is what it is: an affirmation of the worth of the common man, a statement of faith enduring through perplexity and shock in universal brotherhood" (11–12). See Thompson, *The Romantics*, 4–32.

12. The assignation "real and concrete" comes from a letter Eliot wrote to John Blackwood about the confirmation in "Janet's Repentance" in which she

definitively asserts, "Art must be either real and concrete, or ideal and eclectic. Both are good and true in their way, but my stories are of the former kind. I undertake to exhibit some things as they have been or are, seen through such a medium as my own nature gives me." Throughout Eliot's work and writings, she employs the notion of natural history as a model for her realism, as the very language of "[exhibiting] some things as they have been or are" suggests. Wilhelm von Riehl's "The Natural History of German Life" provides an early model for a natural history that relates as much to people as to the animals and plants Eliot observed and wrote about in her journals on trips to the seashore with Lewes. In her essay on Riehl for the *Westminster Review*, Eliot draws a direct parallel between the physical sciences and social science and the need for both to attend to particular details and experience:

> [T]he most complete equipment of theory will not enable a statesman or a political and social reformer to adjust his measures wisely, in the absence of a special acquaintance with the section of society for which he legislates, with the peculiar characteristics of the nation, the province, the class whose well-being he has to consult. In other words, a wise social policy must be based not simply on abstract social science, but on the Natural History of social bodies. (*Selected Essays* 131)

13. In her discussion of the kinship between literary realism and natural history, Amy King notes a similar dynamism in claims to the real. She details how Philip Henry Gosse's descriptions of tide pools "model a pattern of observation and a justification for that observation analogous to literary realism and its commitment to the commonplace and the everyday." Like Eliot's recognition of the dynamic nature of the relations her fiction aims to represent, "Gosse and his tide pools point in fact toward a blurred space between literary effects and scientific claims to the real: to the shoreline, where each version of "realism" depends for its force upon the other" ("Reorienting the Scientific Frontier" 153–54).

14. Eliot humorously concludes this description by imagining one of her female readers objecting: "'An utterly uninteresting character!' I think I hear a lady reader exclaim—Mrs. Farthingale, for example, who prefers the ideal in fiction; to whom tragedy means ermine tippets, adultery, and murder; and comedy, the adventures of some personage who is quite a 'character'" (80).

15. The language of stamps and impressions is common to characteristic writing. As with the language of type, references to characters in terms of their "stamp" or "impression" abound in Eliot's novels. For example, in *The Mill on the Floss*, Eliot writes that "Mr. Glegg, like all men of his stamp, was extremely reticent about his will" (135); in *Felix Holt*, Eliot describes the politics in Treby Magna surrounding the Reform Bill in terms of the "stamp" and "impression" the various political parties have acquired (127–28); and in *Daniel Deronda*, Eliot's narrator asks us to "fancy an assemblage where the men had all that ordinary stamp of the well-bred Englishman, watching the entrance of Herr Klesmer"

(135–36) and describes the "stamp of dignity" that had "always" marked Lydia Glasher's "bearing" and "person" (398).

16. *Silas Marner* also draws on Eliot's childhood experience of the Midlands and the specific situation of handloom weavers at that time, although, as Dolin points out, the actual weavers would have produced for industrial centers not the local population as Silas does (47). In a letter to John Blackwood on January 12, 1861, Eliot writes of how *Silas Marner* "came *across* my other plans by a sudden inspiration"; "a story of old-fashioned village life, which has unfolded itself from the merest millet-seed of thought," the novel, as Blackwood phrases it, "sprang from [Eliot's] childish recollection of a man with a stoop and an expression of face that led her to think that he was an alien from his fellows" (emphasis in original, *George Eliot Letters* 3, 371; 427).

17. Jonathan Lamb sees a similar kind of recalcitrance in the objects that form the subjects of eighteenth- and early- nineteenth-century it-narratives, which he names the "implacability of things": "they are "just there, eying their human adversaries, implacable and meditating affronts" ("The Implacability of Things").

18. Robert Hughes remarks about this figure that "year after year the same proportion held" (163), whether in the early phases of the system of transportation (1787–1810), its peak years (1831–40), or its last stage (1841–50). See *The Fatal Shore*, 158–202.

19. The notion of "dethroning the self" comes from Ludwig Feuerbach and crystallizes the Young Hegelians' radical campaign against "sovereign personhood" as articulated within Christian personalism. Warren Breckman notes as well that this campaign forms the context within which "to understand and assess Marx's critique of individualism" (19).

20. About the preposition *beside*, Eve Kosofsky Sedgwick writes, "*Beside* permits a spacious agnosticism about several of the linear logics that enforce dualistic thinking," including "subject versus object" (*Touching Feeling* 8). But whereas Sedgwick turns to *besideness* and touch as a means of countering what she identifies as the dualistic structure of critique, I see the unsettling of dualisms as part and parcel of critique given its dialectical nature. See Lesjak, "Reading Dialectically."

21. Overall, Staten's analysis compellingly answers his titular, rhetorical question, "Is *Middlemarch* Ahistorical?" by showing "the density of historical specification" (997) in the novel, part of which is to be found in its "unblinkingly materialist substratum" (1000). This substratum demystifies where the country gentry's wealth comes from, be it in the system of inheritance, the handloom weavers having had the life sucked out of them (to paraphrase Mrs. Cadwallader's description of what Vincy's line of work entails), the village laborers poor wages and living conditions, and the particularly dire situation they faced during the 1829–30 economic depression, or the entire system of land management, a central aspect of which was "proper enclosure," which "would over the course of centuries

eliminate the English peasantry and eventually ... secure the English aristocracy's continued dominance through the nineteenth century" (999).

22. For Anderson, Eliot's depiction of Ladislaw and his politics ultimately represents a "political challenge to the primacy of exemplary character," which, in turn, "lights up the complexities that liberal concepts and principles can generate within literary form" (77). As I argue, this move away from "exemplary character," found throughout Eliot's work, is less a sign of a complex liberalism than of a more radical, revolutionary politics grounded in the common good.

23. Importantly, though, this relationship is two-directional: as Bruce Robbins points out, a key aspect of Eliot's cosmopolitanism—ambivalent as it may be—involves inducing a sympathy *in* provincials by cosmopolitan readers. Relating Dorothea's difficulty in coming to terms with "the weight of unintelligible Rome" during her honeymoon and the disorientating effects it has on her with the "ambiguities of cosmopolitanism that were already visible elsewhere in Eliot's fiction," Robbins contends that "[a]s a self-declared novelist of provincial life, Eliot aimed to stretch the social circle by inducing in her readers (assumed to be largely metropolitan) a sympathetic interest in provincials." He goes on to note,

> When she expresses that fondness in a sly Toryism, stubbornly appreciative of tradition that she might elsewhere judge to be backward, she is facing one classic paradox of cosmopolitanism: should one be tolerant of those who, given a choice, would not themselves show tolerance? ("The Cosmopolitan Eliot" 408)

24. For a provocative reading of the relationship between *Daniel Deronda* and *The Spanish Gypsy* in the context of Eliot's cosmopolitanism, see David Kurnick, who prompts us to see Eliot's earlier, generically mixed and messy long poem as "less a dress rehearsal for the ethnic nationalism of *Daniel Deronda* than an anticipatory critique of the blindnesses of such nationalism" (492). As in my reading, the figure of the gypsy for him allows Eliot to grapple with and "work out a model of an affiliative politics that would not be guaranteed by religious, national, or cultural prestige" (504). In short, without taking Eliot's representations of gypsies at face value, we can nevertheless understand her turn to gypsy characters as an attempt to model a collectivity "by definition resistant to the redemptive logics of racial and cultural dignity" (504). See also Hack for the appeal of this poem for African American writers, and Nord, for a reading of Eliot's representation of gypsies in a range of her novels.

25. Eliot describes the players' greed and passion for gambling and the "uniform negativeness of expression" (37) it induces as a distorted (and distorting) form of "human equality":

> Here certainly was a striking admission of human equality. The white bejewelled fingers of an English countess were very near touching a bony, yellow, crab-like hand stretching a bared wrist to clutch a heap of coin—a hand easy

to sort with the square, gaunt face, deep-set eyes, grizzled eyebrows, and ill-combed scanty hair which seemed a slight metamorphosis of the vulture. (36)

Unlike the common grounded in the refusal to "base our life and our reproduction on the suffering of others" (Federici, "Feminism"), the equality that comes by way of the commodity is all about winning at someone else's expense. As I've argued elsewhere, what the players "'share' is a competitive self-interest that paradoxically renders the concept of a shared sociality meaningless" (*Working Fictions* 115).

26. Tracing the connections between Eliot and the eighteenth-century novel, Margaret Anne Doody regards Casaubon as a walled, enclosed self and sees an ironic parallel between him and the character of Bramble in Smollett's *Humphry Clinker*: whereas Bramble, "a crotchedy valetudinarian," ultimately "recovers his health through being willing to share in the world outside his own ego . . . Casaubon, another pompous and complaining elder . . . walls himself up in his overserious self, and dies" (262). In spatial terms, then, Eliot's gypsies and gypsy-like figures counter the ethos of the self-enclosed individual; fittingly, gypsies and wanderers figure centrally in John Clare's unenclosed, circular (rather than linear and fenced), pre-enclosure landscape, as we saw in Chapter 1.

27. This phrase is the title for Fred Moten's recent trilogy and reflects his attempt to articulate an alternative form of subjectivity "about not finishing oneself, not passing, not completing; it's about allowing subjectivity to be unlawfully overcome by others, a radical passion and passivity such that one becomes unfit for subjection, because one does not possess the kind of agency that can hold the regulatory forces of subjecthood" (Harney and Moten, *The Undercommons* 28).

28. Conversely, as Isobel Armstrong argues, we need not automatically equate the plans of Eliot's characters with her own. She makes a strong case for seeing the diverse group of "The Philosophers" who meet at the Hand and Banner as "the most challenging democratic mode of civil society explored in the novel" (178), and a counter vision to Mordecai's messianism and Daniel's proto-Zionist project. See *Novel Politics* 162–81. In general, Armstrong's emphasis on the "democratic imaginations" the nineteenth-century novel actively *produces* usefully allows us to appreciate the open-ended nature of these texts, and how they function as what I am calling thought experiments. See also Dorothea Barrett's early feminist reading of *Daniel Deronda* as an open-ended novel in which Gwendolen's story and "the problems it poses have yet to be solved." Rather, the "question 'what can Gwendolen become?' can only be answered by the future" (*Vocation and Desire* 174).

29. The tension between these two articulations of commonwealth comes to the fore when, earlier in the novel, Mordecai advocates for the founding of a Jewish state, and reasons that "the world will gain as Israel gains." In this version of nationalism, the Jewish state appears inclusive, seemingly co-extensive with the gains of the world. Tellingly, however, Mordecai imagines the new state

as a beacon "amid the despotisms of the East," envisioning a "community in the van of the East which carries the culture and the sympathies of every great nation in its bosom," a polity that will establish a "land set for a halting-place of enmities, a neutral ground for the East as Belgium is for the West" (595). Despite the attempt, then, to square nationalism with a broader vision of an inclusive commonwealth, in which no one loses, Mordecai's account, as I have argued elsewhere, rests on the racist, exclusionary, image of the despotic East, and relies on "a grouping of people joined by exclusive interests separating them from others," which, as Federici clarifies, cannot be the basis for a genuine common ("Feminism"). For more on the representation of the East in the novel, see Lesjak, *Working Fictions*, 123-36.

30. Set in the period of the First Reform Bill refracted through the time just prior to the passing of the Second Reform Bill in 1867, *Felix Holt*'s *mise-en-scène* appears too close for comfort for Eliot, prompting her turn toward "the preservation of order."

31. In *The Victorian Geopolitical Aesthetic*, Goodlad also notes the importance of Machiavelli for Eliot's exploration in *Romola* of the "epic clash between private desire and the public good" (196), but, for her, neither the possibilities within a Machiavellian politics nor the role Savonarola plays are central to the novel; as she weighs the import of Savonarola, "overall *Romola* is less interested in Savonarola's vision than in capturing the multiple factors that undermine it" (197).

32. The lesson to be learned here is made very explicit in Gwendolen's case: "She, whose unquestioning habit it had been to take the best that came to her for less than her own claim, had now to see the position which tempted her in a new light, as a hard, unfair exclusion of others" (380).

33. Julian Corner depicts Tito as "truly the anti-hero [as opposed to his predecessor Hetty], supporting his selfish instinct with proto-utilitarian argument. As such, he asks the rebellious question which the novel is written to answer: 'What was the use of telling the whole?' [99]" (77). Overall, Corner's focus on psychoanalytic trauma and Kierkegaardian faith is quite different from mine, but his emphasis here on "telling the whole" compellingly reflects the need to see the whole (what I refer to as the commonwealth or a global set of relations) and the consequences of looking for self-interested or partial solutions premised on the exclusion of others.

34. On the tradition of Theophrastan character, see Smeed. See also Pinney's headnote to "Poetry and Prose, From the Notebook of an Eccentric," in *Essays of George Eliot*, in which he identifies both compositions as *"moralia"* (13). In his review of Nancy Henry's edition of *Impressions of Theophrastus Such*, John R. Reed points to the resemblance between *Impressions* and "Poetry and Prose" to argue against her claim that *Impressions* represents a "breakthrough document," seeing it instead as potentially a "weary retrogression (170)." As I will argue, it needs to be seen neither as a retrogression nor a breakthrough,

but rather as a continuation of Eliot's experiments with material character. On the significance of the connection between eighteenth-century sketches and the nineteenth-century novel, see Garcha.

35. Frederick Karl's dismissal of it as "one of the least satisfactory of Eliot's publications" (570) exemplifies critical responses to *Impressions of Theophrastus Such*. He singles out "The Modern Hep! Hep! Hep!" as the one exception to this critique. With a bit more punch, the Booklist blurb to the Henry edition refers to the book as "overlooked, underrated, and long out of print in the U.S."

36. As Henry underlines: "'Impressions', 'type', and 'character' work to emphasize the materiality of the printed word, the literal engraving—'impressing' of Theophrastus's impressions and his character on the page for preservation and transmission" (Eliot, *Impressions* xix).

## Chapter 4: The Typical and the Tragic in Hardy's Geopolitical Commons

1. Tim Armstrong calls Hardy's *The Life and Work of Thomas Hardy*, an autobiography written in the third person, "one of the oddest acts of literary ventriloquism ever seen" (*Thomas Hardy: Selected Poems* 3).

2. The synchronicity between the changing landscape and changing social relations is perfectly reflected in *Tess of the d'Urbervilles* in Angel Clare's rise into the ranks of "agriculturists and breeders ... a step in the young man's career which had been anticipated neither by himself nor by others" (131).

3. Hardy did of course utilize maps as he developed his concept of a fictional "Wessex" to define the area of south and southwest England where his major novels are set. But these maps, like Jameson's "ladder," must be "kicked away"; on their own, they only provide a limited view of Hardy's expansive aesthetic. They are also hardly true to life: about the map that is the frontispiece for *The Return of the Native* (as requested by Hardy to emphasize the novel's unity of place), Millgate comments that "it was deliberately disoriented, so that what should be its north-south axis actually appears as east-west." However, for those familiar with Dorchester's environs, clearly "the place whose unity Hardy sought to project was the trace of heathland immediately adjacent to Higher Bockhampton, the position of the fictional Bloom's End roughly approximating to the location of the Hardy cottage" (186).

4. Key evaluations of the provincial novel—of which the regional novel is a variant—associate it with the rural idyll and hence see it as backward-looking, simple, narrowly circumscribed, and historically limited. In this critical tradition, John Plotz identifies Mikhail Bakhtin, Ian Duncan, and Franco Moretti, all of whom share a negative view of the provincial novel, faulted for its "compactness, familiarity, distinctiveness (usually from the metropole), nostalgia-inducing comparative backwardness, and negative definition" (*Semi-Detached* 104). Against this view, Plotz argues that "at the heart of the provincial novel lies not so much a triumph of the local over the cosmopolitan (Little-Englandism), but a fascinating version of *magnum in parvo*, whereby provincial life is desirable for its capacity

to locate its inhabitants at once in a trivial (but chartable) Nowheresville and in a universal (but strangely ephemeral) everywhere" (102).

5. For an account of a postwork society, see Kathi Weeks's *The Problem Of Work*, in which she argues that the label "postwork society" holds open the space for the utopian possibility of an alternative future beyond work. On the other end of the spectrum, Jonathan Crary raises the spectre of work without end made possible by military research into how to keep soldiers awake for long periods of time. As he observes, "24/7 markets and a global infrastructure for continuous work and consumption have been in place for some time, but now a human subject is in the making to coincide with these more intensively" (4).

6. See Lesjak, *Working Fictions*.

7. In his keyword essay "Environment," Nathan K. Hensley identifies the range of meanings the term has come to signify, and distinguishes between Hardy's use of it to refer to "*my* environment, not *the* environment." The latter "world-scaled abstraction," as the OED shows, was a product of the postwar moment and would thus not have been available to Hardy in 1912. As Hensley clarifies, the environment for Hardy "stands to mean not an ontologically complete or total nonhuman world, "*the* environment," but the variable milieus—Flintcomb Ash, the Vale of Froom—that enable and constrain the human actors attempting to flourish in those particular zones" (676).

8. This remark was made at the time Hardy was writing his epic poem *The Dynasts*. He ventures that the idea was "approximately carried out" in the poem rather than in his novels (*Life and Work* 183). But Peter Widdowson argues otherwise, suggesting that this claim on Hardy's part is disingenuous since "the crucial problematic of Hardy's fiction . . . would seem to lie precisely in his attempts to find a form to 'render visible' abstract and analytic 'essences' of contemporary social relations: in particular, the 'fictions' of class and gender hierarchies" (53), an argument I echo.

9. William A. Cohen addresses these entries of Hardy's in his reading of *The Woodlanders*, the novel Hardy was working on in 1886, at the time of the first entry on realism. He too wants to complicate Hardy's novelistic practice, especially in relation to the place of nature in his work.

10. T. H. Huxley and Archibald Geikie promote models of geography that move from the particular locality "upward and outward . . . to realise the shape and dimensions of the earth," as Geikie puts it (quoted in Pite 5). By contrast, Pite points out, "The Oxford school identifies distinct, self-sufficient regions even where they barely exist any longer," and turns to Hardy's Wessex specifically as an exemplar of a "well-marked natural region, with a very considerable regional consciousness and patriotism" (7).

11. For a sustained critique of surface reading and other recent critical turns toward empiricism, see Lesjak, "Reading Dialectically." On the current state of theory today and different potential modes of reading other than surface reading,

see also Bartolovich, "Humanities of Scale"; Kornbluh, "We Have Never Been Critical"; Wegner; and Bewes.

12. George Levine defines Victorian culture as a whole as "a culture committed to the possibility and necessity of knowing the 'real,'" while also recognizing the "Victorians' remarkably creative and troubled recognition of the elusiveness of both the true and the good" (*Realism* vii). For Levine, the true and the good are indissociable since "questions about the possibility of knowing, epistemological questions, were for the Victorians urgent ones, particularly so because they were always also ethical questions" (vi–vii). Hardy's notebook entries and his essays repeatedly invoke truth-telling as the purpose of art.

13. The "grasping of life in history," in turn, allows us to grasp our own present life "in history": "Ultimately, our participation in such imaginative recreation should lead us to view our own societies and our own historical selves as 'other,' as products of history, not nature" (123). Throughout *Narrating Reality*, Shaw draws on Erich Auerbach's account of realism in *Mimesis* to develop this notion of a historicist realism.

14. This has obvious echoes with my discussion of John Clare in Chapter 1, and Linebaugh's identification of Clare's poetry with an epistemology of the unenclosed.

15. He surmises that "[s]uch raw data would not have been found acceptable, or even credible, by many late Victorian readers. There were indeed good reasons for Hardy wishing to keep this 'rough music' in its place" (xxv).

16. For more on Hardy's view of rural depopulation in "The Dorsetshire Labourer," see especially Fred Reid, who infers that Hardy "was well aware that his meditations had virtually global significance. . . . The lifeholders who were being forced from Dorset villages to the towns had their counterparts throughout Europe, not least in Ireland" (185).

17. Significantly, the narrator in *The Mayor of Casterbridge* states that Elizabeth-Jane "had learnt the lesson of renunciation, and was as familiar with the wreck of each day's wishes as with the diurnal setting of the sun. If her earthly career had taught her few book philosophies, it had at least well practised her in this" (137). As we saw with George Eliot, sexual violence and social violence go hand in hand, the need to renounce sexual desire equally the need to renounce social desires, and to similar effect: to keep the laboring class in its place. Although Jude argues that "it is no worse for the woman than for the man" and that "instead of protesting against the conditions, [women] protest against the man"(287), thereby mistaking the real source of "the pressure," Hardy's narratives themselves suggest otherwise. Yes, "the conditions" are the underlying enemy, but the pressures men and women face are shown to be differentially applied. As Tess says, "[T]here are very few women's lives that are not—tremulous" (421).

18. In a well-known set of notes on fiction that Hardy jotted down in July 1881, he addresses the balancing act realism requires between the common or ordinary (the term he uses most frequently to describe his characters) and the uncommon:

"The writer's problem is, how to strike the balance between the uncommon and the ordinary so as on the one hand to give interest, on the other to give reality . . . human nature must never be made abnormal, which is introducing incredulity." Instead for Hardy, the "uncommonness must be in the events, not in the characters; the writer's art lies in shaping that uncommonness while disguising its unlikelihood, if it be unlikely" (*Life and Work* 152). As I am suggesting, the uncommonness of the events in Hardy's novels in fact turns out to tell all too common stories that are not only likely but taken from real-life accounts, as we will see further on.

19. The phrase "beauty is ugliness" comes from Hardy. In *Life and Work* Hardy describes a painting by Giovanni Boldini called "The Morning Walk" and compares it to the opening of *The Return of the Native* and his idea that "the beauty of association is entirely superior to the beauty of aspect, and a beloved relative's old battered tankard to the finest Greek vase. Paradoxically put, it is to see the beauty in ugliness" (April 22, 1878: 124). See also Bullen, *Expressive Eye*, 88–117. Association also determines how one weathers the loneliness of the heath in *The Return of the Native* or Hintock life in *The Woodlanders*, a distinction the narrator thematizes in *The Woodlanders*. Whereas village life begins to wear on Fitzpiers, Winterborne, Melbury, and Grace have "old association" to sustain them, by which the narrator means "an almost exhaustive biographical or historical acquaintance with every object, animate or inanimate, within the observer's horizon" (125).

20. In an oft-quoted comment Hardy makes about the novelist's role, he likens "we tale-tellers" to Ancient Mariners and cautions that "none of us is warranted in stopping Wedding Guests (in other words, the hurrying public) unless he has something more unusual to relate than the ordinary experience of every average man and woman" (*Life and Work* 268). Types, it should be clear, are not equivalent to depictions of "the ordinary experience of every average man and woman," which function like the "simply natural" for Hardy, or an attempt to represent the "exact truth as to material fact" (*Life and Work* 192). This distinction accords with Georg Lukács's elevation of types over description, defined as the difference between the "monotonous commonplace of naturalism, which results from the direct, mechanical mirroring of the humdrum reality of capitalism" (a view Hardy shares without directly referring to naturalism), and a realism that succeeds in "revealing the human and social significance of the struggle for life and lifting it to a higher plan by artistic means" (*Studies in European Realism* 93). See also Lukács, "Narrate or Describe?"

21. The revival of the "casserole protest" today harks back to the skimmington. It is striking, as well, that by characterizing Hardy's "Facts" notebook as "rough music," as we saw above, Greenslade would seem to be likening the notebook to a skimmington. In this regard, the whole set of "facts" might be seen as material ripe for a skimmington.

22. In a note about Hardy's use of "the sort of man" to describe Jude, Dennis Taylor directs our attention to the manuscript and serial versions of the novel,

which read "the coming sort of man," thereby more closely linking Jude to future types, such as Clym and Tess, as well as Angel and "Father Time." See *Jude the Obscure*, fn. 7, p. 413.

23. As Tim Parks encourages us to think about the relation between Hardy's common characters and their tragedies, "rather than repeating the old complaint that Hardy's characters are not 'great' enough for 'real' tragedy, it might be more useful to turn the proposition on its head and say that if we did have 'great' characters the Hardy kind of tragedy could not happen" (10).

24. William Greenslade recounts an entry from Virginia Woolf's diary after a visit to Hardy in which she is struck by his interest in facts: he was, she recalls, "immensely interested in facts; incidents; & somehow, one could imagine, naturally swept off into imagining & creating without a thought of its being difficult or remarkable; becoming obsessed; & living in imagination." Greenslade adds, "She saw Hardy's singular absorption in the local and the oddly contingent as presenting not so much a problem as a creative opportunity. Facts and the transforming pressure of his imagination were in dynamic continuum, not in awkward tension" (xxv).

25. Hardy began the notebook in July 1883 shortly after moving back to Dorchester. He began compiling the news clippings from the *Dorset County Chronicle* in 1884.

26. Apropos this connection, Dickens's "pig-faced lady" makes a surprise appearance in the notebook. She is apparently spotted in Grosvenor Square where "a pig's snout was said to have been seen looking from the window of a carriage under < > poke-bonnet" (228).

27. The notebook ends in April 1913 with a pasted-in periodical cutting of an excerpt from *The Life of Porphyry Bishop of Gaza* describing a strange scene in which a demon dwelling in the statue of Aphrodite, upon seeing Christians carrying a wooden cross, comes out of the statue, breaks the statue into pieces, and in the process strikes down two of the idolaters, one of whom it "clave the head ... in twain," the other "it brake the shoulder and the wrist. For they were both standing and mocking at the holy multitude" (333–34).

28. These news clippings also provided material for *The Mayor of Casterbridge*, the novel Hardy was in the process of writing during this period.

29. Lest we underestimate the role of the sheep, Ivan Kreilkamp's incisive essay on *Far from the Madding Crowd* begins by quoting Henry James's famous remark that "everything human in the book strikes us as factitious and insubstantial; the only things we believe in are the sheep and the dogs," in order to set up an argument in which he asks us "to consider more seriously the implications of a novel in which the most memorable characters, arguably, walk on four legs" (474).

30. This list of phenomena is used by the Midnight Notes Collective to reveal the similarities between the "Old Enclosures" beginning in the late 1400s and the "New Enclosures" occurring since the mid-1970s.

31. Martell usefully draws our attention to a form of industrial agriculture other than the threshing machine in her analysis of the dairy chapters in *Tess of*

*the d'Urbervilles*. "Just as the thresher tears through the narrative structure," she explains, "so industrial milk production oozes its way into the symbolic territory of the pastoral as the ecosystem it mirrors struggles to accommodate the explosive growth of British dairying" (74). See also Meadowsong on the role of machine culture in *Tess of the d'Urbervilles*.

32. In her book *Victorian Pain*, Rachel Ablow also attends to Hardy's "wounded trees" and the "personifying pathos" of the language he uses to describe them in a passage from *The Woodlanders*. For her, these personifications "suggest that [the trees] deserve our attention" (118) and are integral to Hardy's larger view of pain "less as something suffered by other people, animals, trees, or life-forms who deserve our pity, than as a condition of possibility for experiencing ourselves as part of a *universe* that suffers" (134).

33. Egdon Heath is also the fictional name for Hardy's birthplace, Puddletown Heath in Higher Bockhampton. See Bullen, *Thomas Hardy* 49–77, for more on the specific locations in *The Return of the Native* and their connection to Hardy's home.

34. See the *Observer*, January 29, 1879. In a similar vein, Jean R. Brooks argues that

> Egdon Heath, the resistant matter of the cosmos on which the action takes place, bears, shapes, nourishes, and kills conscious organisms possessed of its striving will without its unconsciousness of suffering. The six main characters take their key from Egdon. They all feel its pull through some affinity of temperament. (*Thomas Hardy* 177)

35. The sublime for Hardy is often made into a verb, as in something being "sublimed." The remarks of the stranger Angel Clare meets in *Tess of the d'Urbervilles*, "of whom he knew absolutely nothing beyond a commonplace name, were sublimed by his death, and influenced Clare more than all the reasoned ethics of the philosophers" (422). Similarly, in *Life and Work*, Hardy describes four itinerant musicians, all sisters, who, after appearing old and worn-out during the day, "were sublimed to a wondrous charm" when he sees them again in the evening, "the silvery gleams of Saunders's [silver-smith's] shop shining out upon them" (171).

36. See Bullen's "Appendix: Hardy and the Arctic" in *The Expressive Eye* for an account of this passage and the variety of sources that may have inspired Hardy's fascination with the north and "Northern knowledge," the term he uses to describe the "wild mallard" Venn sees as he crosses the heath to convince Eustacia to give up Wildeve.

37. The full quote for this claim is as follows:

> The conscientiousness and the spring of release in the novel takes always the guise of a leveled insight, without recourse to faith or to any other transcendental signifier. But that insight itself constantly shifts linguistic registers and does not avoid contradictions. She therefore jars her early readers with the

book's closeness to a religious language that yet absolutely debars recourse to faith. Her word is *trust*: the assurance that sustains human—and only human—contact. ("What's Not in *Middlemarch*" 27)

38. Like Miller, I see the relationship between character and environment in Hardy as a dialectical one in which "the environment is determined by the human just as the human is determined by the environment" (701). For an alternative take on this relationship, see John MacNeill Miller, who argues that Hardy's view of nature does "little to promote accurate understanding of ecological interactions" because his narratives "typically portray the nonhuman environment in terms of a single monolithic nature—a monstrous, unfeeling aggregate that overwhelms and ultimately extinguishes the human spirit" (150). For John Miller, Hardy's misreading of nature comes from his inability to see landscapes such as the heath as human-made. Viewing Hardy's landscapes in the context of enclosure, however, calls into question any stark distinction between human and landscape. Elizabeth Miller makes a similar point in her reading of *Under the Greenwood Tree* when she notes how Hardy's references to the woods as a "plantation" or a "copsewood" make clear that they are made by human hands (705).

39. There is comedy in this bed-switching too. When, in *The Mayor of Casterbridge*, Lucetta, Farfrae, and Henchard all end up in the same room, with Elizabeth-Jane looking on, and Lucetta offers more bread to "Henchard and Farfrae equally," they end up in a tug-of-war with a slice of bread with neither letting go and the bread being torn in two. Lucetta cries "Oh—I am so sorry! . . . with a nervous twitter," Farfrae "[tries] to laugh; but he [is] too much in love to see the incident in any but a tragic light," and Elizabeth-Jane, summing up the scene, thinks "'How ridiculous of all three of them!'"(139)—a response that we as onlookers are equally encouraged to echo.

40. For two very different readings of how letters function in Hardy's fiction, see Keen and Koelher, both of whom associate letters with privacy, personal property, and individual rights. They thus see the breaching of privacy as a transgressive act that threatens individuals', and especially women's, autonomy. In this way, privacy and private property are linked and implicitly upheld as positively valued.

41. Eustacia's incompatibility with the heath is brought home when the narrator remarks,

> To dwell on a heath without studying its meanings was like wedding a foreigner without learning his tongue. The subtle beauties of the heath were lost to Eustacia; she only caught its vapours. An environment which would have made a contented woman a poet, a suffering woman a devotee, a pious woman a psalmist, even a giddy woman thoughtful, made a rebellious woman saturnine. (73)

Importantly, the emphasis is on the reciprocity or lack thereof between "Character" and "Environment," to return to Hardy's own description of what his novels are about; in Eustacia's case, the heath affords no such reciprocity and in the end leads to her death as she can imagine no escape from it nor life on it. She is also introduced as a victim of circumstance, having had to leave Budmouth, "her native place, a fashionable seaside resort between twenty and thirty miles distant," when her mother dies, her father leaves "off thriving, drank and died also," and she has no choice but to live with her grandfather, a fate that leaves her bereft: "She hated the change; she felt like one banished; but here she was forced to abide" (70).

42. Drawing on Michael Watts's work *Silent Violence: Food, Famine and Peasantry in Northern Nigeria*, Mike Davis refers to his book *Late Victorian Holocausts* as a "'political ecology of famine' because it takes the viewpoint both of environmental history and Marxist political economy" (15). Jason W. Moore uses the term "world-ecology" to signify the necessity of such a viewpoint, asserting that "as a framework for unifying the production of nature, the pursuit of power, and the accumulation of capital," world-ecology "offers a way of re-reading the diversity of modern human experience as unavoidably, irreducibly, socio-ecological" (291).

43. In a journal entry from 1883, Hardy puts the consequences of adhering to a steadfast self-centeredness that refuses this recognition thus: "Every error under the sun seems to arise from thinking that you are right yourself because you *are* yourself, and other people wrong because they are not you" (*Life and Work* 171). See also Scarry on the intimate "physical continuity of man and his materials" (52) in Hardy's representations of work.

44. Materiality is not limited to selves either. In "Candour in English Fiction," Hardy begins by asserting that "even imagination is the slave of stolid circumstance." "The unending flow of inventiveness," he goes on to say, "is conditioned by its surroundings like a river-stream" (*Thomas Hardy: Selected Poetry and Non-Fictional Prose* 255).

45. Tellingly, Adorno, like Hardy, has been criticized for being too pessimistic.

46. Boumelha concludes that Sue and Jude ultimately end up enforcing the ideal of marriage rather than rejecting it, arguing that

> in the course of the novel they are forced to recognise that their relationship is not transcendent of time, place, and material circumstance, as they have tried to make it; their Romantic delusion gives way, leaving Jude cynical, but in Sue's case leading on into the ideology of legalised and sacramental marriage that her experiences have led her to respect. (149–50)

In this context, the revolutionary nature of the alternative kinship relations that Eliot grants to Romola, as we saw in the previous chapter, can be fully seen. But, again, such relations are not afforded any of her nineteenth-century heroines, underscoring how unattainable such a possibility was given the typical "economic life of the couple."

## Afterword

1. Harvey develops the notion of "accumulation by dispossession" in *The New Imperialism* to describe the means by which neoliberal capitalist politics

work on multiple fronts to enclose the commons. See esp. 137–82.

2. The myth of *terra nullius*, employed by John Locke to establish private property as a natural right, as we saw in Chapter 1, continues to provide the fodder for many of these acts of enclosure. Nowhere, perhaps, is this myth more enduring than in the movement for and resistance to Indigenous rights and recognition today in Canada. As Emma Lowman and Adam Barker state, "[T]*erra nullius* has proven a surprisingly durable and powerful narrative, rising from the grave when least expected" (60) to delegitimize Indigenous land claims.

3. Sometimes they also simply make clear that the past is past, as when Maggie and Tom Tulliver are swept off in a quasi-apocalyptic flood at the end of Eliot's *The Mill on the Floss*.

# References

Ablow, Rachel. *Victorian Pain*. Princeton, NJ: Princeton University Press, 2017.
Adorno, Theodor W. *Minima Moralia: Reflections on Damaged Life*. Trans. E.F.N. Jephcott. New York: Verso, 2005.
———. *Negative Dialectics*. Trans. E. B. Ashton. New York: Continuum, 1987.
———. "Subject and Object." *The Essential Frankfurt School Reader*. Ed. Andrew Arato and Eike Gebhardt, 497–511. New York: Continuum, 1987.
Agathocleous, Tanya, and Jason R. Rudy. "Victorian Cosmopolitanisms: Introduction." *Victorian Literature and Culture* 38.2 (September 2010): 389–97.
Altick, Richard D. *Victorian People and Ideas*. New York: W.W. Norton, 1973.
Anderson, Amanda. *Bleak Liberalism*. Chicago: University of Chicago Press, 2016.
———. *The Powers of Distance: Cosmopolitanism and the Cultivation of Detachment*. Princeton: Princeton University Press, 2001.
Anderson, Robert. "Ruinous Mixture: Godwin, Enclosure and the Associated Self." *Studies in Romanticism* 39.4 (Winter 2000): 617–45.
Anger, Suzy. "George Eliot and Philosophy." *Cambridge Companion to George Eliot*. Ed. George Levine. New York: Cambridge University Press, 2001.
Armstrong, Isobel. *Novel Politics: Democratic Imaginations in Nineteenth-Century Fiction*. New York: Oxford University Press, 2016.
Auerbach, Erich. *Mimesis: The Representation of Reality in Western Literature*. Trans. Willard R. Trask. Princeton: Princeton University Press, 1953.
Banner, Stuart. *Possessing the Pacific: Land, Settlers, and Indigenous People from Australia to Alaska*. Cambridge, MA: Harvard University Press, 2007.
Barrell, John. *The Idea of Landscape and the Sense of Place 1730–1840: An Approach to the Poetry of John Clare*. Cambridge, UK: Cambridge University Press, 2011.
Barrett, Dorothea. *Vocation and Desire: George Eliot's Heroines*. New York: Routledge, 1989.
Bartlett, Neil. *Who Was That Man? A Present for Oscar Wilde*. London: Serpent's Tail, 1989.
Bartolovich, Crystal. "Humanities of Scale: Marxism, Surface Reading—and Milton." *PMLA* 127.1 (2012): 115–21.
———. "Organizing the (Un) Common." *Angelaki* 12.3 (2007): 81–104.

# REFERENCES

Bate, Jonathan. *John Clare: A Biography*. London: Picador, 2003.
Beaumont, Matthew, ed. *Adventures in Realism*. Malden, MA: Blackwell, 2007.
———. *Nightwalking: A Nocturnal History of London*. New York: Verso, 2015.
Beer, Gillian. *Darwin's Plots: Evolutionary Narrative in Darwin, George Eliot and Nineteenth-Century Fiction*. Cambridge, UK: Cambridge University Press, 2009.
———. "What's Not in *Middlemarch*." *Middlemarch in the Twenty-First Century*. Ed. Karen Chase. New York: Oxford University Press, 2006. 15–35.
Belsey, Catherine. *Critical Practice*. New York: Routledge, 1980.
Benjamin, Walter. *Illuminations*. Ed. Hannah Arendt. Trans. Harry Zohn. New York: Schocken, 1969.
Bernstein, Susan David, and Elsie B. Michie, eds. *Victorian Vulgarity: Taste in Verbal and Visual Culture*. Burlington, VT: Ashgate, 2009.
Bewes, Timothy. "Reading with the Grain: A New World in Literary Criticism." *Differences: A Journal of Feminist Cultural Studies* 21. 3 (2010): 1–33.
Bhandar, Brenna. *Colonial Lives of Property: Law, Land, and Racial Regimes of Ownership*. Durham, NC: Duke University Press, 2018.
Bigelow, Gordon. *Fiction, Famine, and the Rise of Economics in Victorian Britain and Ireland*. Cambridge, UK: Cambridge University Press, 2003.
Blackwell, Mark, ed. *The Secret Life of Things: Animals, Objects, and It-Narratives in Eighteenth-Century England*. Lewisburg: Bucknell University Press, 2007.
Blomley, Nicholas. "Enclosure, Common Right and the Property of the Poor." *Social & Legal Studies* 17.3 (2008): 311–31.
Bollier, David. *Silent Theft: The Private Plunder of Our Common Wealth*. New York: Routledge, 2002.
———. *Think Like a Commoner: A Short Introduction to the Life of the Commons*. Gabriola Island, BC: New Society, 2014.
Boumelha, Penny. *Thomas Hardy and Women: Sexual Ideology and Narrative Form*. Sussex, UK: Harvester Press, 1982.
Bowlby, Rachel. Foreword. *Adventures in Realism*. Ed. Matthew Beaumont, xi–xviii. Malden, MA: Blackwell, 2007.
Braddon, Mary Elizabeth. *Lady Audley's Secret*. New York: Oxford University Press, 2012.
Brantlinger, Patrick. *The Reading Lesson: The Threat of Mass Literacy in Nineteenth-Century British Fiction*. Bloomington: Indiana University Press, 1998.
Braudel, Fernand. *On History*. Trans. Sarah Matthews. Chicago: University of Chicago Press, 1980.
Breckman, Warren. *Marx, The Young Hegelians, and the Origins of Radical Social Theory: Dethroning the Self*. Cambridge, UK: Cambridge University Press, 1998.
Bresnihan, Patrick. "John Clare and the Manifold Commons." *Environmental Humanities* 3 (2013): 71–91.

# REFERENCES

Brooks, Jean R. *Thomas Hardy: The Poetic Structure*. Ithaca, NY: Cornell University Press, 1971.

Brownlow, Timothy. *John Clare and Picturesque Landscape*. Oxford, UK: Clarendon Press, 1983.

Brundage, Anthony. *The English Poor Laws, 1700–1930*. New York: Palgrave, 2002.

Bullen, J. B. *The Expressive Eye: Fiction and Perception in the Work of Thomas Hardy*. Oxford, UK: Clarendon Press, 1986.

———. *Thomas Hardy: The World of His Novels*. London: Frances Lincoln, 2013.

Butler, Judith. *Gender Trouble: Feminism and the Subversion of Identity*. 2nd Ed.. New York: Routledge, 1999.

———. *Precarious Life: The Powers of Mourning and Violence*. London: Verso, 2004.

Buzard, James. "'The Country of the Plague': Anticulture and Autoethnography in Dickens's 1850s." *Victorian Literature and Culture* 38 (2010): 413–19.

Chesterton, G. K. *Appreciations and Criticisms of the Works of Charles Dickens*. London: J. M. Dent & Sons, 1911.

———. *Charles Dickens*. London: Methuen and Co., 1906.

Christophers, Brett. *The New Enclosure: The Appropriation of Public Land in Neoliberal Britain*. New York: Verso, 2019.

Clare, John. *"I AM": The Selected Poetry of John Clare*. Ed. Jonathan Bate. New York: Farrar, Straus and Giroux, 2003.

———. *John Clare: Major Works*. Ed. Eric Robinson and David Powell. New York: Oxford University Press, 2004.

———. *The Poems of John Clare*. Ed. J. W. Tibble. London: J. M. Dent & Sons, 1935.

Clark, Alice. *The Working Life of Women in 17th Century England*. London: Frank Cass and Co., 1968.

Cobbett, William. *Rural Rides*. New York: Penguin, 2001.

Cohen, William A. "Arborealities: The Tactile Ecology of Hardy's *Woodlanders*." *Interdisciplinary Studies in the Long Nineteenth Century* 19 (2014): 1–19.

Colligan, Colette, and Margaret Linley, eds. *Media, Technology, and Literature in the Nineteenth Century: Image, Sound, Touch*. Burlington, VT: Ashgate, 2011.

Collins, Wilkie. *The Woman in White*. New York: Penguin, 2003.

Collis, Stephen. *The Commons*. Vancouver, BC: Talonbooks, 2008.

Connor, Steven. *Charles Dickens*. Oxford, UK: Blackwell, 1985.

Corner, Julian. "'Telling the Whole': Trauma, Drifting and Reconciliation in *Romola*." *From Author to Text: Re-reading George Eliot's* Romola. Ed. Caroline Levine and Mark W. Turner. Brookfield, VT: Ashgate, 1998.

Corrigan, Philip, and Derek Sayer. *The Great Arch: English State Formation as*

*Cultural Revolution*. New York: Basil Blackwell, 1985.
Coupe, Laurence, ed. *The Green Studies Reader: From Romanticism to Ecocriticism*. New York: Routledge, 2000.
Cowper, William. *The Task, and Other Poems*. Philadelphia: Carey and Hart, 1845. https://catalog.hathitrust.org/Record/011602279. Accessed July 17, 2018.
Crary, Jonathan. *24/7: Late Capitalism and the Ends of Sleep*. New York: Verso, 2013.
[Dallas, E. S.]. "Our Mutual Friend." *The Times* (November 29, 1865): 6.
Daly, Nicholas. *Literature, Technology, and Modernity, 1860–2000*. Cambridge, UK: Cambridge University Press, 2004.
Davis, Mike. *Late Victorian Holocausts: El Niño Famines and the Making of the Third World*. New York: Verso, 2001.
———. *Planet of Slums*. New York: Verso, 2006.
Dickens, Charles. *Bleak House*. New York: Penguin, 2003.
———. *A Child's History of England*. London: Chapman and Hall, 1876.
———. *A Christmas Carol and Other Christmas Writings*. New York: Penguin, 2003.
———. *David Copperfield*. New York: Penguin, 1996.
———. *Hard Times*. New York: Penguin, 1985.
———. *The Old Curiosity Shop*. New York: Penguin, 2000.
———. *Our Mutual Friend*. New York: Penguin, 1997.
———. *The Pickwick Papers*. New York: Penguin, 2000.
———. "Railway Waifs and Strays." *Household Words*, December 20, 1850, 319–22.
Dienst, Richard. *The Bonds of Debt*. New York: Verso, 2011.
Dingwall, E. J. *Some Human Oddities: Studies in the Queer, the Uncanny and the Fanatical*. London: Horne and Van Tal, 1947.
———. *Very Peculiar People: Portrait Studies in the Queer, the Abnormal and the Uncanny*. London: Rider, 1950.
Dolin, Tim. *George Eliot*. New York: Oxford University Press, 2005.
Doody, Margaret Anne. "George Eliot and the Eighteenth-Century Novel." *Nineteenth-Century Fiction* 35.3 (1980): 260–91.
Dunn, John. *Locke: A Very Short Introduction*. New York: Oxford University Press, 2003.
Dvorak, Wilfred P. "Charles Dickens' *Our Mutual Friend* and Frederick Somner Merryweather's *Lives and Anecdotes of Misers*." *Dickens Studies Annual* 9 (1981): 117–41.
Dyck, Ian. *William Cobbett and Rural Popular Culture*. Cambridge, UK: Cambridge University Press, 1992.
Eagleton, Terry. "Buried in the Life: Thomas Hardy and the Limits of Biographies." Rev. of *Thomas Hardy* by Claire Tomalin, and *Thomas Hardy: The Guarded Life* by Ralph Pite. *Harpers Magazine* (November 2007): 89–94.

———. "The Critic as Clown." *Marxism and the Interpretation of Culture.* Ed. Cary Nelson and Lawrence Grossberg. Urbana: University of Illinois Press, 1988.
———. *The English Novel: An Introduction.* Malden, MA: Blackwell, 2005.
———. *Literary Theory: An Introduction.* Minneapolis: University of Minnesota Press, 2008.
Eliot, George. *Adam Bede.* New York: Penguin, 1987.
———. *Daniel Deronda.* New York: Penguin, 1986.
———. *Felix Holt, The Radical.* New York: Penguin, 1984.
———. *The George Eliot Letters.* Ed. Gordon S. Haight. 9 vols. New Haven: Yale University Press, 1954–78.
———. *Impressions of Theophrastus Such.* Ed. Nancy Henry. Iowa City: University of Iowa Press, 1994.
———. *Middlemarch.* New York: Penguin, 1994.
———. *The Mill on the Floss.* New York: Penguin, 2003.
———. *Romola.* New York: Penguin, 1980.
———. *Scenes of Clerical Life. Novels of George Eliot.* Vol. IV. Edinburgh: William Blackwood and Sons, n.d.
———. *Selected Essays, Poems and Other Writings.* Ed. A. S. Byatt and Nicholas Warren. New York: Penguin, 1990.
———. *Silas Marner.* New York: Penguin, 1980.
Fairholt, Frederick. *Eccentric and Remarkable Characters. A Series of Biographical Memoirs of Persons Famous for Extraordinary Actions or Singularities.* London: Richard Bentley, 1849.
Federici, Silvia. *Caliban and the Witch: Women, the Body and Primitive Accumulation.* Brooklyn, NY: Autonomedia, 2004.
———. "Feminism and the Politics of the Commons." *The Commoner.* http://www.thecommoner.org, January 24, 2011.
———. *Re-enchanting the World: Feminism and the Politics of the Commons.* Oakland, CA: PM Press, 2018.
Felski, Rita. "After Suspicion." *Profession* (2009): 28–35.
———. "The Invention of Everyday Life." *New Formations* 39 (1999): 15–31.
Festa, Lynn. *Sentimental Figures of Empire in Eighteenth Century Britain and France.* Baltimore: Johns Hopkins University Press, 2006.
Forster, E. M. *Aspects of the Novel.* New York: Harcourt, Brace, 1927.
Forster, John. *The Life of Charles Dickens. Volume 3: 1852–1870.* Cambridge, UK: Cambridge University Press, 2011.
Freedgood, Elaine. *The Ideas in Things: Fugitive Meaning in the Victorian Novel.* Chicago: University of Chicago Press, 2006.
———. "What Objects Know: Circulations, Omniscience and the Comedy of Dispossession in Victorian It-Narratives." *Journal of Victorian Culture* 15.1 (2010): 83–100.
Friedman, Stanley. "The Motif of Reading in *Our Mutual Friend.*" *Nineteenth-Century Fiction* 28.1 (June 1973): 38–61.

Gagnier, Regenia. *The Insatiability of Human Wants: Economics and Aesthetics in Market Society*. Chicago: University of Chicago Press, 2000.
Gallagher, Catherine. *The Body Economic: Life, Death, and Sensation in Political Economy and the Victorian Novel*. Princeton: Princeton University Press, 2006.
———. "Formalism and Time." *Modern Language Quarterly* 61.1 (2000): 229–51.
Garcha, Amanpal. *From Sketch to Novel: The Development of Victorian Fiction*. Cambridge, UK: Cambridge University Press, 2009.
Gaskell, Elizabeth. *North and South*. New York: Penguin, 2003.
———. *Ruth*. New York: Oxford University Press, 1998.
Gatrell, Simon. *Thomas Hardy and the Proper Study of Mankind*. London: Macmillan, 1993.
Goldberg, Jonathan. "On the Eve of the Future." *PMLA* 125.2 (2010): 374–77.
Goodlad, Lauren M. E. "Afterword." "Television for Victorianists." Special issue of *Romanticism and Victorianism on the Net* 63 (April 2013).
———. "Cosmopolitanism's Actually Existing Beyond; Toward a Victorian Geopolitical Aesthetic." *Victorian Literature and Culture* 38 (2010): 399–411.
———. *The Victorian Geopolitical Aesthetic: Realism, Sovereignty, and Transnational Experience*. New York: Oxford University Press, 2015.
———. *Victorian Literature and the Victorian State: Character and Governance in a Liberal Society*. Baltimore: John Hopkins University Press., 2003.
Grass, Sean. *Charles Dickens's Our Mutual Friend: A Publishing History*. New York: Routledge, 2016.
Greenslade, William. "Thomas Hardy's Notebooks." *A Companion to Thomas Hardy*. Ed. Keith Wilson. Malden, MA: Blackwell, 2013.
Gregory, James. "Eccentric Biography and the Victorians." *Biography* 30.3 (Summer 2007): 342–76.
———. "Eccentric Lives: Character, Characters and Curiosities in Britain, c. 1760–1900." *Histories on the Normal and the Abnormal: Social and Cultural Histories of Norms and Normativity*. Ed. Waltraud Ernst. New York, Routledge, 2006.
Grossman, Jonathan. *Charles Dickens's Networks: Public Transport and the Novel*. New York: Oxford University Press, 2012.
Hack, Daniel. *Reaping Something New: African American Transformations of Victorian Literature*. Princeton: Princeton University Press, 2017.
Haiven, Max. "On Capitalism, Colonialism, Women and Food Politics: An Interview with Silvia Federici." *Politics and Culture* 2 (2009).
Hammond, J. L., and Barbara Hammond. *The Village Labourer 1760–1832*. New York: Augustus M. Kelley, 1967.
Hannay, James. *A Course of English Literature*. London: Tinsley Brothers, 1866.

Hansard. Ministerial Declarations: House of Lords Debate, November 22, 1830. Vol. 1. http://hansard.millbanksystems.com/lords/1830/nov/22/ministerial-declarations. Accessed July 5, 2013.

Hapgood, Lynne. *Margins of Desire: The Suburbs in Fiction and Culture 1880–1925*. New York: Manchester University Press, 2005.

Hardin, Garrett. "The Tragedy of the Commons." *Science* 162.3859 (1968): 1243–48.

Hardt, Michael, and Antonio Negri. *Commonwealth*. Cambridge, MA: Harvard University Press, 2009.

———. *Empire*. Cambridge, MA: Harvard University Press, 2000.

———. *Multitude: War and Democracy in the Age of Empire*. New York: Penguin, 2004.

Hardy, Barbara. *The Novels of George Eliot: A Study in Form*. London: Athlone Press, 1963.

Hardy, Thomas. *The Collected Letters of Thomas Hardy, 1893–1901*. Vol. 2. Ed. Richard L. Purdy and Michael Millgate. Oxford, UK: Oxford University Press, 1980.

———. "The Dorsetshire Labourer." *Thomas Hardy's Public Voice: The Essays, Speeches, and Miscellaneous Prose*. Ed. Michael Millgate. Oxford, UK: Clarendon Press, 2001.

———. *Jude the Obscure*. New York: Penguin, 1998.

———*The Life and Work of Thomas Hardy*. Ed. Michael Millgate. New York: Macmillan, 1984.

———. *The Mayor of Casterbridge*. New York: W.W. Norton, 1977.

———. *The Return of the Native*. New York: Penguin, 1999.

———. *Tess of the d'Urbervilles*. London: Penguin, 1985.

———. *Thomas Hardy: Selected Poems*. Ed. Tim Armstrong. London: Longman, 1993.

———. *Thomas Hardy: Selected Poetry and Non-Fictional Prose*. Ed. Peter Widdowson. London: Macmillan, 1997.

———. *Thomas Hardy's "Facts" Notebook: A Critical Edition*. Ed. William Greenslade. Burlington, VT: Ashgate, 2004.

———. *Under the Greenwood Tree*. New York: Penguin, 1998.

———. *The Woodlanders*. New York: Penguin, 1998.

Harney, Stefano, and Fred Moten. *The Undercommons: Fugitive Planning and Black Study*. Brooklyn, NY: Minor Compositions, 2013.

Harvey, David. "*Commonwealth*: An Exchange." *Artforum International* 48.3 (2009): 210–62.

———. *The New Imperialism*. New York: Oxford University Press, 2003.

Haughton, Hugh. "Progress and Rhyme: The 'Nightingale's Nest' and Romantic Poetry." *John Clare in Context*, eds. Hugh Haughton, Adam Phillips, and Geoffrey Summerfield. Cambridge, UK: Cambridge University Press, 1994.

Haughton, Hugh, Adam Phillips, and Geoffrey Summerfield, eds. *John Clare in Context*. Cambridge, UK: Cambridge University Press, 1994.

Hensley, Nathan K. "Environment." *Victorian Literature and Culture* 46.3–4 (Fall/Winter 2018): 676–81.

———. *Forms of Empire: The Poetics of Victorian Sovereignty*. New York: Oxford University Press, 2016.

Hensley, Nathan K., and Philip Steer. "Introduction: Ecological Formalism; or, Love Among the Ruins." *Ecological Form: System and Aesthetics in the Age of Empire*. Ed. Nathan K. Hensley and Philip Steer. New York: Fordham University Press, 2018.

Hill, Christopher. *The Century of Revolution 1603–1714*. New York: Routledge, 1980.

*The Historic Gallery of Portraits and Paintings, and Biographical Review*. London: Vernor, Hood and Sharpe, 1810.

Hitchens, Christopher. "In Defense of *Daniel Deronda*." *Threepenny Review* 39 (1989): 9–12.

Hobsbawm, Eric. *The Age of Capital: 1848–1875*. New York: Vintage, 1975.

———. *The Age of Empire: 1875–1914*. New York: Vintage, 1989.

———. "Introduction." *The Communist Manifesto*. New York: Verso, 1998.

Hobsbawm, Eric, and George Rudé. *Captain Swing*. New York: W.W. Norton, 1975.

Hughes, Linda K., and Michael Lund. *The Victorian Serial*. Charlottesville: University of Virginia Press., 1991.

Hughes, Robert. *The Fatal Shore: The Epic of Australia's Founding*. New York: Vintage, 1988.

Jaffe, Audrey. *The Victorian Novel Dreams of the Real: Conventions and Ideology*. New York: Oxford University Press, 2016.

[James, Henry]. "*Our Mutual Friend*," *The Nation* (December 21, 1865): 786–87.

Jameson, Fredric. "Cognitive Mapping." *Marxism and the Interpretation of Culture*. Ed. Cary Nelson and Lawrence Grossberg. Urbana: University of Illinois Press, 1988.

———. *The Geopolitical Aesthetic: Cinema and Space in the World System*. Bloomington: Indiana University Press, 1992.

———. *Jameson on Jameson: Conversations on Cultural Marxism*. Ed. Ian Buchanan. Durham, NC: Duke University Press, 2007.

———. "A New Reading of *Capital*." *Mediations* 25.1 (2010): 5–14.

———. *The Political Unconscious: Narrative as a Socially Symbolic Act*. Ithaca, NY: Cornell University Press, 1981.

———. "The Politics of Utopia." *New Left Review* 25 (2004): 35–54.

John, Juliet. *Dickens and Mass Culture*. New York: Oxford University Press, 2010.

Karl, Frederick. *George Eliot, Voice of a Century: A Biography*. New York: W.W. Norton, 1995.

# REFERENCES

Keen, Suzanne. *Victorian Renovations of the Novel: Narrative Annexes and the Boundaries of Representation*. New York: Cambridge University Press, 1998.

Kelley, D. G. "A Poetics of Anticolonialism." *Monthly Review* 51.6 (1999): 1–21.

Kincaid, James. *Annoying the Victorians*. New York: Routledge, 1995.

King, Amy M. "Dilatory Description and the Pleasures of Accumulation: Towards a History of Novelistic Length." *Narrative Middles: Navigating the Nineteenth-Century British Novel*. Ed. Caroline Levine and Mario Ortiz-Robles. Columbus: Ohio State University Press, 2011.

———. "Reorienting the Scientific Frontier: Victorian Tide Pools and Literary Realism." *Victorian Studies* 47.2 (Winter 2005): 153–63.

Klein, Naomi. "Reclaiming the Commons." *New Left Review* 9 (May/June 2001): 81–89.

Kluge, Alexander, and Oskar Negt. *History and Obstinacy*. Trans. Richard Langston. Cambridge, MA: MIT Press, 2014.

Knoepflmacher, U. C. *George Eliot's Early Novels: The Limits of Realism*. Berkeley: University of California Press, 1968.

Koehler, Karin. *Thomas Hardy and Victorian Communication: Letters, Telegrams and Postal Systems*. London: Palgrave Macmillan, 2016.

Kornbluh, Anna. *The Order of Forms: Realism, Formalism, and Social Space*. Chicago: University of Chicago Press, 2019.

———. *Realizing Capital: Financial and Psychic Economies in Victorian Form*. New York: Fordham University Press, 2014.

———. "We Have Never Been Critical: Toward the Novel as Critique." *Novel: A Forum on Fiction* 50.3 (2017): 397–408.

Koven, Seth. *The Matchgirl and the Heiress*. Princeton, NJ: Princeton University Press, 2014.

Kreilkamp, Ivan. "Pitying the Sheep in *Far from the Madding Crowd*." *Novel: A Forum on Fiction* 42.3 (2009): 474–81.

Kurnick, David. "Unspeakable George Eliot." *Victorian Literature and Culture* 38.2 (September 2010): 489–509.

Lamb, Jonathan. "The Implacability of Things." *Public Domain Review*, 2012. https://publicdomainreview.org/2012/10/03/the-implacability-of-things. Accessed August 9, 2020.

———. *The Things Things Say*. Princeton, NJ: Princeton University Press, 2016.

Langert, Christina Bosco. "Hedgerows and Petticoats: Sartorial Subversion and Anti-Enclosure Protest in Seventeenth-Century England." *Early Theatre* 12.1 (2009): 119–35.

Langland, Elizabeth. *Telling Tales: Gender and Narrative Form in Victorian Literature and Culture*. Columbus: Ohio State University Press, 2002.

Ledger, Sally. *Dickens and the Popular Radical Imagination*. New York: Cambridge University Press, 2007.

Lees, Lynn Hollen. *The Solidarities of Strangers: The English Poor Laws and the People, 1700–1948.* New York: Cambridge University Press, 1998.

Lesjak, Carolyn. "All or Nothing: Reading Franco Moretti Reading." *Historical Materialism* 24.3 (2016): 185–205.

———. "Reading Dialectically." *Criticism* 55.2 (Spring 2013): 233–77.

———. *Working Fictions: A Genealogy of the Victorian Novel.* Durham, NC: Duke University Press, 2006.

Levine, Caroline. *Forms: Whole, Rhythm, Hierarchy, Network.* Princeton, NJ: Princeton University Press, 2015.

Levine, Caroline, and Mario Ortiz-Robles, eds. *Narrative Middles: Navigating the Nineteenth-Century British Novel.* Columbus: Ohio State University Press, 2011.

Levine, George. *Realism, Ethics and Secularism: Essays on Victorian Literature and Science.* Cambridge, UK: Cambridge University Press, 2008.

Linebaugh, Peter. "Enclosures from the Bottom Up." *Radical History Review* 108 (Fall 2010): 11–27.

———. *The Magna Carta Manifesto: Liberties and Commons for All.* Berkeley: University of California Press, 2008.

———. *Stop, Thief! The Commons, Enclosures, and Resistance.* Oakland, CA: PM Press, 2014.

Litvak, Joseph. "Vulgarity, Stupidity, and Worldliness in *Middlemarch*." *Victorian Vulgarity: Taste in Verbal and Visual Culture*, eds. Susan David Bernstein and Elsie B. Michie. Burlington, VT: Ashgate, 2009.

Lloyd, William Foster. *Two Lectures on the Checks to Population.* Oxford, UK: Oxford University Collection, 1833. https://archive.org/details/twolecturesonchoolloygoog. Accessed August 9, 2020.

Locke, John. *Second Treatise of Government.* Ed. C. B. Macpherson. Indianapolis: Hackett, 1980.

Lodge, David. "The Making of 'George Eliot': *Scenes of Clerical Life*." *The Year of Henry James; or, Timing Is All: The Story of a Novel.* London: Harvill Secker, 2006.

Lowman, Emma Battell, and Adam J. Barker. *Settler: Identity and Colonialism in 21st Century Canada.* Winnipeg, MB: Fernwood, 2015.

Lukács, Georg. *History and Class Consciousness: Studies in Marxist Dialectics.* Trans. Rodney Livingstone. Boston: MIT Press, 1972.

———. "Narrate or Describe?" *Essays on Realism*, ed. Rodney Livingstone. Boston: MIT Press, 1983.

———. *Studies in European Realism.* Trans. Edith Bone. New York: Grosset & Dunlap, 1964.

Lupton, Christina. *Knowing Books: The Consciousness of Mediation in Eighteenth-Century Britain.* Philadelphia: University of Pennsylvania Press, 2011.

Lynch, Deidre. *The Economy of Character: Novels, Market Culture, and the*

*Business of Inner Meaning*. Chicago: University of Chicago Press, 1998.
MacCormack, Justin. "ART. II.—ROMOLA." *The Westminster Review* 24.2 (October 1863): 344–52. *British Periodicals*.
MacDuffie, Allen. "Charles Darwin and the Victorian Pre-History of Climate Denial." *Victorian Studies* 60.4 (2018): 543–64.
———. *Victorian Literature, Energy, and the Ecological Imagination*. Cambridge, UK: Cambridge University Press, 2014.
Macpherson, C. B. *The Political Theory of Possessive Individualism: Hobbes to Locke*. Oxford, UK: Clarendon Press, 1962.
Malcolm, Robert, ed. *Curiosities of Biography, or, Memoirs of Wonderful and Extraordinary Characters*. London: Richard Griffen and Co., 1855.
Malm, Andreas. *Fossil Capital: The Rise of Steam Power and the Roots of Global Warming*. New York: Verso, 2016.
Malthus, Thomas Robert. *An Essay on the Principle of Population*. 2nd Ed. Ed. Philip Appleman. New York: W.W. Norton, 2004.
Mann, Geoff, and Joel Wainwright. *Climate Leviathan: A Political Theory of Our Planetary Future*. New York: Verso, 2018.
Martell, Jessica. "The Dorset Dairy, the Pastoral, and Thomas Hardy's *Tess of the d'Urbervilles*." *Nineteenth-Century Literature* 68.1 (June 2013): 64–89.
Marx, Karl. *Capital*. Vol. I. Trans. Ben Fowkes. New York: Vintage, 1976.
———. *Capital*. Vol. III. Trans. David Fernbach. New York: Penguin, 1981.
———. *Surveys from Exile. Political Writings: Volume 2*. New York: Penguin, 1992.
Marx, Karl, and Frederick Engels. *The Communist Manifesto*. New York: Verso, 1998.
McCabe, Colin. "Realism and the Cinema." *Tracking the Signifier*. Minneapolis: University of Minnesota Press, 1985.
McKusik, James C. *Green Writing: Romanticism and Ecology*. New York: Palgrave Macmillan, 2010.
Meadowsong, Zena. "Thomas Hardy and the Machine: The Mechanical Deformation of Narrative Realism in *Tess of the d'Urbervilles*." *Nineteenth-Century Literature* 64.2 (2009): 225–48.
Menke, Richard. *Telegraphic Realism: Victorian Fiction and Other Information Systems*. Stanford, CA: Stanford University Press, 2007.
Michie, Helena, and Ronald R. Thomas, eds. *Nineteenth-Century Geographies: The Transformation of Space from the Victorian Age to the American Century*. New Brunswick, NJ: Rutgers University Press, 2002.
Midnight Notes Collective. "Introduction to the New Enclosures." *Midnight Notes* 10 (1990). http://www.midnightnotes.org/newenclos.html. Accessed August 9, 2020.
Mill, J. S. *On Liberty*. New York: W.W. Norton, 1975.
Miller, Andrew H. *Novels Behind Glass: Commodity Culture and Victorian Narrative*. Cambridge, UK: Cambridge University Press, 1995.

Miller, Elizabeth Carolyn. "Dendrography and Ecological Realism." *Victorian Studies* 58.4 (Summer 2016): 696–718.
Miller, J. Hillis. *Charles Dickens: The World of His Novels*. Cambridge, MA: Harvard University Press, 1958.
Miller, John MacNeill. "Mischaracterizing the Environment: Hardy, Darwin, and the Art of Ecological Storytelling." *Texas Studies in Literature and Language* 62.2 (Summer 2020): 149–77.
Millgate, Michael. *Thomas Hardy: A Biography Revisited*. New York: Oxford University Press, 2004.
Moore, Jason W. *Capitalism in the Web of Life: Ecology and the Accumulation of Capital*. New York: Verso, 2015.
Moretti, Franco. *Atlas of the European Novel 1800–1900*. New York: Verso, 1999.
"Mr. Dickens's Romance of a Dust-Heap." *Eclectic and Congregational Review* 9 (November 1865): 455–76.
Neeson, J. M. *Commoners: Common Right, Enclosure and Social Change in England, 1700–1820*. Cambridge, UK: Cambridge University Press, 1993.
Nef, John U. *The Rise of the British Coal Industry*. Hamden, CT: Archon, 1966.
Nixon, Rob. *Slow Violence and the Environmentalism of the Poor*. Cambridge, MA: Harvard University Press, 2011.
Nord, Deborah Epstein. *Gypsies and the British Imagination, 1807–1930*. New York: Columbia University Press, 2006.
Ostrom, Elinor. *Governing the Commons: The Evolution of Institutions for Collective Action*. Cambridge, UK: Cambridge University Press, 2015.
Parks, Tim. "Bitten by an Adder." *London Review of Books* 36.4 (July 2014): 8–12.
Pindar, Paul. *Remarkable Biography; or, The Peculiarities and Eccentricities of the Human Character Displayed*. London: H. Rowe, 1821.
Pite, Ralph. *Hardy's Geography: Wessex and the Regional Novel*. New York: Palgrave Macmillan, 2002.
Plietzsch, Birgit. *The Novels of Thomas Hardy as a Product of Nineteenth-Century Social, Economic, and Cultural Change*. Berlin: Tenea Verlag., 2004.
Plotz, John. *Portable Property: Victorian Culture on the Move*. Princeton, NJ: Princeton University Press, 2010.
———. *Semi-Detached: The Aesthetics of Virtual Experience Since Dickens*. Princeton, NJ: Princeton University Press, 2017.
Polanyi, Karl. *The Great Transformation: The Political and Economic Origins of Our Time*. Boston: Beacon Press, 2001.
Powers, Richard. *The Overstory*. New York: W.W. Norton, 2018.
Prendergast, Christopher. *The Order of Mimesis*. Cambridge, UK: Cambridge University Press, 1988.
Price, Leah. *How to Do Things with Books in Victorian Britain*. Princeton, NJ: Princeton University Press, 2012.

# REFERENCES

Purdy, Jedediah. *This Land Is Our Land: The Struggle for a New Commonwealth.* Princeton, NJ: Princeton University Press, 2019.

R. S. Kirby's *Wonderful and Eccentric Museum; or, Magazine of Remarkable Characters, Including All the Curiosities of Nature and Art, From the Remotest Period to the Present Time, Drawn from Every Authentic Source.* London: R.S. Kirby, 1820.

Reed, John R. Review of *Impressions of Theoprastus Such.* Ed. Nancy Henry. *Criticism* 38.1 (Winter 1996): 169–71.

Reid, Fred. "The Dorsetshire Labourer." *Thomas Hardy in Context.* Ed. Phillip Mallett. Cambridge, UK: Cambridge University Press, 2013.

"Reviews—*Our Mutual Friend.*" *Saturday Review* (November 11, 1865): 612–13.

Richards, Thomas. *The Commodity Culture of Victorian England: Advertising and Spectacle 1851–1914.* Stanford, CA: Stanford University Press, 1990.

Riquelme, John Paul, ed. *Tess of the d'Urbervilles.* Boston: Bedford/St. Martins, 1998.

Robbins, Bruce. "The Cosmopolitan Eliot." *A Companion to George Eliot.* Ed. Amanda Anderson and Harry E. Shaw. New York: John Wiley & Sons, 2013.

———. "Introduction Part I: Actually Existing Cosmopolitanism." *Cosmopolitics: Thinking and Feeling Beyond the Nation.* Ed. Pheng Cheah and Bruce Robbins. Minneapolis: University of Minnesota Press, 1998.

———. "On Amanda Anderson's *The Way We Argue Now.*" *Mediations* 24, no. 2 (2009): 265–74.

———. *The Servant's Hand: English Fiction from Below.* Durham, NC: Duke University Press, 1993.

Rosenman, Ellen. "On Enclosure Acts and the Commons." *BRANCH: Britain, Representation and Nineteenth-Century History.* Ed. Dino Franco Felluga. Extension of *Romanticism and Victorianism on the Net.* http://www.branchcollective.org/?ps_articles=ellen-rosenman-on-enclosure-acts-and-the-commons. Accessed August 10, 2020.

Ross, Kristin. *Communal Luxury: The Political Imaginary of the Paris Commune.* New York: Verso, 2015.

Roth, Marco. "Letters of Resignation from the American Dream." *Occupy! Scenes from Occupied America.* Ed. Astra Taylor, Keith Cassen, et al. New York: Verso, 2011.

Ryan, Alan. *J. S. Mill.* New York: Routledge, 1974.

Saville, Julia F. "Eccentricity as Englishness in *David Copperfield.*" *Studies in English Literature 1500–1900* 42.4 (2002): 781–97.

Scarry, Elaine. *Resisting Representation.* Oxford, UK: Oxford University Press, 1994.

Scholl, Lesa. *Hunger Movements in Early Victorian Literature: Want, Riots, Migration.* New York: Routledge, 2016.

Sedgwick, Eve Kosofsky. *Touching Feeling: Affect, Pedagogy, Performativity.* Durham, NC: Duke University Press, 2003.
Sen, Sambudha. *London, Radical Culture, and the Making of the Dickensian Aesthetic.* Columbus: Ohio State University Press, 2012.
Shaw, Harry E. *Narrating Reality: Austen, Scott, Eliot.* Ithaca, NY: Cornell University Press, 1999.
Sicher, Efraim. "Acts of Enclosure: The Moral Landscape of Dickens' *Hard Times.*" *Dickens Studies Annual* 22 (1993): 195–216.
Sinclair, Iain. *Edge of the Orison: In the Traces of John Clare's 'Journey Out of Essex'.* New York: Penguin, 2006.
Sitwell, Edith. *The English Eccentrics: A Gallery of Weird and Wonderful Men and Women.* London: Penguin, 1971 [1933].
Smeed, J. W. *The Theophrastan Character: The History of a Literary Genre.* Oxford, UK: Oxford University Press, 1985.
Smith, Grahame. *Dickens and the Dream of Cinema.* Manchester, UK: Manchester University Press, 2003.
Snell, K. D. M. *Parish and Belonging: Community, Identity, and Welfare in England and Wales, 1700–1950.* Cambridge, UK: Cambridge University Press, 2006.
Staten, Henry. "Is *Middlemarch* Ahistorical?" *PMLA* 115.3 (October 2000): 991–1005.
Stengers, Isabelle. *In Catastrophic Times: Resisting the Coming Barbarism.* Trans. Andrew Goffey. London: Open Humanities Press, 2015.
Stewart, Susan. *On Longing: Narratives of the Miniature, the Gigantic, the Souvenir, the Collection.* Durham, NC: Duke University Press, 1993.
Stocking, George W., ed. *Objects and Others: Essays on Museums and Material Culture.* Madison: University of Wisconsin Press, 1985.
Storey, Mark. *John Clare: A Critical Introduction.* London: Macmillan, 1974.
Taylor, Jesse Oak. *The Sky of Our Manufacture: The London Fog in British Fiction from Dickens to Woolf.* Charlottesville: University of Virginia Press, 2016.
Thackeray, W. M. "Jerome Paturot; With Considerations on Novels in General." *Complete Works.* Vol. 25. New York: Harper and Brothers, 1903.
Thompson, E. P. *The Making of the English Working Class.* New York: Vintage, 1966.
———. *The Romantics: England in a Revolutionary Age.* New York: New Press, 1997.
Trollope, Anthony. *The Way We Live Now.* New York: Penguin, 1994.
Tucker, Herbert F. "In the Event of a Second Reform." *BRANCH: Britain, Representation and Nineteenth-Century History.* Ed. Dino Franco Felluga. Extension of *Romanticism and Victorianism on the Net.* http://www.branchcollective.org/?ps_articles=herbert-f-tucker-on-event. Accessed August 10, 2020.
Tucker, Robert C., ed. *The Marx-Engels Reader.* 2nd Ed. New York: W.W. Norton, 1972.

Turner, Michael. *English Parliamentary Enclosure: Its Historical Geography and Economic History.* Hamden, CT: Archon, 1980.
Underdown, David. "Popular Politics Before the Civil War." *Reformation to Revolution: Politics and Religion in Early Modern England.* Ed. Margo Todd. New York: Routledge, 1995.
Uglow, Jennifer. *George Eliot.* London: Virago Press, 1987.
Van Ghent, Dorothy. *The English Novel: Form and Function.* New York: Holt, Rinehart and Winston, 1953.
Vrettos, Athena. "Defining Habits: Dickens and the Psychology of Repetition," *Victorian Studies* 42.3 (2000): 399–426.
Wall, Derek. *The Commons in History: Culture, Conflict, and Ecology.* Cambridge, MA: MIT Press, 2014.
Waters, Catherine. *Commodity Culture in Dickens's* Household Words: *The Social Life of Goods.* Burlington, VT: Ashgate, 2008.
Weber, Max. *The Protestant Ethic and the Spirit of Capitalism.* Trans. Talcott Parsons. London: Unwin Hyman, 1930.
Weeks, Kathi. *The Problem with Work: Feminism, Marxism, Antiwork Politics, and Postwork Imaginaries.* Durham, NC: Duke University Press, 2011.
Wegner, Phillip E. *Invoking Hope: Theory and Utopia in Dark Times.* Minneapolis: University of Minnesota Press, 2020.
Whipple, Edwin P. "The Genius of Dickens." *Atlantic Monthly* 19 (May 1867): 546–54.
Widdowson, Peter. *On Thomas Hardy: Late Essays and Earlier.* New York: St. Martin's Press, 1998.
Wihl, Gary. "Republican Liberty in George Eliot's *Romola.*" *Criticism* 51.2 (2009): 247–62.
Williams, Raymond. *The Country and the City.* New York: Oxford University Press, 1973.
———. *The English Novel: From Dickens to Lawrence.* New York: Oxford University Press, 1970.
———. *Keywords: A Vocabulary of Culture and Society.* New York: Oxford University Press, 1983.
———. *The Long Revolution.* New York: Penguin, 1984.
———. *Writing in Society.* London: Verso, 1985.
Wilson, G. H. *The Eccentric Mirror: Reflecting a Faithful and Interesting Delineation of Male and Female Characters, Ancient and Modern, Collected and Re-Collected, From the Most Authentic Sources.* London: J. Cundee, 1807.
Wilson, Henry, and James Caulfield. *The Book of Wonderful Characters: Memoirs and Anecdotes of Remarkable and Eccentric Persons in All Ages and Countries.* London: Reeves and Turner, 1869 [reprint; original 1829].
Witemeyer, Hugh. *George Eliot and the Visual Arts.* New Haven, CT: Yale University Press, 1979.

Woloch, Alex. *The One vs. the Many: Minor Characters and the Space of the Protagonist in the Novel.* Princeton, NJ: Princeton University Press, 2003.

Wood, Ellen Meiksins. *Empire of Capital.* New York: Verso, 2005.

Wright, John. *A Natural History of the Hedgerow: and Ditches, Dykes and Dry Stone Walls.* London: Profile, 2016.

Young, Phoebe S. K. "'Bring Tent': The Occupy Movement and the Politics of Public Nature." *Rendering Nature: Animals, Bodies, Places, Politics.* Ed. Marguerite S. Shaffer and Phoebe S. K. Young. Philadelphia: University of Pennsylvania Press, 2015.

Žižek, Slavoj. *Enjoy Your Symptom! Jacques Lacan in Hollywood and Out.* New York: Routledge, 2001.

———. *In Defense of Lost Causes.* New York: Verso, 2008.

# Index

Note: page numbers in italics refer to figures. Those followed by n refer to notes, with note number.

Ablow, Rachel, 207n32
Adam Bede (Eliot): Arthur's guilt in, 102–3; common characters in, 8, 100, 101–4; commons envisioned by, as radical transformation, 101–3; dialectical relation of local with global in, 195n5; Dinah Morris's preaching on Hayslope Green, 106, *107*; echoes of Wordsworth in, 96; on Eliot's realism, 94, 95; on enclosure, 101–4, 186n35; enclosure resistance in, 173; Hetty's fate, class overtones of, 102; and manufacturing district as new common, 106; materiality of character in, 103; Mrs. Poyser's rebuttal of Squire in, 101–2, 104; narrative pause in, 94, 195–96n7; outsiders in, and yearning for cosmopolitanism, 111–12; web of indebtedness in, 103, 104
Adorno, Theodor, 12, 83, 165, 166–67, 209n45
afterlife of enclosure: in Hardy, 135–36, 140–44, 146–47, 148; in indirect representations of enclosure, 11; suburbs and, 21
afterlife of enclosure resistance, 3–4, 6, 11

afterlife of utopian spirit in British realism, 3, 11, 13
agricultural workers, importance to reform, 186n35
Anderson, Amanda, 109, 175–76n5, 193n36, 199n22
Armstrong, Isobel, 2, 175n4, 176n6, 200n28
Auerbach, Erich, 84–85, 194n45, 194n56, 204n13

Bacon, Francis, 23, 52
Balzac, Honoré de, 74–75, 92, 192n34
Bate, Jonathan, 10, 17, 37, 177n16, 185n32
Beaumont, Matthew, 67, 195n5
Beer, Gillian, 110–11, 153, 165, 207–8n37
Benjamin, Walter, 1, 3
Bennett, Arnold, 84–85
Bleak House (Dickens): call for readers' action in, 82–83; constraints of current order in, 76–79; cover of, profusion of characters in, 67, 68; publication in *Frederick Douglass' Paper*, 186–87n3; repetition in, 76, 191n28
Bollier, David, 7, 32, 43, 183n20, 183n21

227

*The Book of Wonderful Characters*
  (Wilson and Caulfield), 52, 53,
  54, 55, 57, 59, 62–63, 188n14
bottom-up history, 1–2, 28, 171–72
Boumelha, Penny, 155, 168, 209n46
Bowlby, Rachel, 2, 104, 175n3
Bresnihan, Patrick, 37–38, 184n30
British Empire, legacy of, 40–41
Brooks, Jean R., 207n34
Brundage, Anthony, 33–34, 184n25
Butler, Judith, 65–66, 189n16,
  190n23

"Candour in English Fiction"
  (Hardy), 209n44
capital, workers' right to reclaim, 30
*Capital I* (Marx), 21–24
capitalism: centrality of land in,
  173; constitutive violence of, 7–
  8, 176–77n13; and destruction
  of commons, 6, 176n11;
  globalization, and real *vs.* visible,
  131; green, as class fantasy,
  173–74; industrial, and climate
  change, as intertwined, 40–42,
  180n6; mapping of global system
  of, as representational problem,
  126; modern relevance of realist
  concerns about, 14; necessity of
  resistance to, 178n22; resistance
  to, feminists and, 29; violence of,
  in history of enclosure, 26
Carlyle, Thomas, 188n12
Caulfield, James, 53, 54, 55, 57, 59,
  61–63, 187n7, 199n14
character, as material: in Dickens,
  12, 188n13; in eccentric
  biographies, 51, 54, 197–98n15;
  in Eliot, 4–5, 92, 94, 98–99, 103,
  112–13, 120; Mill on, 50–51
character books/characteristic
  writing. *See* eccentric biographies
character portrayals: in eighteenth
century, as about quantity rather
  than quality, 69; turn from focus
  on legibility to distinction, 69–70
*Characters* (Caulfield), 54, 187n7
*Characters* (Theophrastus), 122
*Characters* (Wilson), 187n7
character types in realism, 11–
  12; as embrace of equivalent
  selves, 5, 12–13, 178n20; as
  expression of common, 98–
  99, 135; flat *vs.* round, 11–
  12, 47, 177–78n18; need for
  understanding contemporary
  views on, 47; nineteenth-century
  critics' comfort with, 47; origin
  in eighteenth-century eccentric
  biographies, 12, 47–48. *See
  also* Dickens, Charles; eccentric
  biographies; Eliot, George;
  Hardy, Thomas
Charter of the Forest, 29–30, 151
Chesterton, G. K., 79–80, 83, 85
*A Child's History of England*
  (Dickens), 186n1
China, urbanization in, 15, 178n1
*A Christmas Carol* (Dickens), 33,
  189n18
Christophers, Brett, 176n12
*Chrysal, or the Adventures of a
  Guinea* (Johnstone), 95, 98,
  196n9
Clare, John: alternative epistemology
  of, 17, 36; critique of enclosure,
  38–39; different form of
  identity in, 40; Eliot and, 90; on
  enclosure, 10, 17, 25, 177n16;
  and future commons, 39–40,
  184–85n31; "Helpstone Green,"
  38; "Helpstone," 38; on joys
  of common life, 36–38, 42–43;
  "The Lament of Swordy Well,"
  38–39; life of, 184n28, 184n30;
  "The Moors," 37, 38, 39; politics

of commons in, 39–40; and
possibilities of commons, 39–40;
"The Village Minstrel," 36–37,
184n29
class consciousness, Occupy
movement and, 6
climate change: effects of, as
attritional catastrophe, 7; and
enclosure on global scale, as
intertwined, 40–42, 180n6;
and global significance of local,
163; and modern relevance of
realist concerns, 14; necessity of
resistance to, 178n22
Cobbett, William, 10, 19–21, 25, 28,
81–82, 180n7, 180n8
Cohen, William A., 163, 165, 203n9
colonialism/imperialism: and
climate change, as intertwined,
40–42, 180n6; and enclosure
and deforestation, 16; and
teleological view of history, 11;
and *terra nullius* doctrine, 11,
31–32, 182n16, 210n2
common characters: depiction of
commons through, 3; and pejorative
senses of commonness, 8
commonness: associations with,
196n8
common rights: current relevance of,
30; loss of, with enclosure, 6–7,
16–17, 22–23, 176n12, 180n9;
need for reassertion of, 30;
and political rights, connection
between, 29–30
commons/common: alternative
worldview envisioned by,
16–17; ambivalent terms
used to describe, 177n15; in
British realist novels, 2, 3,
13, 178n21; Clare on joys of,
36–38, 42–43; desire for, as
more than nostalgia, 5, 29;

181–82n14; Diggers' defense
of, 173; enclosure as antonym
of, 1; and English Poor Laws,
177n17; eradication of memory
of, through enclosure, 42–
43; etymology of, 8, 177n14;
everyday life and, 85, 194n45;
future of, 7, 9, 13, 29, 39–40,
43, 174, 184–85n31, 193n38;
invisibility to modern view, 7;
loss of, 5, 6–7, 28–29; provisions
for management of, 184nn26–27;
rights of usufruct and estover,
184n26; and sociality, 28; terms
for, 187–88n9; in Woolf, 85. See
*also under* Dickens, Charles;
Eliot, George; Hardy, Thomas
commonwealth ideal, 9; narrow *vs.*
expansive views of, 113, 200–
201n29; as ongoing project, 9
*Communal Luxury* (Ross), 3
Corbould, Edward Henry, 106, *107*
cosmopolitanism: as always
imperfect, 113; definition of,
112–13; Eliot and, 110–13,
121–22, 126, 199n23, 199n24,
200n26; existence in nineteenth
century, 8, 110, 177n15
*The Country and the City*
(Williams), 18–19, 44, 94, 100,
104, 106, 128–29, 180–81n10
countryside, English, disappearance
of, 15–16, *16*
Cowper, William, 95–96, 196n10
Crary, Jonathan, 182–83n19, 203n5
Cruikshank, George, 15–16, *16*, 81

Dallas, E. S., 46, 187n5
Dancer, Daniel, 48, 52, 54–56, *57*
*Daniel Deronda* (Eliot): character
types in, 120, 124, 197–98n15;
and commonwealth ideal, 113,
200–201n29; Deronda's narrow

nationalism and, 199n24;
Eliot on interrelatedness of all
parts of, 109–10; and Eliot's
discomfort with commonness,
94–95; globalization as backdrop
of, 110; on one's gain as loss
by another, 121, 199–200n25;
outsiders in, and yearning for
cosmopolitanism, 111–12;
"philosophers" meeting at Hand
and Banner, as debate on social
change, 120–21, 200n28; on
realism, and changing conditions,
97; on social change, necessity
of, 121
Darwin, Charles, 165, 186n37
Davis, Mike, 15, 40, 44, 175n1,
178n1, 209n42
Defoe, Daniel, 33, 180n7
Dickens, Charles: aggregate of
social determinants in novels of,
75; celebration of eccentricity
within collective, 63; characters
in, 44, 45–47, 48–49, 66–
69; character types in, 12, 44,
47–48, 65–67, 75, 84, 187n8;
cinematic effects in, 191–92n31;
and common, 48–49, 66–69,
173; common characters, work
against pejorative view of, 8;
constraints of current order in,
75–81, 82; on contemporary
hostility to imagination, 188n12;
disease as common in, 77; and
divide of high and low culture,
transcending of, 81; and eccentric
biographies, 48–49, 64–65,
187n7, 190n24; on enclosure,
3, 10, 76, 186n1, 186n2; and
equivalent selves, embrace of, 13;
on global commons, 8–9;
habit-obsessed characters in,
189n17; imagination of, as
dialectical, 193n38; importance
of city and crowds to, 44, 67,
190–91n26; and individualism,
challenge to, 5–6; influence on
large audience as goal of, 49;
as literature of protest, 82; and
melodramatic mode, 81–82,
193–94n43; on misers, imbalance
of subjects and objects in, 56;
moral universe of, vs. Eliot's, 88–
90, 91–92; and new culture of
commons, 7, 44, 49–50, 66–67,
80, 84, 85–86, 188n10, 193n38,
193n39; new subject inseparable
from the collective as goal of,
60; novels of, as both too real
and too pleasant, 86; ongoing
engagement with enclosure, 10;
optimism about possibilities, 74;
on politics, 74, 80, 81–82, 91–
92; on politics of commons, 78;
popularity of, 49; radical content
in materialist view of character,
188n13; readers of, familiarity
with eccentric biographies, 61;
repetition in, 70–71, 191n28,
191n30; reputation of, 47;
sentimentalism of, 81; and social
unity, as ongoing challenge, 5–
6; on social utopia, 13; sources
of inspiration for, 67–69,
187n6; structural critique and
call to action in, 82–84; and
subject, rethinking of, 58; and
subject-object relations, 58–60;
subjunctive mode in, 49–50, 74,
80, 188n10; and synecdochal
linking of people and objects,
64–65; and typographical
culture of eighteenth century, 48,
66, 69–70, 178n20; unsettled
meaning of individual lives in,
87; utopian impulse in, 48–49,

73, 82–83, 86. *See also specific works*
Dienst, Richard, 101, 109
Diggers, 173
"Dinah Morris Preaching on the Common" (Corbould), 106, *107*
Dolin, Tim, 90–91, 96, 195n4, 198n16
*Dombey and Son* (Dickens), 67
Doody, Margaret Anne, 124, 200n26
"The Dorsetshire Labourer" (Hardy), 19, 127, 133, 204n16
Dunn, John, 182n18
Dvorak, Wilfred, 60–61
Dyck, Ian, 19
*The Dynasts* (Hardy), 127, 203n8

Eagleton, Terry, 5, 81, 88, 92, 98, 144, 161, 175n5, 193n40, 195n6
eccentric biographies, 50–63; celebration of eccentricity within collective, 63; character as collective and material in, 51, 52–54, 58–60, 197–98n15; characters in, as revivified through reification, 60, 63; and construction of self through repetition, 189n16; copies owned by Dickens, 48, 187n7; described, 48; Eliot and, 98; engraved portraits in, 51–52, *55*, *57*, *59*, *61*; familiarity of characters to public, 48; modern loss of individuality as theme in, 62–63; and museums, 52; notable titles, 188–89n14; and objectification, 52–54; origin of realist fiction character types in, 12, 47–48; popularity of, 60–61, 189–90n20, 190n22; and possibility of other social space, 60; preservation of individuality in, 54, 58–60; turn from focus on character legibility to distinction, 69; vignettes of eccentric characters in, 51–52, 54–56
eccentricity, as individuality, Mill on, 50–51
Eliot, George: on character, 92, 93, 95, 98–99, 103, 112–13; characters in, 8, 58, 65, 88, 98, 122–24; character types in, 12, 98–100, 104, 120–24, 139, 197–98n15, 201n32; on common, 5–6, 13, 88–89, 91, 93–100, 105–6, 121, 201n32; and commonness, 94–95, 100, 108; commonplace as focus of works, 94, 95, 100–101; commons envisioned by, 4–5, 7–9, 12, 13, 93, 101–5, 108–14, 121–24, 200n28; and cosmopolitanism, 110–13, 121–22, 199n23, 199n24, 200n26; on empathy with others, 91, 93–94, 96–98, 121, 179n5, 201n32; on enclosure, 3, 5, 10, 89–90, 91, 105–6; ethics in, 4–5, 12, 13, 89, 91, 93–94, 96–97, 100, 103; fictional world of, 89–91; on French Revolution, 105; and globalization, awareness of, 195n4; Ilfracombe journal, 88–89, 104, 195nn2–3; and individualism, 5–6, 98; and interpretations, effort to control, 89; and liberalism, 98, 199n22; on life as inescapably economic, 104–5; life of, 89–90; and local, dialectical relation with global, 91, 93, 97, 195n5; on misers, imbalance of subjects and objects in, 56–58; moral universe *vs.* Dickens's, 88–90, 91–92; narrative pauses in, 195–96n7; outsiders in, and yearning

for cosmopolitanism, 111–12, 200n26; on physical *vs.* social science, 197n12; on political, 91–93; politics of commons in, 106–9, 110, 114, 118, 119; precedents for, 95–96; and precise control of language, 88–89; realism of, 94, 95–97, 196–97n12, 197nn12–13; relevance to modern readers, 94; style of, 89, 92, 194–95n1, 195n3; *Westminster Review* essays, 194–95n1, 197n12; "Worldliness and Other-Worldliness," 95–96. *See also specific works*
enclosure, 20–21; advocates of, 31–36; and common rights, loss of, 6–7, 16–17, 22–23, 176n12, 180n9; commons as antonym of, 1; and concentration of land ownership, 183n20; contemporary critics of, 20–21, 38–39; and countryside, global disappearance of, 15–16; and depopulation of countryside, 20; and dialectical imagination, 167, 172–73; and difficulty of representation, 17, 22, 30–31; displacements in, 26; dissolution of Catholic monasteries and, 24; early informal process of, 21–22; effect of, as well known, 25–26; effect on both country and city, 18, 20; eighteenth century as turning point in, 22, 24; Gaskell on, 185n33; on global scale, 16, 40–42, 178n1, 180n6; and great houses of England, 180–81n10; and hedgerows, 132, 179n2; Henry VII's resistance to, 23; importance of local stories in, 25; and industrial capitalism, 20, 23; joint rural and urban workers' activism against, 20; later legal forms of, 22, 24; as long and complex, 7–8, 22, 25; *longue durée* of, 18–30; and market dependence of property rights, 24; Marx on, 21–22; as massive cultural change, 179n2; and memory of commons, eradication of, 42–43; and mineral rights, 41–42, 186n36; modern forms of, 172; multiple and diffuse effects, 7–8; new research on, 24–25; and new vision of future commons, 7, 29, 43; in nineteenth-century works, 9–11, 18; as not historically inevitable, 11, 28, 177n17, 181–82n14; old and new forms, similarities in, 173; as ongoing, 7, 18, 22; peak events within, 23–24, 25; percentage enclosed, 24; political ecology of, 164, 173, 209n42; realist authors as witness to, 5, 6–7; as redefinition of agrarian property, 22; resistance to, 3–4, 6, 11, 18, 25–28, 34, 137–38, 144–45, 171, 179n3, 181n12; as slow violence, 7, 22, 26, 128, 132; synchronic and diachronic analysis of, 25; and violence of capitalism, 26; as well documented, 25
enclosure of the self. *See* Hardy, enclosure of the self in
Engels, Frederick, 19–20
*The English Eccentrics* (Sitwell), 60, 188n14
environment, as term, 203n7
environmental battles, presaging of, in Hardy, 151–52, 162–63, 208n38
environmental crisis, as crisis of imagination and ideology, 164
environmental movements, as

INDEX

resistance to enclosure, 3–4

"Facts" notebook (Hardy): attention to detail in, 142; controversial nature of facts in, 204n15; on economic distress of countryside, 143–44; entries from *Dorset County Chronicle* in, 142–45; events from, used in novels, 146, 147–48; on forgery of relief passes, 144; Greenslade introduction to, 143; local noteworthy events recorded in, 145–46; mundane details recorded in, 141–42; record of Dorset as crime-ridden, 148; record of violence of enclosure in, 132, 134, 142; on sale of wives, 147; subtitle of, 142; on violent responses to economic change, 144–45

*Far From the Madding Crowd* (Hardy): closed village in, 125; events from "Facts" notebook used in, 146; reviews of, 206n29

Federici, Silvia: and common, collapse of personal and political in, 29; on common, and exclusion of groups, 201n29; on common, ethics informing, 13, 91, 157, 200n5; on common as social relations, 174; on Hardt and Negri's commons, 13, 178n21; on land, capitalist monetization of, 185–86n35; on rural unrest, 179–80n5; and women, importance of commons to, 28–29; on women's economic power, destruction of, 185n35

*Felix Holt* (Eliot): "Address to Working Men" in, 113–14; character types in, 197n15; incipient industrialization in, 90–91; local life in, influence of larger global politics on, 91; real-life political context of, 201n30

feminists, and resistance to capitalism, 29

Forster, E. M., 47, 177–78n18

Forster, John, 67, 86

*Fossil Capital* (Malm), 41–42, 186n36

fossil fuels, access to, through enclosure, 41–42

Freedgood, Elaine, 16, 89, 189n19

functionality, superseding of other relations in modern world, 166–167

Gaskell, Elizabeth, 9, 185n33, 192n35

Geikie, Archibald, 130, 203n10

Goodlad, Lauren, 2, 3, 110, 112, 131, 175n4, 175–76n5, 178n20, 185n34, 191n27, 201n31

*Great Expectations* (Dickens), constraints of current order in, 76, 193n36

green capitalism, as class fantasy, 173–74

Greenslade, William, 132, 143–147, 205n21, 206n24

Gregory, James, 52, 60, 190n21, 190n22

Hack, Daniel, 186–87n3, 199n24

Hardin, Garrett, 35–36, 38, 184n27

Hardt, Michael, 13, 99–100, 105, 117, 177n15, 178n21, 193n38

*Hard Times* (Dickens), 76, 77, 188n12

Hardy, Barbara, 106–8

Hardy, Emma, 141, 146, 147

Hardy, Thomas: on abstract realism, 129–30; on afterlife of enclosure in, 135–36, 140–41, 142–44,

233

146–47, 148; autobiography of, 125; on beauty in ugliness, 205n19; characters in, 136–37, 206n23; character types in, 12, 135–37, 139–40, 205n20; common characters in, 8, 135; and common humanity, commons implied by, 140; on commons, 5–9, 13–14, 126–28, 139–40, 161–62, 164–66, 170, 173; and convention, implacable force of, 168–69, 170; and deeper reality, portrayal of, 130; and effects of capitalism, difficulty of figuration, 126; on enclosure, 3, 125, 127, 128, 132–35, 141, 144, 147–52, 160, 164, 167; enclosure of the self in, 132, 153, 154–63, 164, 169; and equivalent selves, embrace of, 13; and facts, great interest in, 206n24; fatalism in, 160; geopolitical in, 126–27, 133–35, 140–41, 146–47, 163–64, 167, 202n3; human-landscape interactions in, 135, 151, 153, 163, 208–9n41, 208n38; on imagination's conditioning by surroundings, 209n44; and individualism, challenge to, 5–6; interconnectedness of place in, 130; land in, as animating feature of novels, 127; letters in, 157–60, 164, 166, 208n40; and modern environmental battles, presaging of, 152, 162–63, 208n38; on new human type, 167–68; on new work relations, and necessity of itinerancy, 127; on novelist's role, 205n20; "Preface to the Fifth and Later Editions," 133; and provincial novel, 127, 202–3n4; realism of, 127, 129–30, 162–64, 173–74, 204–5n18; and real *vs.* visible, 130–31; relevance to modern readers, 127–28; research on local life, 146; on rural laborers, 19, 179n4; on self-centeredness, 209n43; self in, 157–60, 161–62, 164–66; and subject-object relations, revision of, 164–65; and "sublime" as verb, 207n35; tactile ecology of, 163; typical and tragic, oscillation between, 127; universe in, as evidenced only figurally, 162; on utopian-emancipatory possibilities in, 127, 161, 170; on women, social pressure on, 204n17; on woodland commons, connection with Marx, 170; work in, visible and invisible forms of, 128–29; world of, as peripatetic, 134–35. *See also specific works*

Harvey, David, 105, 172, 209–10n1

hedgerows, and enclosure, 8, 132, 179n2

Hensley, Nathan K., 40–41, 175n1, 203n7

history; and real *vs.* visible, 131; teleological view of, 11, 177n17; writing of, 17–18

History Workshop, 1

Hitchens, Christopher, 110

Hobsbawm, Eric, 20, 126, 181n12

Hone, William, 81–82

*Household Words* (Dickens), 70, 189n19, 191n29

Huxley, T. H., 130, 203n10

*Impressions of Theophrastus Such* (Eliot), 122–24; critics' response to, 123, 201–2nn34–35; Henry's introduction to, 123; and materiality of character, 201–2n34; and Theophrastan

# INDEX

character types, 65, 122–24; title of, 123

Indigenous movements, and resistance to enclosure, 3, 32, 40, 172–73, 201n2

individuality, loss of: Mill on, 50–51; railroads and, 62; as theme in eccentric biographies, 54, 58–60, 62–63; Victorian concerns about, 51

itinerancy: modern forms of, 172; as norm in Hardy, 134–35, 172

James, Henry, 8, 46–47, 63, 87, 206n29

Jameson, Fredric: analysis of contemporary world system, 162; on cognitive mapping, 129; on collective struggle for freedom, 6; on effects of capitalism, difficulty of figuration, 126; on effort to imagine a different economic system, 161; on the geopolitical aesthetic, 131, 202n3; on problems of global economy, first impact of, 110; on representation of the collective, 187–88n9; on universal equality, 119–20; on utopian impulse, 80, 83, 161

John, Juliet, 49, 67, 82, 193n38

*Jude the Obscure* (Hardy): character types in, 135, 139; and contrast of real life *vs.* desired life, 139–40; on enclosure, helplessness of characters against, 134; enclosure of the self in, 154–55, 168–69, 170; and Jude and Sue, social constraints on, 154–55, 157, 168–69, 170, 209n46; and possession of others, 156–57, 169; on subject-object relations, 165; world of, as peripatetic, 134

Ket's Rebellion, 142, 186n1

Kincaid, James, 66–67, 86, 88

King, Amy, 195–96n7, 197n13

Kirby, R. S., 48, 54, 187n7, 190n22

Kluge, Alexander, 21

Knoepflmacher, U. C., 95, 100, 115–16

Kornbluh, Anna, 2, 3, 175n4, 193n37, 203–4n11

Kreilkamp, Ivan, 206n29

Kurnick, David, 199n24

labor, productive and reproductive, gendered division of, 28–29

Lacan, Jacques, 159–60

land: capitalist monetization of, 185–86n35; centrality in global capitalism, 173; importance in politics of commons, 172–74

Ledger, Sally, 81–82, 187n6

legal rights, economic foundation necessary for, 173

Levine, Caroline, 76, 192–93n35

liberalism: challenges to, in realist novels, 5; Eliot's alternatives to, 117–118; and realism, Eliot's disruption of pairing of, 94, 98, 199n22; reductive analyses of 175–76n5

*The Life and Work of Thomas Hardy* (Hardy), 125, 129–30, 202n1, 204–5n18, 205nn19–20

Linebaugh, Peter: on Clare, 17, 36, 204n14; on Cobbett, 180n7; on common rights, 29–30; demand to commonize city, 44; on enclosure, bottom-up history of, 1, 11; on enclosure, old and new, 173; on enclosure and fossil economy, 42; on links from commons to communism, 169–70; on Magna Carta, 182n15; on peaks in history of enclosure, 23–24; on politics of commons, usefulness of past to, 127–28; and resistance to enclosure, renewed focus on, 171

*Little Dorrit* (Dickens): constraints of current order in, 76, 77, 193n36; disease in, 77; repetition in, 191n28

*Lives and Anecdotes of Misers* (Merryweather), 48, 54–56, 58–61

Lloyd, William Foster, 34–35, 38

Locke, John, 5, 31–35, 38, 69–71, 132, 182–83nn18–19, 183n21, 210n2

"London Going Out of Town, or the March of Bricks & Mortar" (Cruikshank), 15–16, 16

*Lost Illusions* (Balzac), Lukács on, 74–75, 192n34

Lukács, Georg, 6, 12, 47, 60, 74–75, 92–93, 109, 176n11, 192n34, 205n20

Lynch, Deidre, 48, 60, 69–70, 189–90n20

MacDuffie, Allen, 33, 186n37

Machiavelli, Niccolo, 117–118, 201n31

Magna Carta, 29–30, 182n15

Malm, Andreas, 41–42, 186n36

Malthusianism, 32–35, 38, 83, 183n22

Martell, Jessica, 148, 206–7n31

*Martin Chuzzlewit* (Dickens), 65, 189

Marx, Karl: on Bacon's arguments against enclosure, 23; on capitalism's power to create world in its own image, 169; on collective struggle for freedom, 6; on enclosure and primitive accumulation, 21–23; on enclosure of the self, 162; on freeing of labor, 21; on material recalcitrance, 100–101; on rights of usufruct, 184n26; on rural laborers, 19–20; on unrest in agricultural workers, 181n13

*The Mayor of Casterbridge* (Hardy): character types in, 135, 139; enclosure of the self in, 155; events from "Facts" notebook used in, 147; Henchard's sale of wife in, 134, 147, 156; Henchard's will in, 166; letters in, 159–60, 166; Mixen Lane residents as refuse of new system, 136–37, 138–39; Mixen Lane skimmington, 137–39; shifting relationships in, 155, 208n39; and social pressure on women, 204n17; and subject-object relations, 164–65; work in, visibility of, 129; world of, as peripatetic, 134

McKusick, James C., 184–85n31

Merryweather, F. Somner, 48, 54–56, 58–62, 187n7

*Middlemarch* (Eliot): character in, materiality of, 12, 103; character types in, 12, 123–24; on common, empathy with others as basis of, 93, 99; and commonness, Eliot's discomfort with, 94–95; and commonness, rejection of, in future common, 108; and cosmopolitanism of readers, 199n23; discrepancy in urbanity between book and town, 110–11; ethics of equivalent selves (worldly ethics) in, 4–5, 12, 103; on interpretations, as limitless, 89; Ladislaw as counterpoint to Lydgate in, 109; and liberation from small self, as goal, 88; on life as inescapably economic, 104–5, 108, 198–99n21; outsiders in, and yearning for cosmopolitanism, 111; and pairing of liberalism with realism, 98; web of social obligation in, 109

Midnight Notes Collective, 135, 147, 172, 206n30

Mill, J. S., 50–51, 117, 124, 165, 188nn12–13, 189n16

Miller, Andrew, 104–5, 189n19

Miller, Elizabeth, 127, 153, 208n38

Millgate, Michael, 141, 146, 202n3

*The Mill on the Floss* (Eliot): character types in, 197n15; on common, empathy with others as basis of, 99; and common characters, creation of empathy for, 179n5; echoes of Wordsworth in, 96; and Eliot's discomfort with commonness, 94; focus on real and concrete in, 97; outsiders in, and yearning for cosmopolitanism, 111

*Mimesis* (Auerbach), 84–85

misers: in eccentric biographies, 54–56; misbalance of subjects and objects in, 56–58

modernism, Auerbach on, 84–85

Moretti, Franco, 81, 193n39, 193n41, 202n4

Neeson, J. M., 24, 26–28, 171, 179n3, 181n12

Negri, Antonio, 13, 99–100, 105, 117, 177n15, 178n21, 193n38

neoliberalism, and enclosure, 4, 26, 131, 172

new human type, emergence of, 166–68

*New Wonderful Museum*, 48, 60

*Nicholas Nickleby* (Dickens), 65, 189n18

nineteenth century, cultural and economic similarities to current times, 172

nineteenth-century novels: collective political aspirations in, 5, 176n6; democratic imagination in, 176n6; and resistance to enclosure, bottom-up history of, 171–72; as venue for considering alternative collective future, 171

Nixon, Rob, 7–8, 22, 26, 128, 132, 153

novels: and closure, 192–93n35; development, teleological model of, 65

Occupy movement: on 99%, 80; and creation of class consciousness, 6; as resistance to enclosure, 3, 163; history of, 176n9

*The Old Curiosity Shop* (Dickens): characters in, and eccentric biographies, 48–49, 65, 187n8; Thackeray on, 45, 49–50

*Oliver Twist* (Dickens): Chesterton's reading of, 80; constraints of current order in, 76. 79; cover of, profusion of characters on, 67; on forced mobility of poor, 183–84n24; melodrama in, 193–94n43; and poor children's loss of childhood, 194n44; social critique in, 83–84, 172

ontology, as common, 99–100

Ostrom, Elinor, 184n27

*Our Mutual Friend* (Dickens): accident as predominant in early books, 72; balance of subjects and objects in, 56; characters in, 48, 70–72, 73, 191n28; constraints of current order in, 77; cover of, profusion of characters on, 67; critics on characters in, 45–46, 187n5; inescapability of accidental and contingent in, 72, 192n32; mutually constitutive relationship of things and characters in, 74; Noddy Boffin in, 48, 54–56, 60–61, 69, 72–73; plots and ruses, accumulation of, 72; Postscript's conflation of Dickens and novel, 74; ruses as predominant in final book, 72–73; utopian possibilities opened up in, 73–74

Peterloo Massacre, 81

*The Pickwick Papers* (Dickens): as both pleasant and real, 86; celebration of fat in, 86; character types in, and eccentricity, 66–67; connection to others as essential in, 86–87; on politics, as encompassing everything, 91–92; references to eccentric biographies in, 64–65; Sam Weller's listing of inn guests by shoe type, 63–64

Pite, Ralph, 130, 203n10

political rights: and common rights, connection between, 29–30; economic foundation necessary for, 173

politics of the commons: in Clare, 39–40; current focus on, 3–4; in Dickens, 78; in Eliot, 106–9, 110, 114, 118, 119; and land, importance of, 172–74; and new vision of past, 127–28. *See also Romola*, politics of commons envisioned in

Poor Laws, English: collective perspective on, 177n17; efforts to exclude undeserving poor, 34; fear of overpopulation and, 33–34; historians' debate on, 183n23; and in-door *vs.* out-door relief, 183n23; and mobility of workers, control of, 24, 181n11

primitive accumulation: and attacks on commons, 34; British realism's attention to, 7–8; mineral rights and, 41–42, 186n36; as ongoing process, 21–22

Private Enclosure Act of 1791, protest against, 20

property as basis of status in Victorian England, 182n17

propertylessness: and forced mobility of poor, 183–84n24; state interventions to maintain system, 24, 34; as system, 76

property rights: Locke on, 31–32, 183n21; shaping of society by, 12, 23–24, 28, 31–2, 34, 38, 41–43, 76, 102, 152, 182n17; shifting of, in Hardy, 152

Queen Caroline Affair, 81

"Railway Waifs and Strays" (Dickens), 70, 191n29

realist novels, British: bottom-up literary history and, 1–2; criticisms of status quo in, 3; critiques of, 2, 175n2, 175–76n5; and disappearing commons, ability to comment on, 43; exposure of green capitalism as fantasy, 173–74; and liberalism, Eliot's disruption of pairing of, 98; and new culture of commons, work toward, 7, 43; and nostalgia about commons, avoidance of, 5, 29, 127–28, 152, 174; recent political accounts of, 2; reinvention of commons in, 5, 174; relevance of concerns in,

2, 14, 175n3; and ties between ordinary and the commons, 171; as venue for considering alternative collective future, 171–72; and Victorian geopolitical aesthetic, 110. *See also* character types in realism

reciprocity: in Dickens, of selves, 192n32; in Eliot, between characters and things, 95; as hallmark of new commons, 9; in Hardy, in human-landscape interactions, 135, 151, 153, 163, 208–9n41; in Hardy, of selves, 164

reproduction of everyday life, address of, in realist novels, 13, 178n21

*The Return of the Native* (Hardy): character types in, 135; on economic change, and extinction of livelihoods, 151; on enclosure, slow violence of, 148–52, 167; enclosure of the self in, 155, 156, 162; heath in, 149, 150–51, 207–8n41, 207n34; and impossibility of return to past, 153; on invisibility of larger movements of history, 141; letters in, as characters, 158; possession of others in, 156; on right to subsistence, loss of, 151; storm-lashed trees in, as type of enclosure violence, 148–49, 167; on subject-object relations, 165; work in, visibility of, 129

right to subsistence: in Forest Charter, 28–30, 147, 151, 172, 180n7, 182n15, 184n26; loss of, in *Return of the Native*, 151

Robbins, Bruce, 112, 121–22, 194n46, 199n23

*Romola* (Eliot): on common created by procession of Cross, 113; and Eliot's materialist standards, 115–16; familiar themes from other novels in, 115; Machiavelli's influence on, 117–118, 201n31; politics of commons envisioned in, 13, 114–20, 201n33; recognition of inequality in, 13; Tito's rejection of commons in, 122; web of indebtedness creating common in, 116–17

Ross, Kristin, 3, 163, 176n7

rural ideal, as class-specific, 181–82n14

rural laborers: and common, independence derived from, 28; and enclosure, 20–21, 24–26, 28, 134, 172; joint activism with industrial laborers, 20; political apathy, false stereotypes of, 19–20

*Rural Rides* (Cobbett), 10, 39

"The Sad Fortunes of Amos Barton" (Eliot), 99, 100, 197n14

Saville, Julia F., 188n13, 189n16

*Scenes of Clerical Life* (Eliot), 93, 105–6

self, construction through repetition, 189n16

serialization of nineteenth-century novels, 191n27

Shaw, Harry, 131, 175n5, 204n13

*Silas Marner* (Eliot), 56–58, 100, 198n16

skimmington (skimmity-rides), 137–38, 155, 205n21

social change, psychological change necessary for, 193n38

social utopia, envisioning of, in realism: and incorporation of both individual and hemispheric registers, 13–14; modern

relevance of concerns in, 14
*The Spanish Gypsy* (Eliot), 199n24
Staten, Henry, 108–109, 198–99n21
Steer, Philip, 40–41
suburbs, and afterlife of enclosure, 21
Swing Riots (1830), 25, 26, 27, 34, 106, 137, 145, 181n12

Taylor, Jesse Oak, 190–91n26, 194n47
technology, new human created by, 166–67
*terra nullius* doctrine, 11, 31–32, 182n16, 210n2
*Tess of the D'Urbervilles* (Hardy): character types in, 135, 139; and contrast of real life vs. desired life, 139; enclosure in, 125, 132–33, 145, 167, 202n2; events from "Facts" notebook used in, 148; impossibility of self-enclosure in, 161; letters in, 158–59, 161; questioning of accepted social law in, 153–54; and Tess's retreat from self in woods, 152–53; Tess's tragedy as tragedy of Tess's world, 133; work in, visibility of, 128–29; world of, as peripatetic, 134
Thackeray, William, 45, 49–50, 65
Theophrastan character types, 66, 98, 122–24, 201–2n34, 202n36
Thompson, E. P., 17, 22, 28, 180n9, 185n32, 196n11
*To the Lighthouse* (Woolf), 85
tragedy of the commons, 34–36, 184nn26–27
*Two Lectures on the Checks to Population* (Lloyd), 34–35
typographical culture of eighteenth century, Dickens and, 48, 66
Uglow, Jennifer, 89, 195n2

*Under the Greenwood Tree* (Hardy), 152, 153
urbanization: as class-specific ideal, 182n14; effects of, nineteenth-century writers' anticipation of, 179n1; and enclosure, 15–16; rapid, in modern capitalism, 178n1
utopian impulse: in British realist novels, afterlife of, 3; as ultimately economic, 83

Victorian culture, definition of, 204n12
Victorian geopolitical aesthetic, 110
Victorian literature, African Americanization of, 186–87n3
Victorian period: and capitalist world order, consolidation of, 1, 175n1; and individuality, concerns about loss of, 51; property as basis of status in, 182n17; workers' chattel-like status in, 182n17
violence, constituted vs. constitutive, 176–77n13
von Riehl, Wilhelm, 196–97n12
Vrettos, Athena, 54, 58, 189n17

Wall, Derek, 36, 152, 184n26
Weber, Max, 6, 171, 176n11
Wihl, Gary S., 117–118
Williams, Raymond: on city-country division, 18–19; on common, etymology of, 177n14; on community through struggle, 106; on derogatory associations of the common, 8; on Dickens's and Lukács's model of realism, 75; on Dickens's focus on city life, 44, 67; on Eliot's discomfort with commonness, 94, 100; on enclosure, as part of larger change, 104; on enclosure and

community, 176n8; on extending relationships, 176n7; on great houses of England, 180–81n10; on Hardy's focus on life and work, 128–29; on *Middlemarch*'s common, 109; on subjunctive mode, 49–50, 188n10
Wilson, Henry, 53, 54, 55, 57, 58–63, 59, 187n7, 188n14
Woloch, Alex, 5, 49, 190n24
women: and future commons, 29; and loss of commons, impact of, 28–29; possession by others, in Hardy, 156
*Wonderful and Eccentric Museum* (Kirby), 48, 54, 187n7
Wood, Ellen Meiksins, 24, 76, 181n11
*The Woodlanders* (Hardy): character types in, 135; on enclosure, 152; enclosure of the self in, 155, 156, 158; and global interconnectedness, 127; letters in, 158; and ownership of others, 156, 165–66; personifications of trees in, 207n32; reciprocal relationship between humans and non-humans, 163; and self-enclosure, impossibility of, 160–61; sharing of selves in, and possibility of commons, 157; on web of humanity, 140; work in, visibility of, 129
Woolf, Virginia, 2, 84–85, 193n38, 206n24
Wordsworth, William, 95–97, 184–85n31, 196n11
workers: chattel-like status in Victorian England, 182n17; laziness of, and need for pressure of necessity, 33; market dependence on, 24, 34; state support of reserve of, 24, 181n11. *See also* rural laborers
workhouses, poor conditions in, as incentive to work, 33–34, 183n23, 184n25
World Bank, 30, 185–86n35
Young, Arthur, 180n9, 181n12
Young, Edward, 95–96

Zapatista's Forest People's Manifesto (1985), 173
Žižek, Slavoj, 159–60, 176–77n13

The authorized representative in the EU for product safety and compliance is:
Mare Nostrum Group
B.V Doelen 72
4831 GR Breda
The Netherlands

www.ingramcontent.com/pod-product-compliance
Lightning Source LLC
Chambersburg PA
CBHW031807220426
43662CB00007B/553